SIMON SPURRIER × MATÍAS BERGARA

CODA ™

VOLUME ONE

BOOM! ™
STUDIOS

CODA Volume One, March 2019.
Published by BOOM! Studios, a division of
Boom Entertainment, Inc. Coda is ™ &
© 2019 Simon Spurrier, Ltd. & Matías
Bergara. Originally published in single
magazine form as CODA No. 1-4. ™ &
© 2018 Simon Spurrier, Ltd. & Matías Bergara. All rights reserved. BOOM!
Studios™ and the BOOM! Studios logo are trademarks of Boom Entertainment,
Inc., registered in various countries and categories. All characters, events, and
institutions depicted herein are fictional. Any similarity between any of the
names, characters, persons, events, and/or institutions in this publication to
actual names, characters, and persons, whether living or dead, events, and/
or institutions is unintended and purely coincidental. BOOM! Studios does not
read or accept unsolicited submissions of ideas, stories, or artwork.

BOOM! Studios, 5670 Wilshire Boulevard, Suite 400, Los Angeles, CA 90036-
5679. Printed in China. First Printing.

ISBN: 978-1-68415-321-3, eISBN: 978-1-64144-174-2

CODA™

CREATED BY **SIMON SPURRIER & MATÍAS BERGARA**

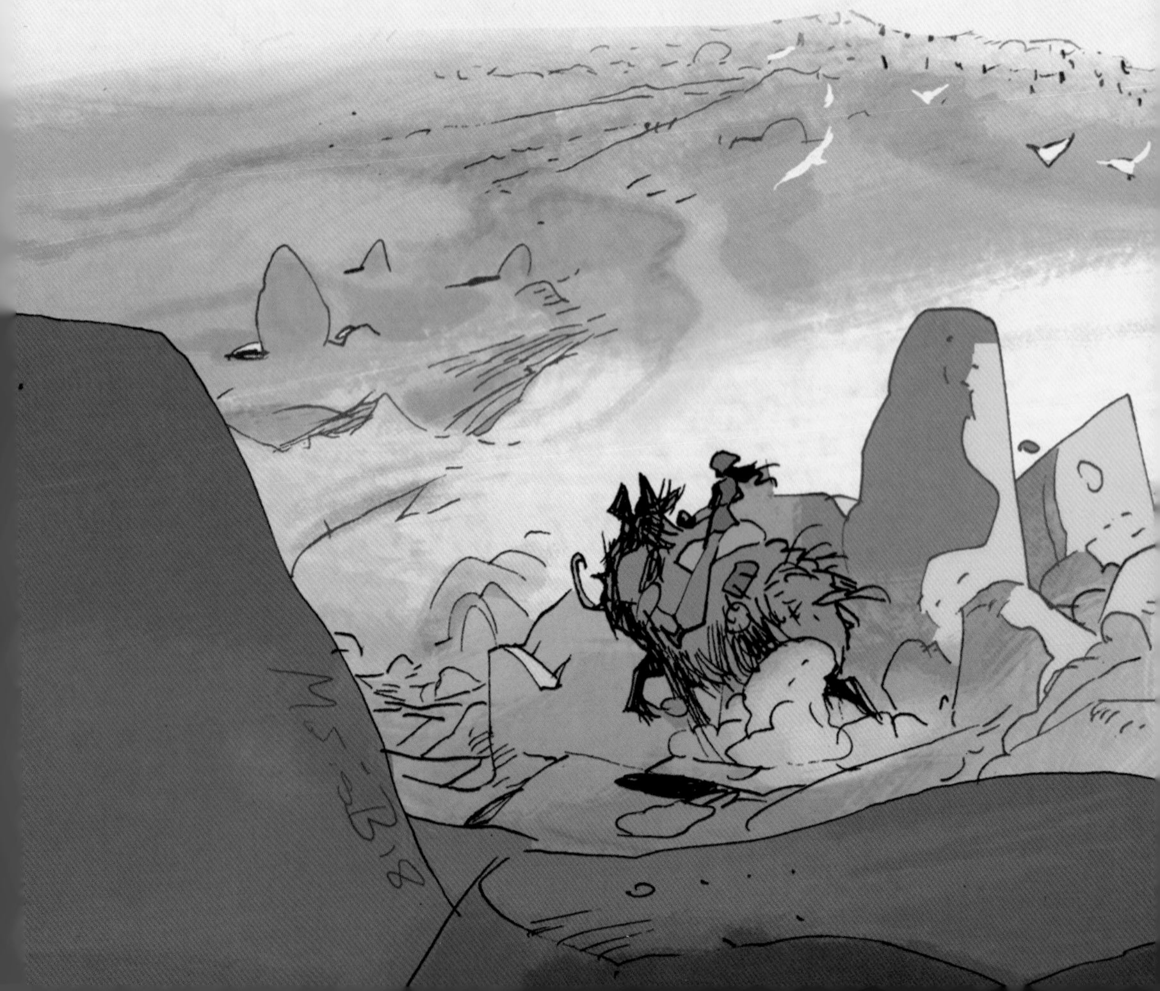

WRITTEN BY **SIMON SPURRIER**
ILLUSTRATED BY **MATÍAS BERGARA**
WITH COLOR ASSISTS BY **MICHAEL DOIG**
LETTERED BY **JIM CAMPBELL & COLIN BELL**

COVER BY **MATÍAS BERGARA**

SERIES DESIGNER **MARIE KRUPINA**
COLLECTION DESIGNER **CHELSEA ROBERTS**
ASSISTANT EDITOR **GAVIN GRONENTHAL**
EDITOR **ERIC HARBURN**

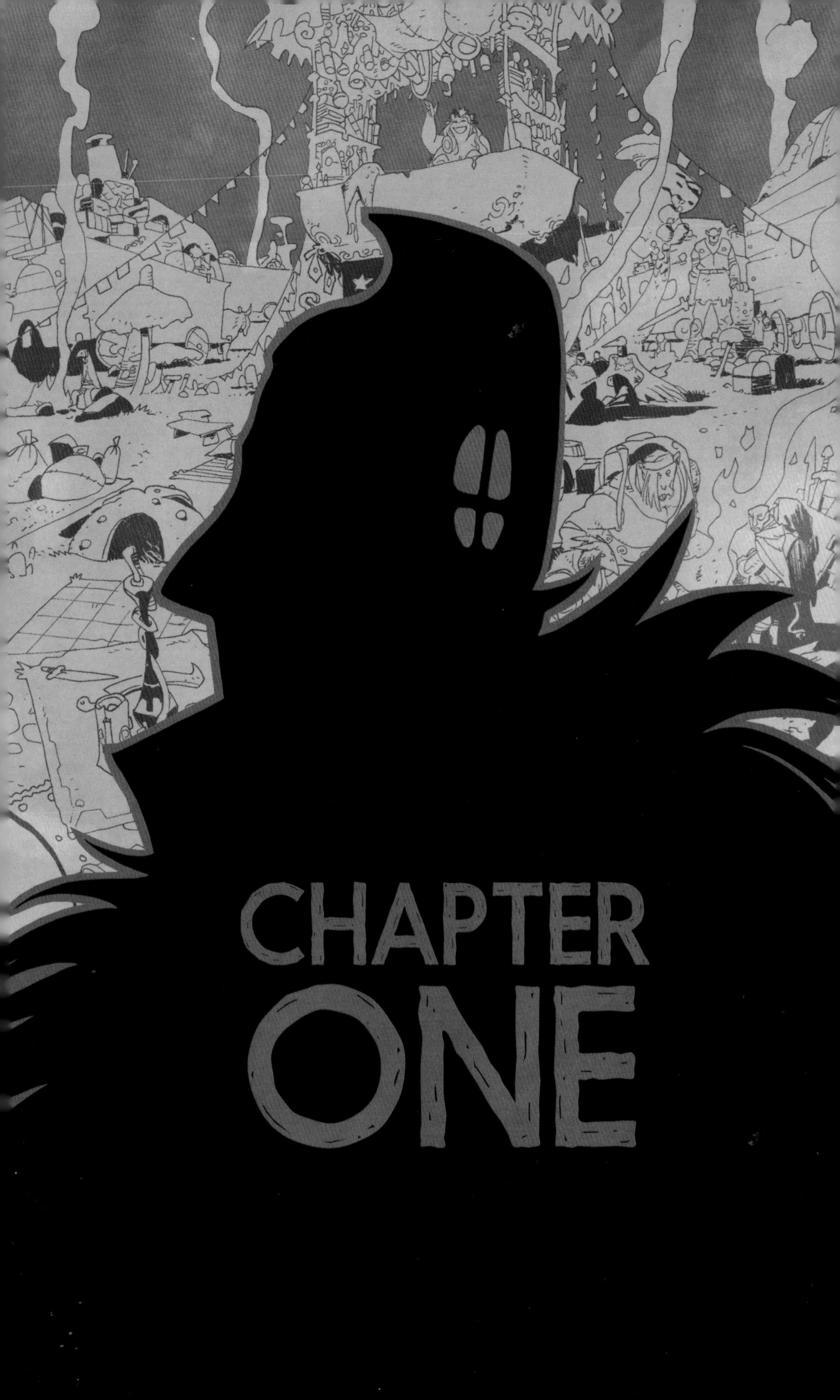
CHAPTER
ONE

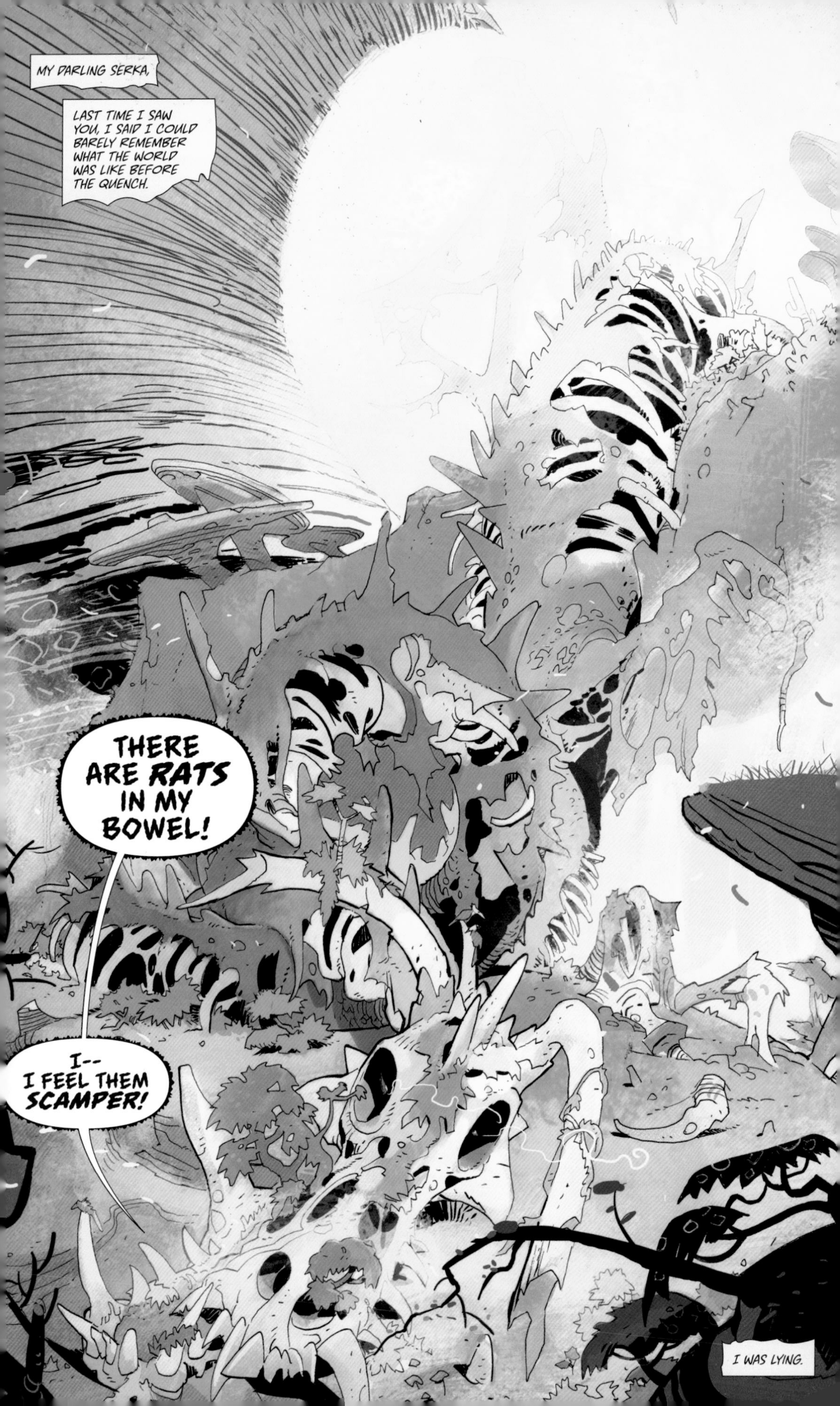
MY DARLING SERKA,
LAST TIME I SAW YOU, I SAID I COULD BARELY REMEMBER WHAT THE WORLD WAS LIKE BEFORE THE QUENCH.
THERE ARE RATS IN MY BOWEL!
I-- I FEEL THEM SCAMPER!
I WAS LYING.

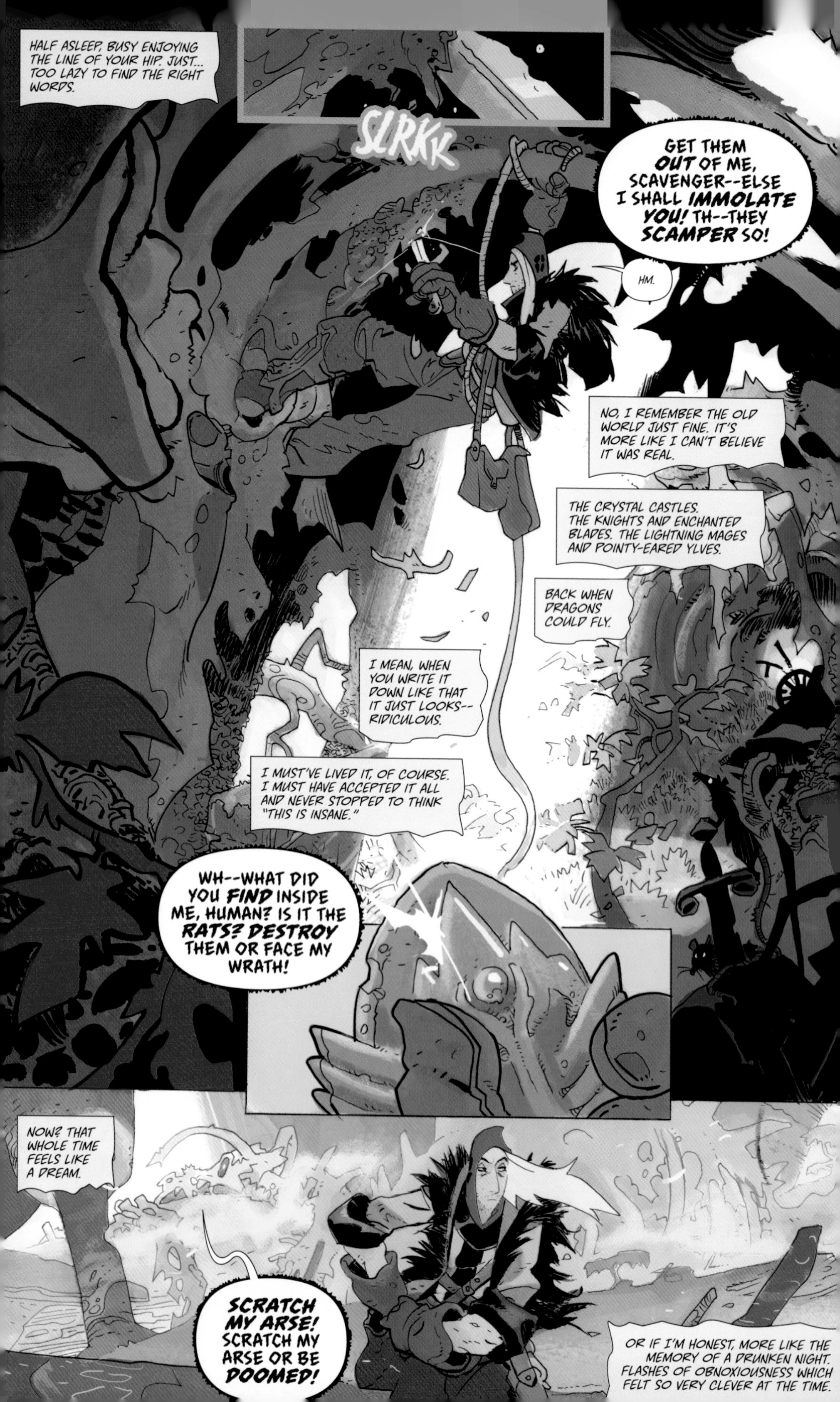
HALF ASLEEP, BUSY ENJOYING THE LINE OF YOUR HIP. JUST... TOO LAZY TO FIND THE RIGHT WORDS.
SLRKK
GET THEM OUT OF ME, SCAVENGER--ELSE I SHALL IMMOLATE YOU! TH--THEY SCAMPER SO!
HM.
NO, I REMEMBER THE OLD WORLD JUST FINE. IT'S MORE LIKE I CAN'T BELIEVE IT WAS REAL.
THE CRYSTAL CASTLES. THE KNIGHTS AND ENCHANTED BLADES. THE LIGHTNING MAGES AND POINTY-EARED YLVES.
BACK WHEN DRAGONS COULD FLY.
I MEAN, WHEN YOU WRITE IT DOWN LIKE THAT IT JUST LOOKS--RIDICULOUS.
I MUST'VE LIVED IT, OF COURSE. I MUST HAVE ACCEPTED IT ALL AND NEVER STOPPED TO THINK "THIS IS INSANE."
WH--WHAT DID YOU FIND INSIDE ME, HUMAN? IS IT THE RATS? DESTROY THEM OR FACE MY WRATH!
NOW? THAT WHOLE TIME FEELS LIKE A DREAM.
SCRATCH MY ARSE! SCRATCH MY ARSE OR BE DOOMED!
OR IF I'M HONEST, MORE LIKE THE MEMORY OF A DRUNKEN NIGHT. FLASHES OF OBNOXIOUSNESS WHICH FELT SO VERY CLEVER AT THE TIME.

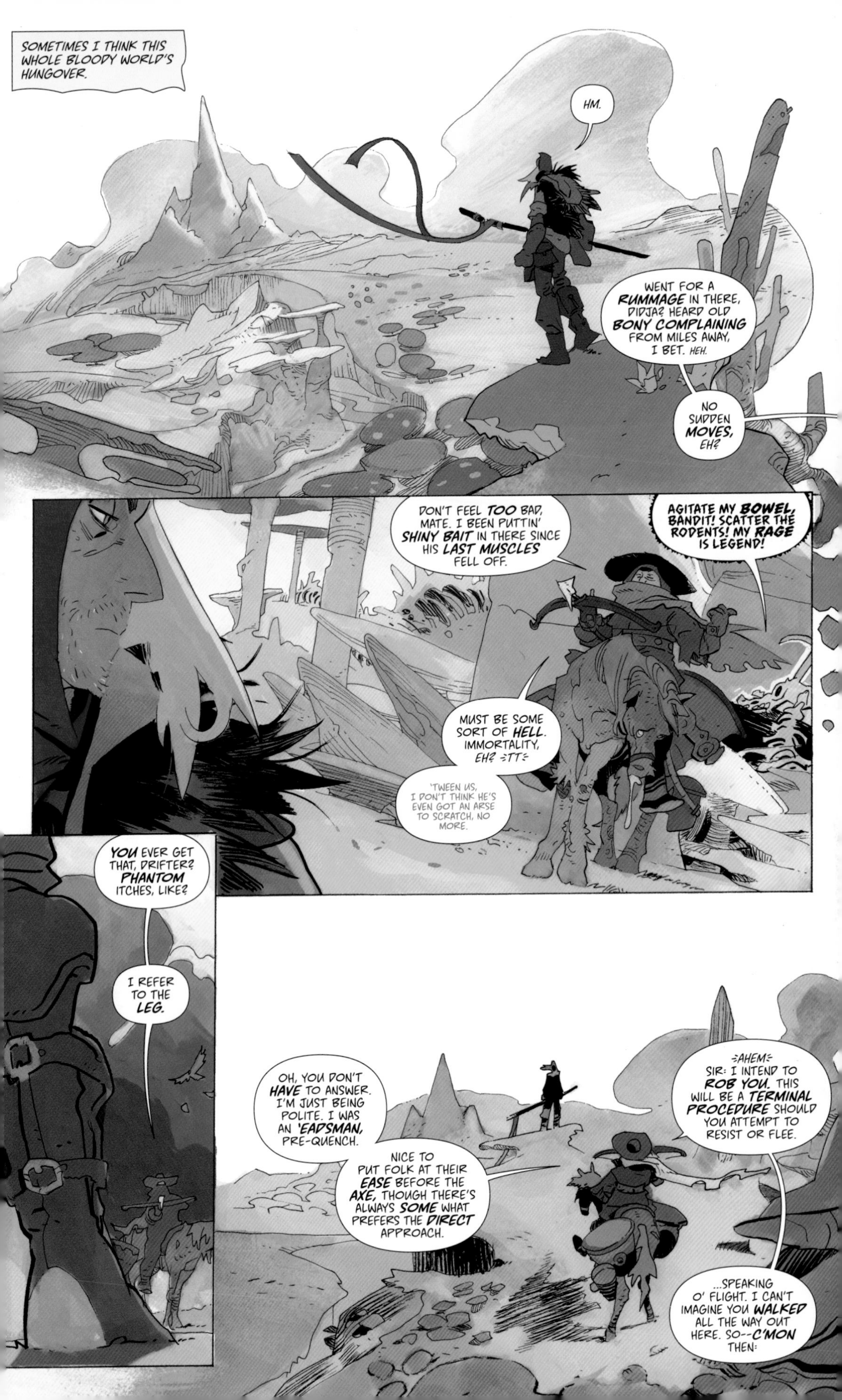

SOMETIMES I THINK THIS WHOLE BLOODY WORLD'S HUNGOVER.
HM.
WENT FOR A RUMMAGE IN THERE, DIDJA? HEARD OLD BONY COMPLAINING FROM MILES AWAY, I BET. HEH.
NO SUDDEN MOVES, EH?
DON'T FEEL TOO BAD, MATE. I BEEN PUTTIN' SHINY BAIT IN THERE SINCE HIS LAST MUSCLES FELL OFF.
AGITATE MY BOWEL, BANDIT! SCATTER THE RODENTS! MY RAGE IS LEGEND!
MUST BE SOME SORT OF HELL. IMMORTALITY, EH? =TT=
'TWEEN US, I DON'T THINK HE'S EVEN GOT AN ARSE TO SCRATCH, NO MORE.
YOU EVER GET THAT, DRIFTER? PHANTOM ITCHES, LIKE?
I REFER TO THE LEG.
OH, YOU DON'T HAVE TO ANSWER. I'M JUST BEING POLITE. I WAS AN 'EADSMAN, PRE-QUENCH.
NICE TO PUT FOLK AT THEIR EASE BEFORE THE AXE, THOUGH THERE'S ALWAYS SOME WHAT PREFERS THE DIRECT APPROACH.
=AHEM= SIR: I INTEND TO ROB YOU. THIS WILL BE A TERMINAL PROCEDURE SHOULD YOU ATTEMPT TO RESIST OR FLEE.
...SPEAKING O' FLIGHT. I CAN'T IMAGINE YOU WALKED ALL THE WAY OUT HERE. SO--C'MON THEN:

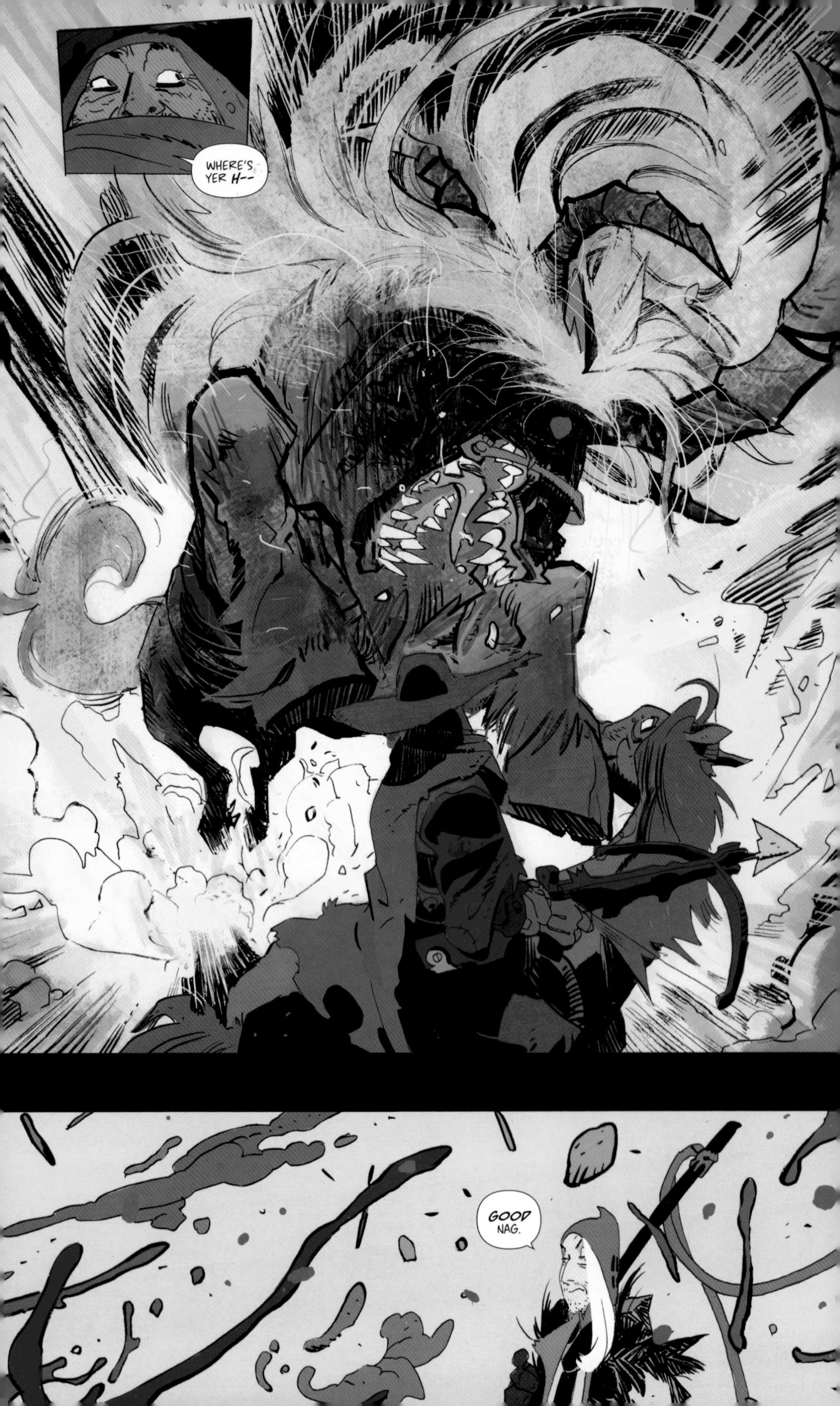
WHERE'S YER H--
GOOD NAG.

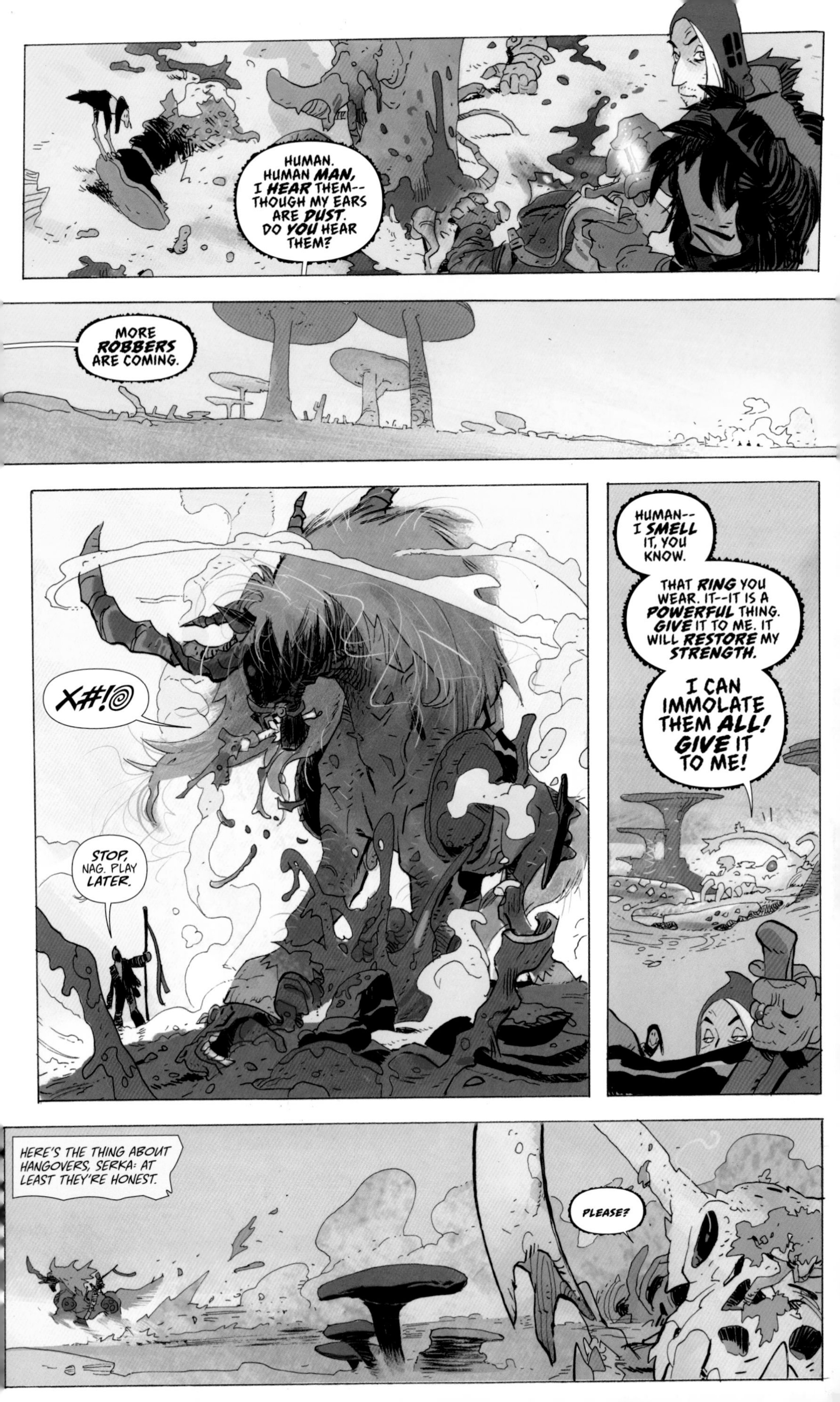
HUMAN. HUMAN MAN, I HEAR THEM-- THOUGH MY EARS ARE DUST. DO YOU HEAR THEM?
MORE ROBBERS ARE COMING.
X#!@
STOP, NAG. PLAY LATER.
HUMAN-- I SMELL IT, YOU KNOW.
THAT RING YOU WEAR. IT--IT IS A POWERFUL THING. GIVE IT TO ME. IT WILL RESTORE MY STRENGTH.
I CAN IMMOLATE THEM ALL! GIVE IT TO ME!
HERE'S THE THING ABOUT HANGOVERS, SERKA: AT LEAST THEY'RE HONEST.
PLEASE?

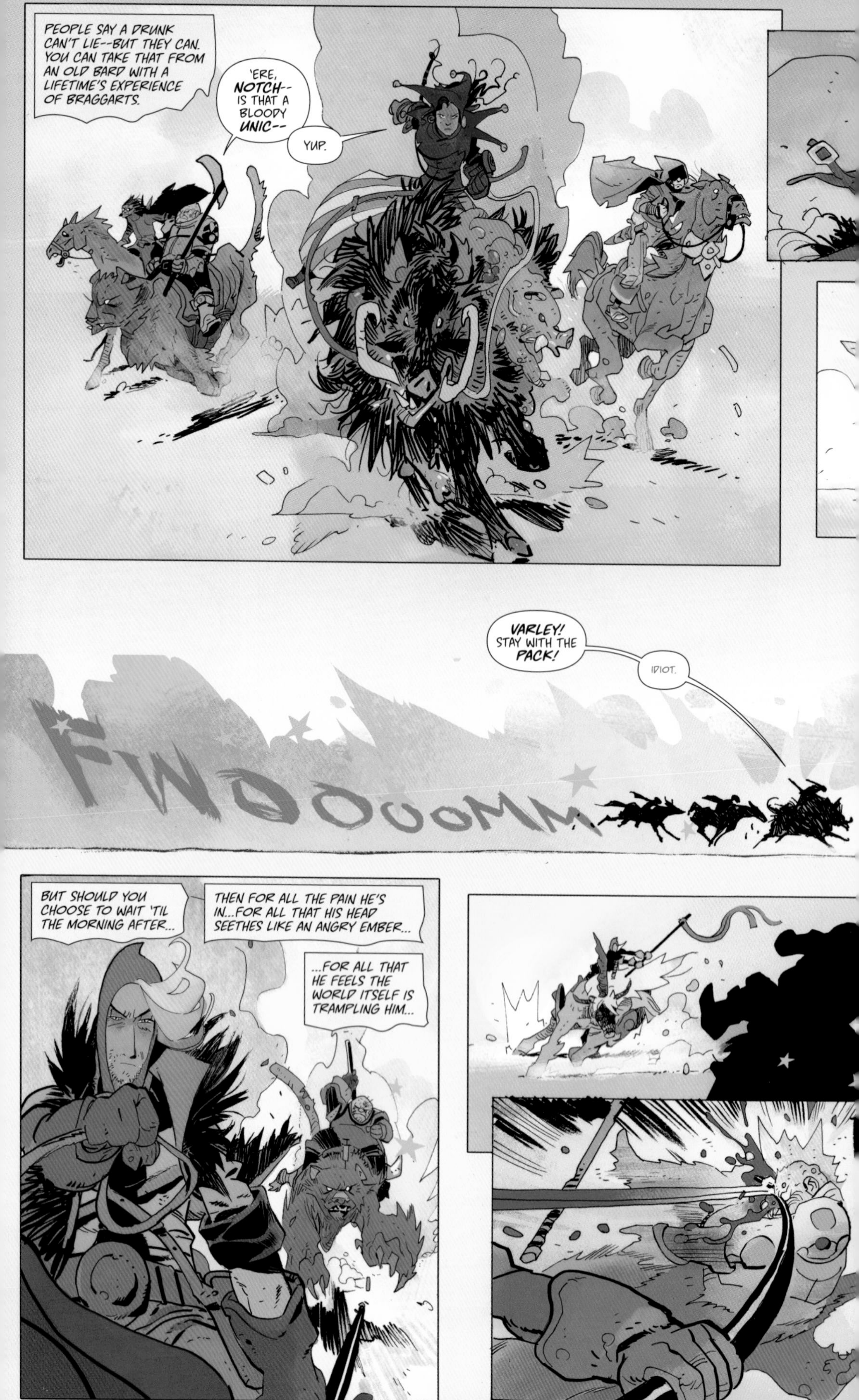
PEOPLE SAY A DRUNK CAN'T LIE--BUT THEY CAN. YOU CAN TAKE THAT FROM AN OLD BARD WITH A LIFETIME'S EXPERIENCE OF BRAGGARTS.
'ERE, NOTCH-- IS THAT A BLOODY UNIC--
YUP.
VARLEY! STAY WITH THE PACK!
IDIOT.
FWOOOOMM
BUT SHOULD YOU CHOOSE TO WAIT 'TIL THE MORNING AFTER...
THEN FOR ALL THE PAIN HE'S IN...FOR ALL THAT HIS HEAD SEETHES LIKE AN ANGRY EMBER...
...FOR ALL THAT HE FEELS THE WORLD ITSELF IS TRAMPLING HIM...

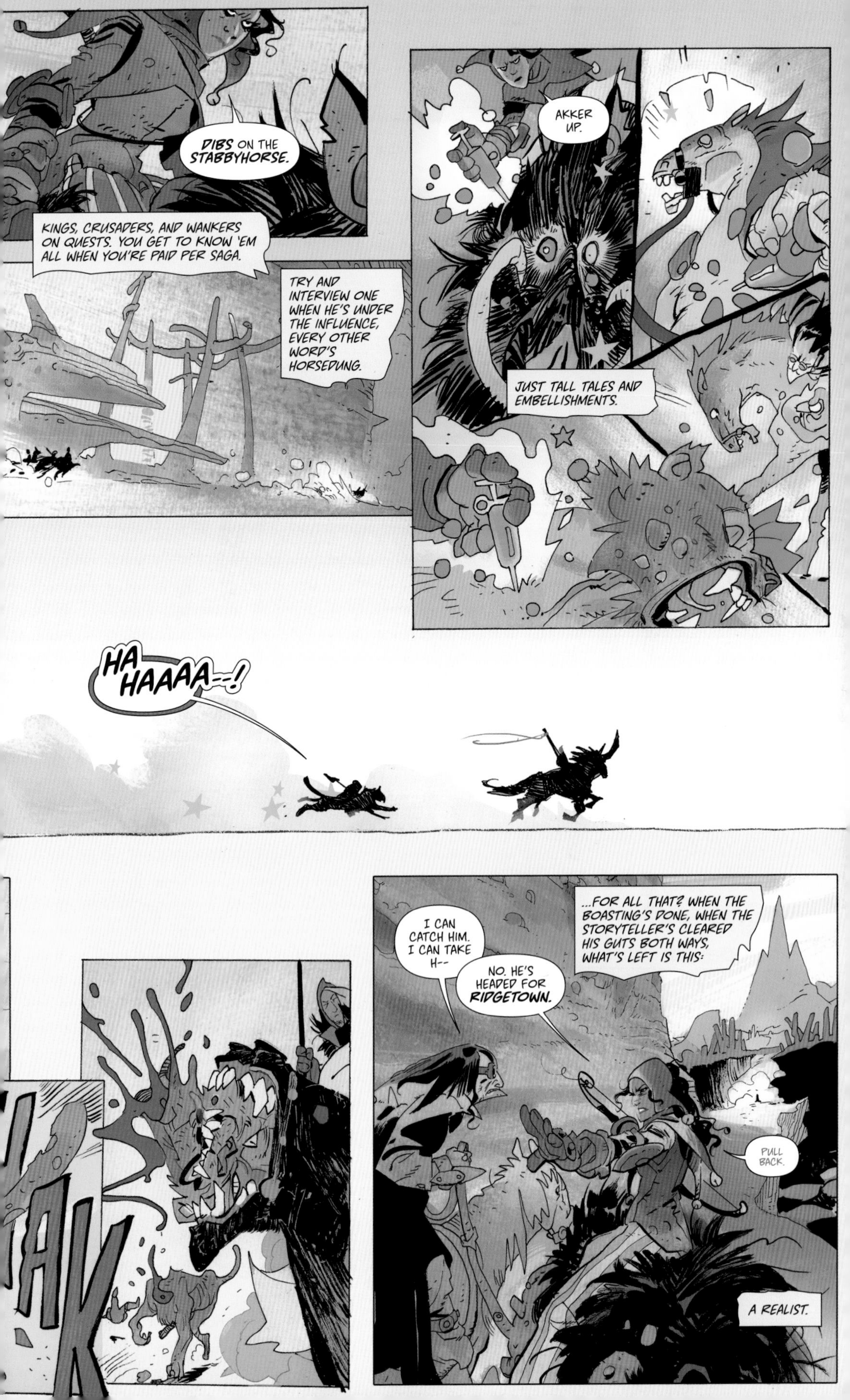
DIBS ON THE STABBYHORSE.
KINGS, CRUSADERS, AND WANKERS ON QUESTS. YOU GET TO KNOW 'EM ALL WHEN YOU'RE PAID PER SAGA.
TRY AND INTERVIEW ONE WHEN HE'S UNDER THE INFLUENCE, EVERY OTHER WORD'S HORSEDUNG.
AKKER UP.
JUST TALL TALES AND EMBELLISHMENTS.
HA HAAAA--!
I CAN CATCH HIM. I CAN TAKE H--
NO. HE'S HEADED FOR RIDGETOWN.
...FOR ALL THAT? WHEN THE BOASTING'S DONE, WHEN THE STORYTELLER'S CLEARED HIS GUTS BOTH WAYS, WHAT'S LEFT IS THIS:
PULL BACK.
A REALIST.

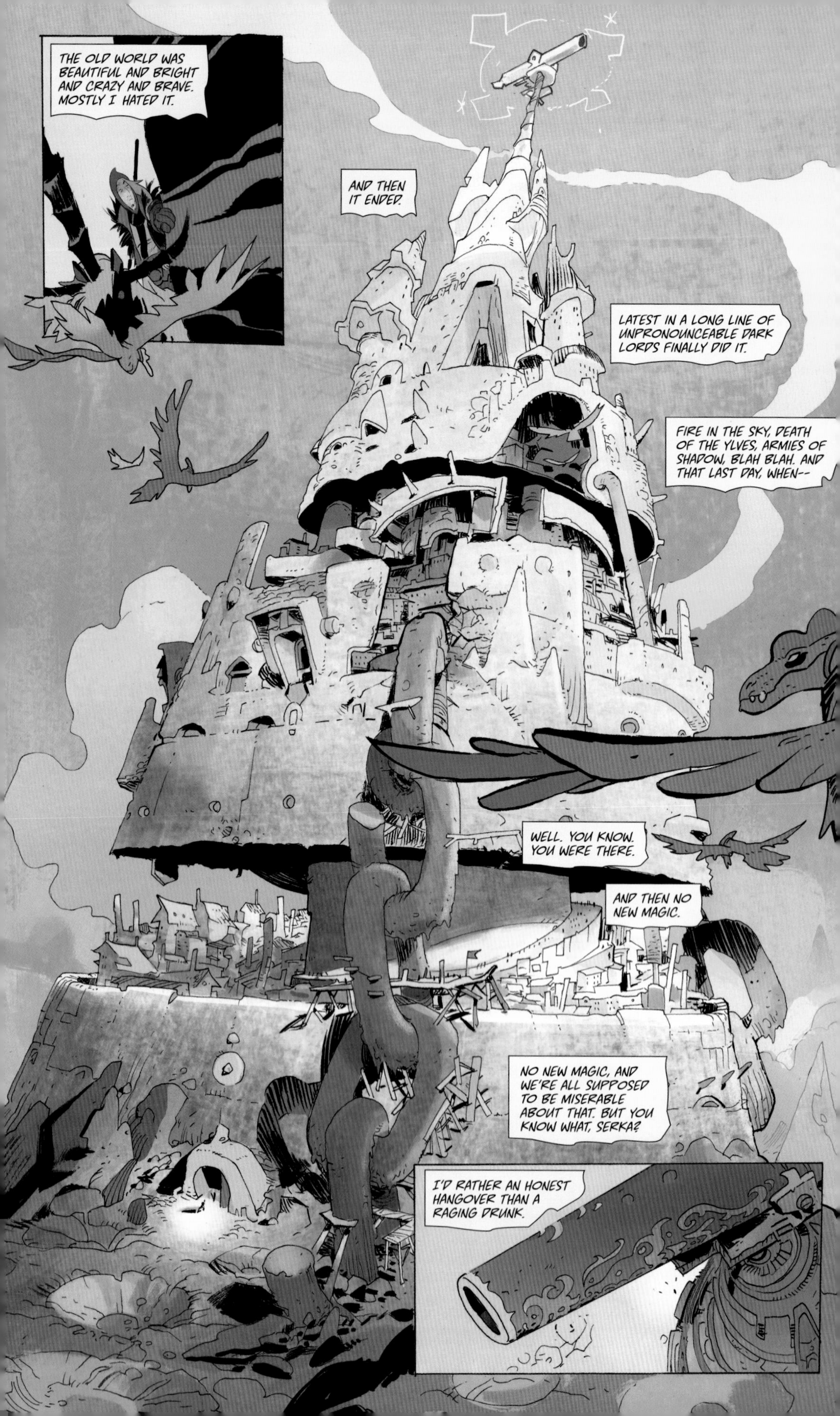
THE OLD WORLD WAS BEAUTIFUL AND BRIGHT AND CRAZY AND BRAVE. MOSTLY I HATED IT.
AND THEN IT ENDED.
LATEST IN A LONG LINE OF UNPRONOUNCEABLE DARK LORDS FINALLY DID IT.
FIRE IN THE SKY, DEATH OF THE YLVES, ARMIES OF SHADOW, BLAH BLAH. AND THAT LAST DAY, WHEN--
WELL. YOU KNOW. YOU WERE THERE.
AND THEN NO NEW MAGIC.
NO NEW MAGIC, AND WE'RE ALL SUPPOSED TO BE MISERABLE ABOUT THAT. BUT YOU KNOW WHAT, SERKA?
I'D RATHER AN HONEST HANGOVER THAN A RAGING DRUNK.

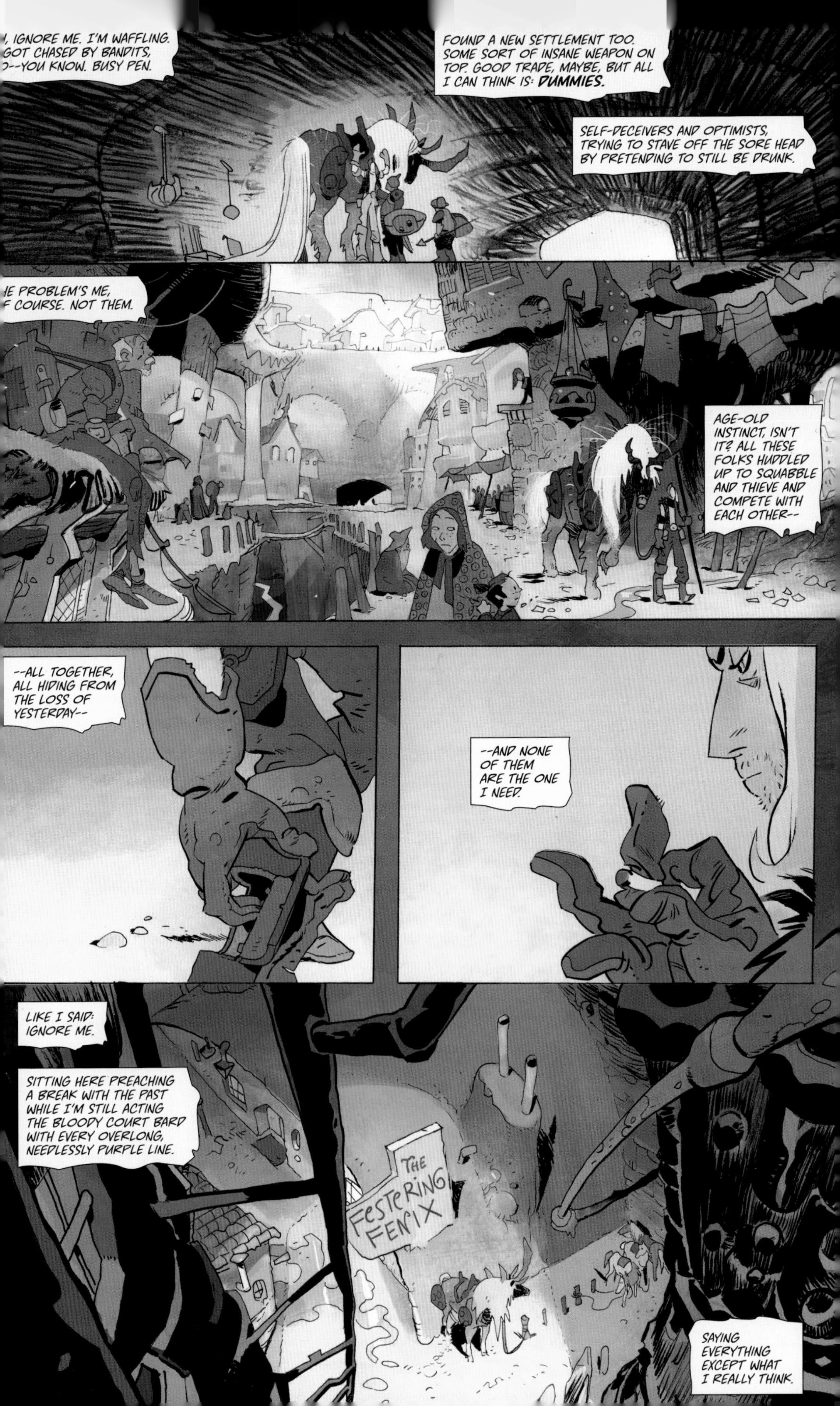
IGNORE ME. I'M WAFFLING. GOT CHASED BY BANDITS, --YOU KNOW. BUSY PEN.
FOUND A NEW SETTLEMENT TOO. SOME SORT OF INSANE WEAPON ON TOP. GOOD TRADE, MAYBE, BUT ALL I CAN THINK IS: DUMMIES.
SELF-DECEIVERS AND OPTIMISTS, TRYING TO STAVE OFF THE SORE HEAD BY PRETENDING TO STILL BE DRUNK.
PROBLEM'S ME, COURSE. NOT THEM.
AGE-OLD INSTINCT, ISN'T IT? ALL THESE FOLKS HUDDLED UP TO SQUABBLE AND THIEVE AND COMPETE WITH EACH OTHER--
--ALL TOGETHER, ALL HIDING FROM THE LOSS OF YESTERDAY--
--AND NONE OF THEM ARE THE ONE I NEED.
LIKE I SAID: IGNORE ME.
SITTING HERE PREACHING A BREAK WITH THE PAST WHILE I'M STILL ACTING THE BLOODY COURT BARD WITH EVERY OVERLONG, NEEDLESSLY PURPLE LINE.
THE FESTERING FENIX
SAYING EVERYTHING EXCEPT WHAT I REALLY THINK.

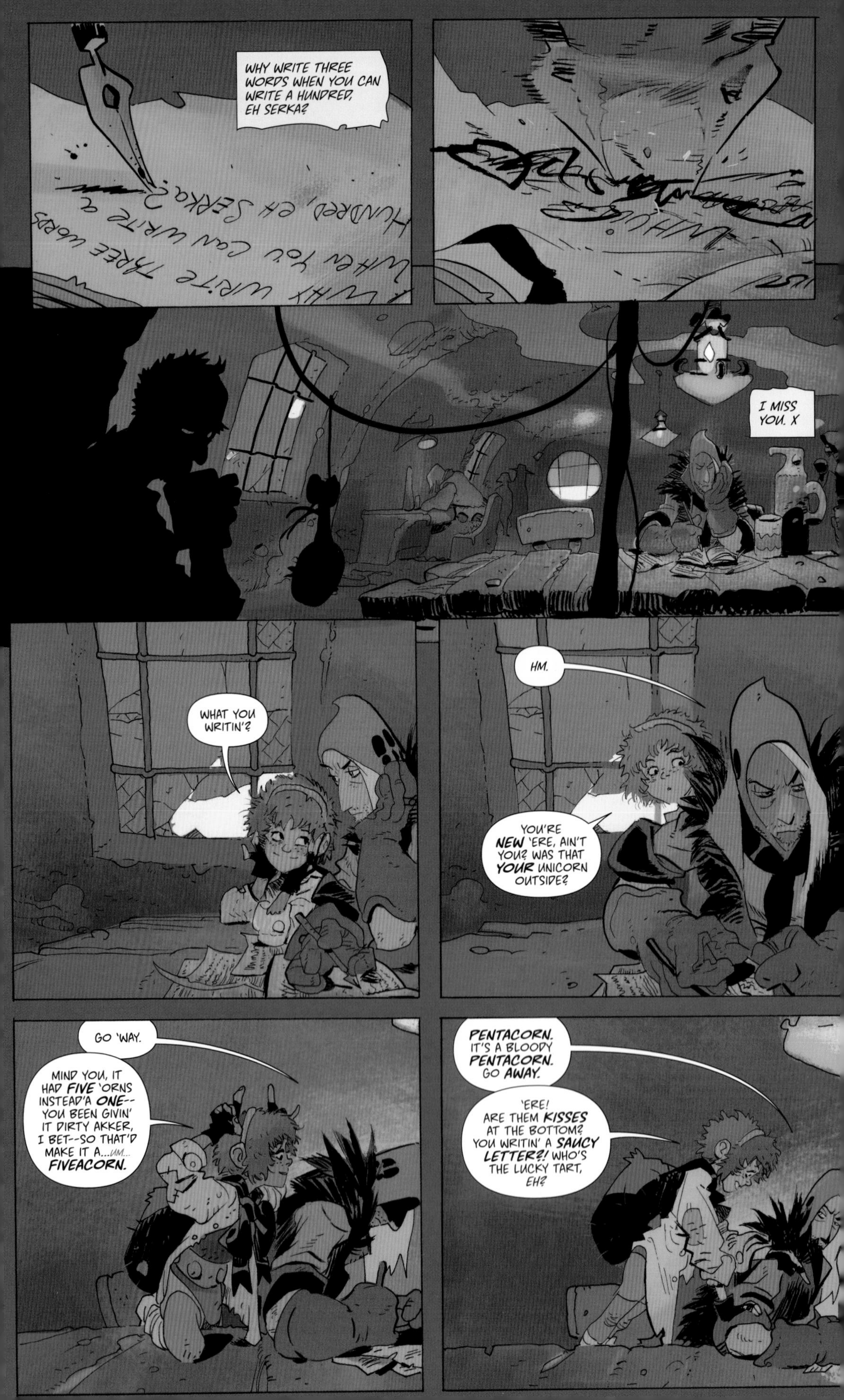

WHY WRITE THREE WORDS WHEN YOU CAN WRITE A HUNDRED, EH SERKA?
WHY WRITE THREE WORDS WHEN YOU CAN WRITE A HUNDRED, EH SERKA?
I MISS YOU. X
WHAT YOU WRITIN'?
HM.
YOU'RE NEW 'ERE, AIN'T YOU? WAS THAT YOUR UNICORN OUTSIDE?
GO 'WAY.
MIND YOU, IT HAD FIVE 'ORNS INSTEAD'A ONE--YOU BEEN GIVIN' IT DIRTY AKKER, I BET--SO THAT'D MAKE IT A...UM... FIVEACORN.
PENTACORN. IT'S A BLOODY PENTACORN. GO AWAY.
'ERE! ARE THEM KISSES AT THE BOTTOM? YOU WRITIN' A SAUCY LETTER?! WHO'S THE LUCKY TART, EH?

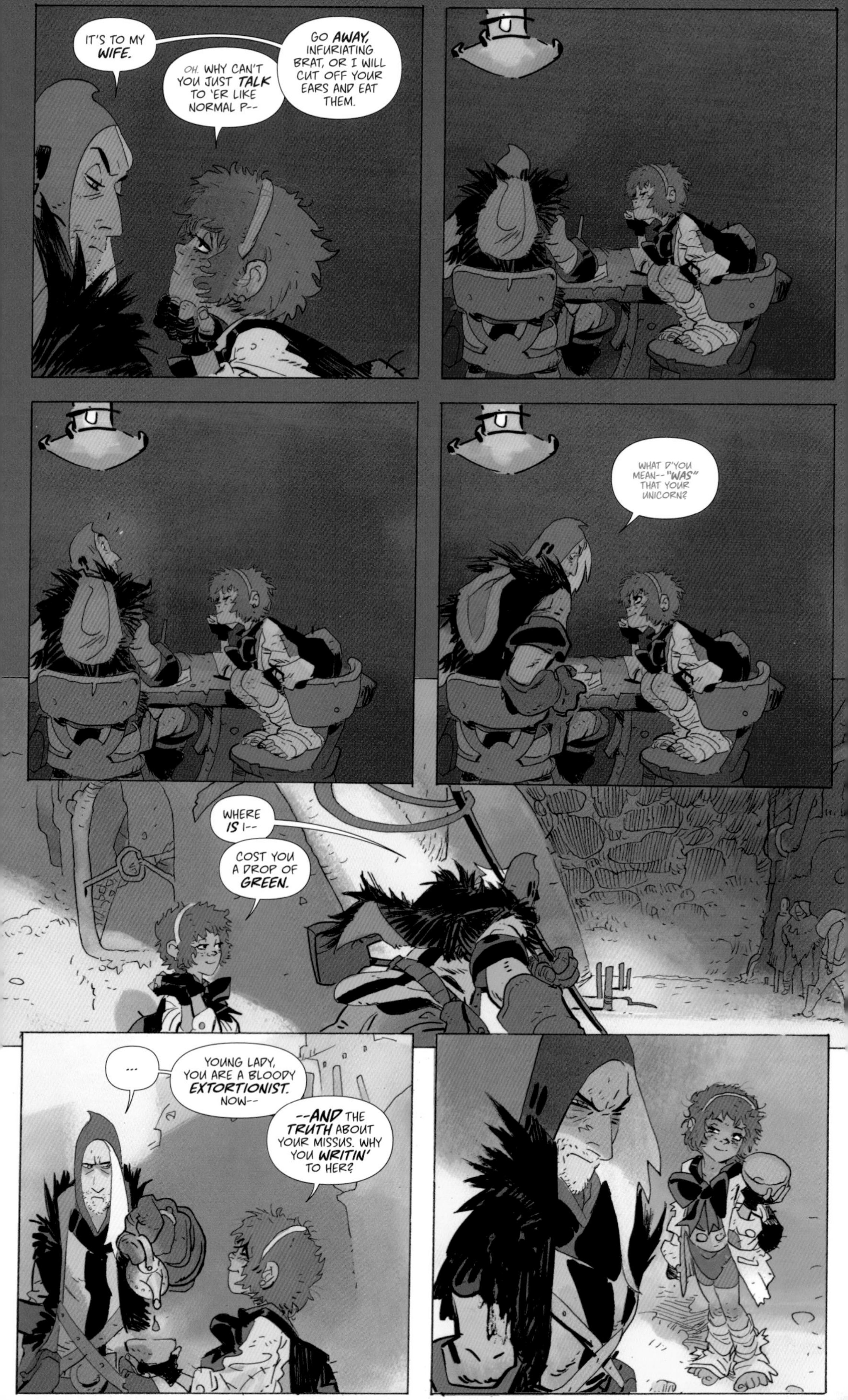
IT'S TO MY WIFE.
OH. WHY CAN'T YOU JUST TALK TO 'ER LIKE NORMAL P--
GO AWAY, INFURIATING BRAT, OR I WILL CUT OFF YOUR EARS AND EAT THEM.
WHAT D'YOU MEAN--"WAS" THAT YOUR UNICORN?
WHERE IS I--
COST YOU A DROP OF GREEN.
...
YOUNG LADY, YOU ARE A BLOODY EXTORTIONIST. NOW--
--AND THE TRUTH ABOUT YOUR MISSUS. WHY YOU WRITIN' TO HER?

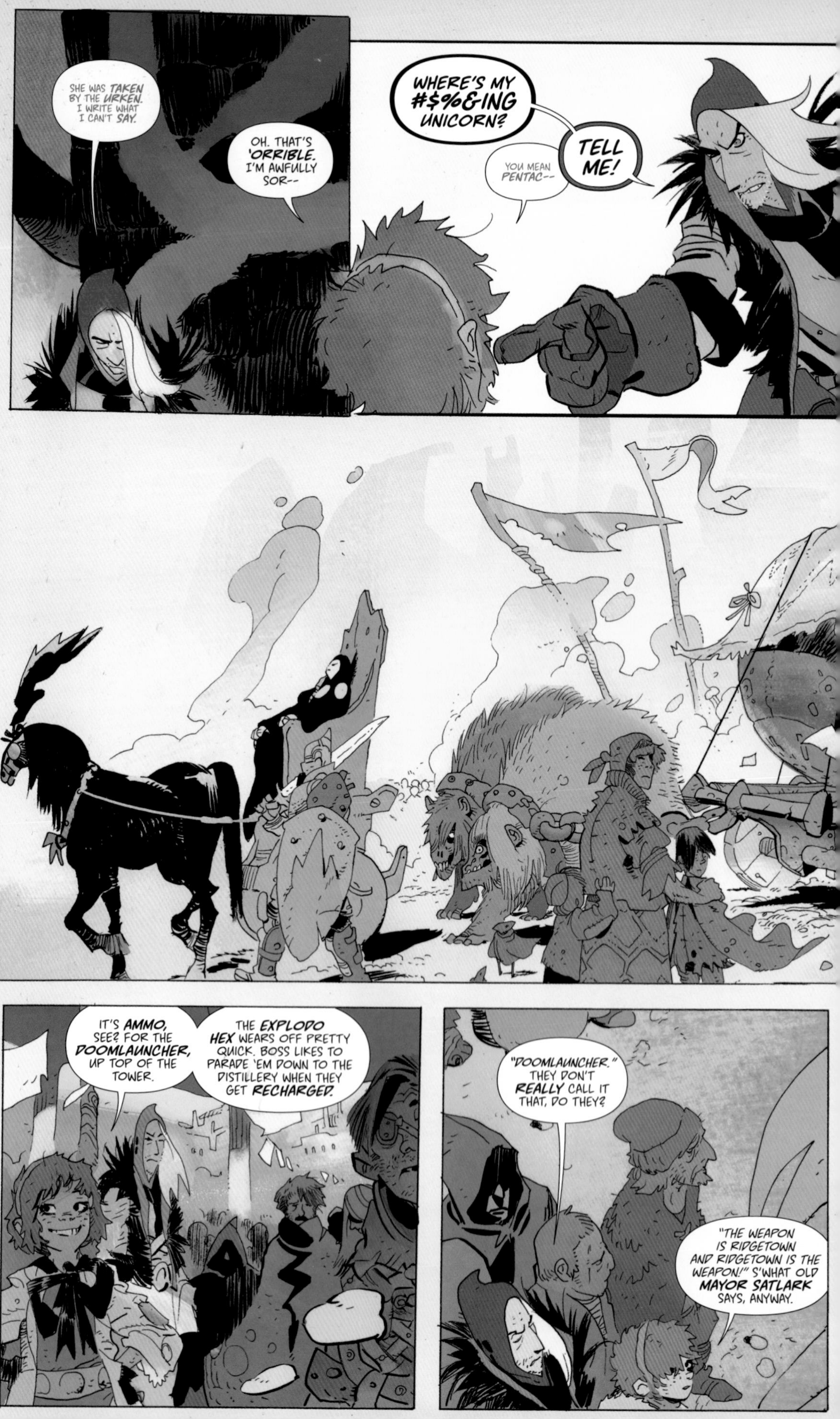

SHE WAS TAKEN BY THE URKEN. I WRITE WHAT I CAN'T SAY.
OH. THAT'S 'ORRIBLE. I'M AWFULLY SOR--
WHERE'S MY #$%&ING UNICORN?
TELL ME!
YOU MEAN PENTAC--
IT'S AMMO, SEE? FOR THE DOOMLAUNCHER, UP TOP OF THE TOWER.
THE EXPLODO HEX WEARS OFF PRETTY QUICK. BOSS LIKES TO PARADE 'EM DOWN TO THE DISTILLERY WHEN THEY GET RECHARGED.
"DOOMLAUNCHER." THEY DON'T REALLY CALL IT THAT, DO THEY?
"THE WEAPON IS RIDGETOWN AND RIDGETOWN IS THE WEAPON!" S'WHAT OLD MAYOR SATLARK SAYS, ANYWAY.

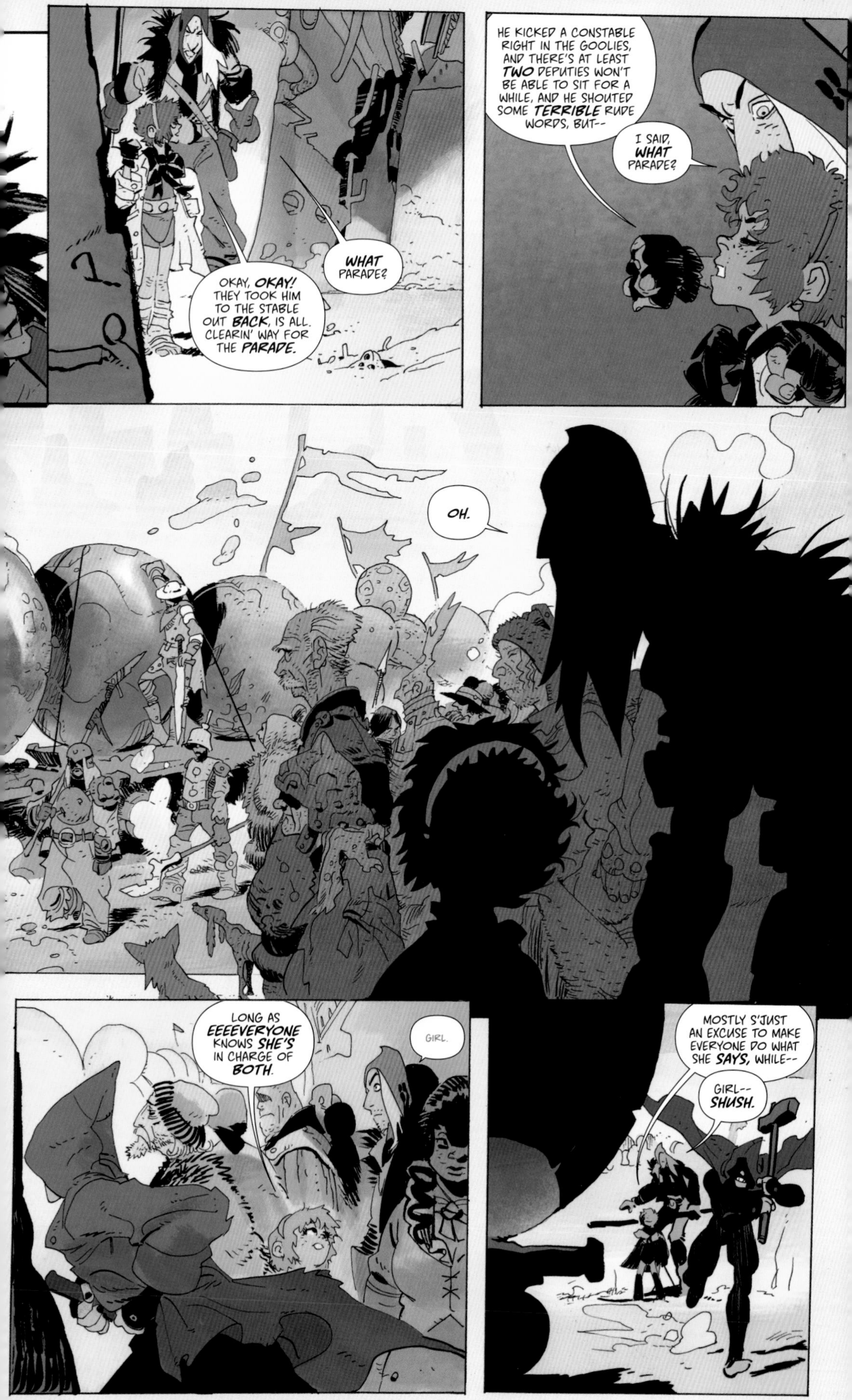
WHAT PARADE?
OKAY, OKAY! THEY TOOK HIM TO THE STABLE OUT BACK, IS ALL. CLEARIN' WAY FOR THE PARADE.
HE KICKED A CONSTABLE RIGHT IN THE GOOLIES, AND THERE'S AT LEAST TWO DEPUTIES WON'T BE ABLE TO SIT FOR A WHILE, AND HE SHOUTED SOME TERRIBLE RUDE WORDS, BUT--
I SAID, WHAT PARADE?
OH.
LONG AS EEEEVERYONE KNOWS SHE'S IN CHARGE OF BOTH.
GIRL.
MOSTLY S'JUST AN EXCUSE TO MAKE EVERYONE DO WHAT SHE SAYS, WHILE--
GIRL-- SHUSH.

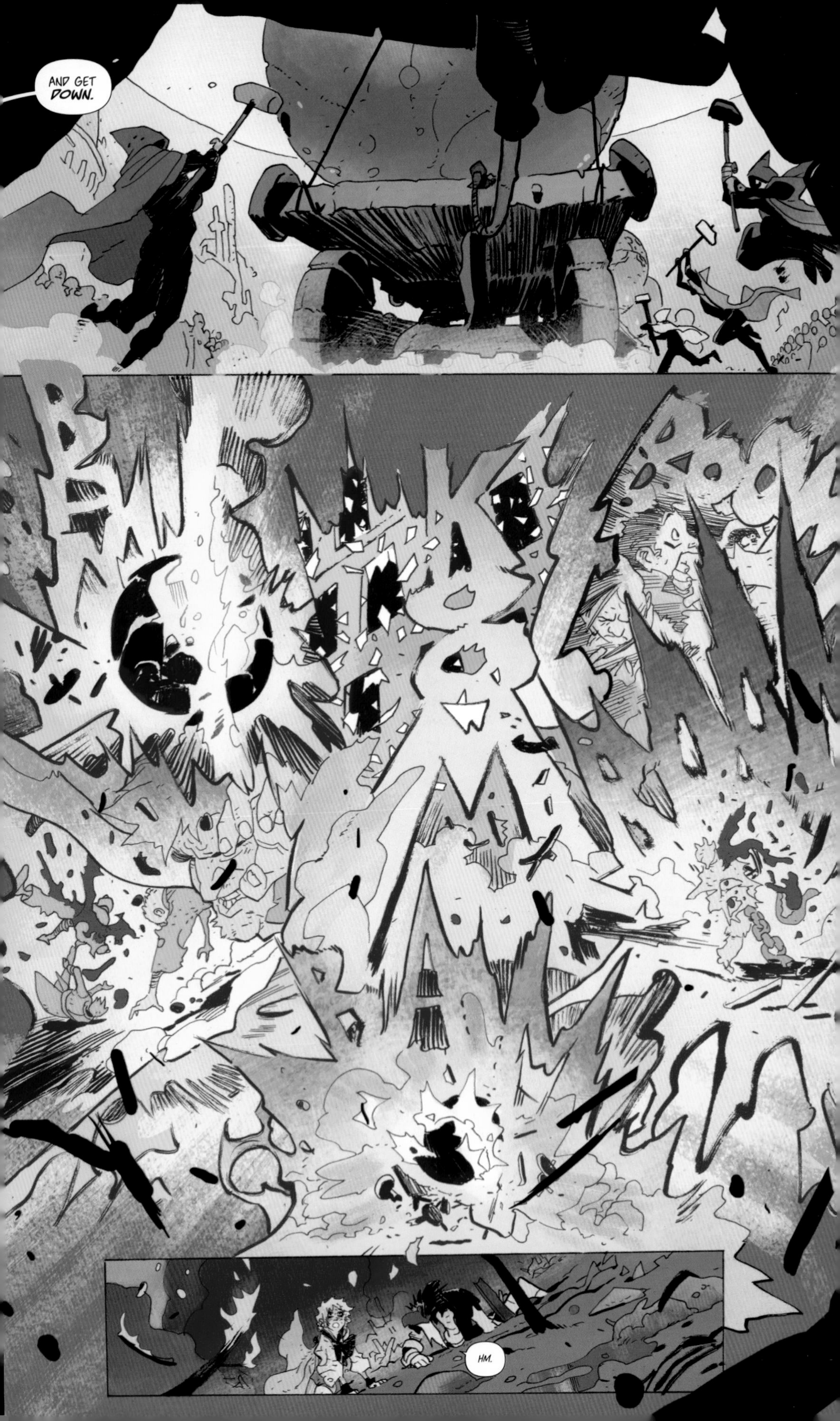
AND GET DOWN.
HM.

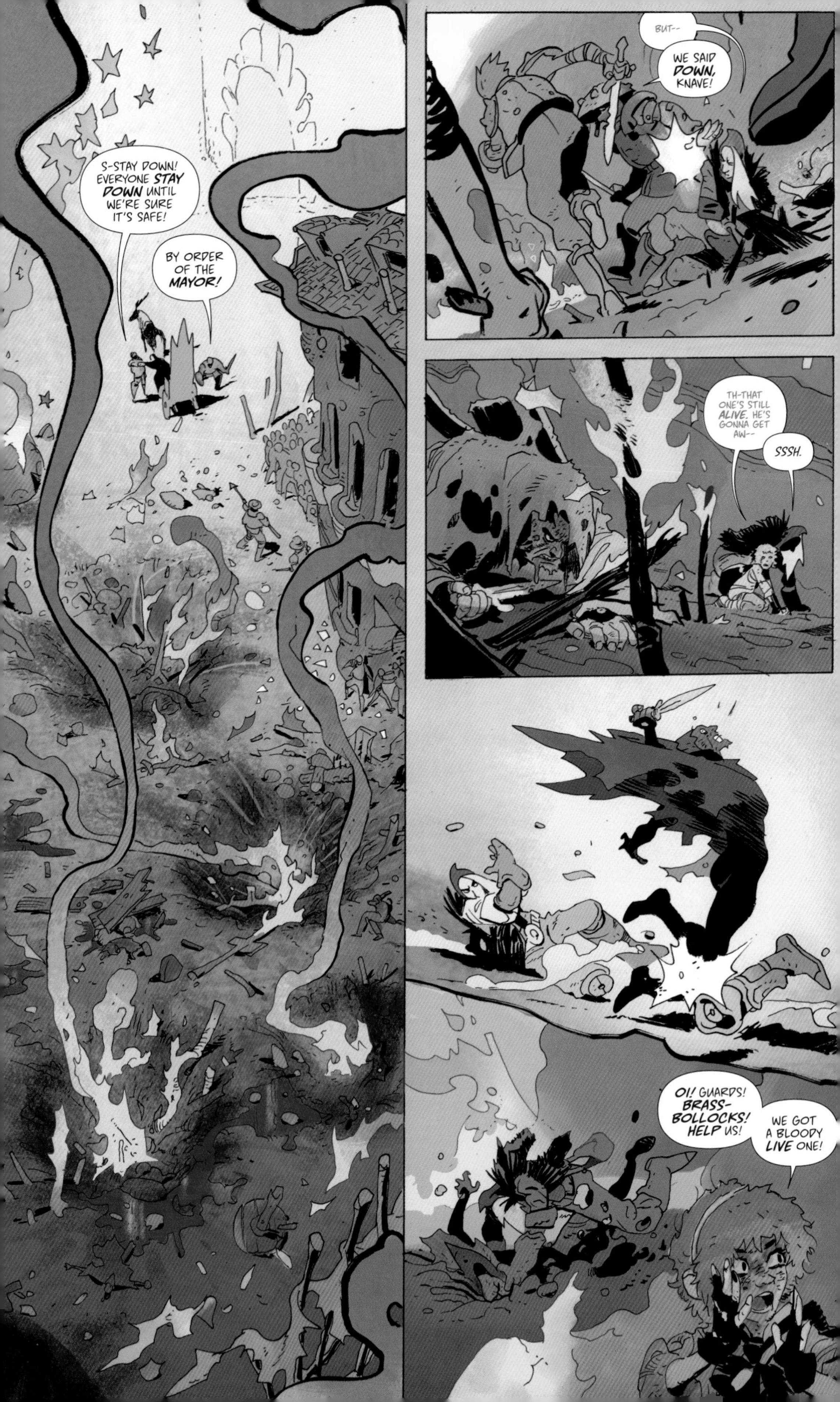

S-STAY DOWN! EVERYONE **STAY DOWN** UNTIL WE'RE SURE IT'S SAFE!
BY ORDER OF THE ***MAYOR!***
BUT--
WE SAID ***DOWN,*** KNAVE!
TH-THAT ONE'S STILL *ALIVE.* HE'S GONNA GET AW--
SSSH.
OI! GUARDS! ***BRASS-BOLLOCKS! HELP*** US!
WE GOT A BLOODY ***LIVE*** ONE!

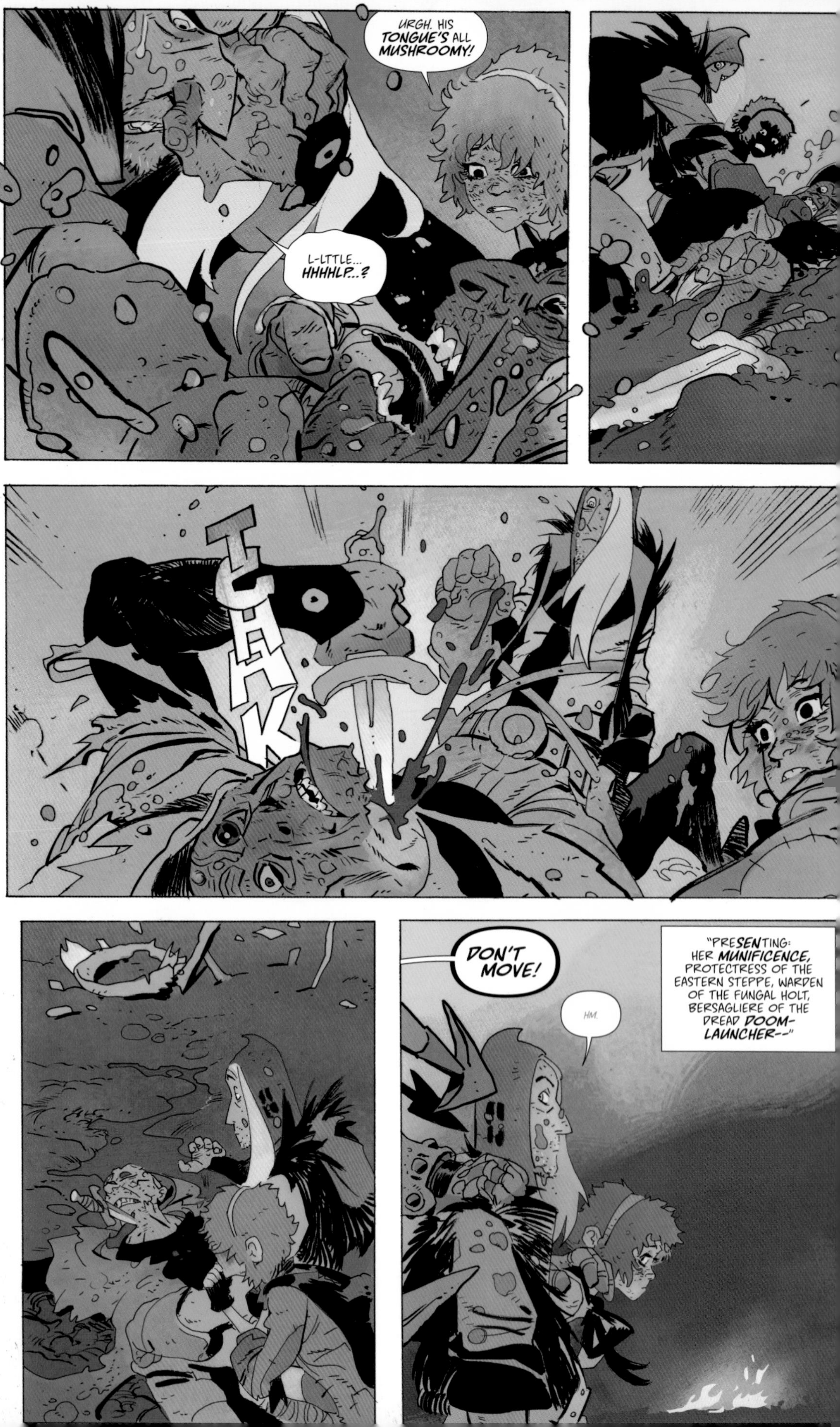
URGH. HIS TONGUE'S ALL MUSHROOMY!
L-LTTLE... HHHHLP...?
TCHAK
DON'T MOVE!
HM.
"PRESENTING: HER MUNIFICENCE, PROTECTRESS OF THE EASTERN STEPPE, WARDEN OF THE FUNGAL HOLT, BERSAGLIERE OF THE DREAD DOOM-LAUNCHER--"

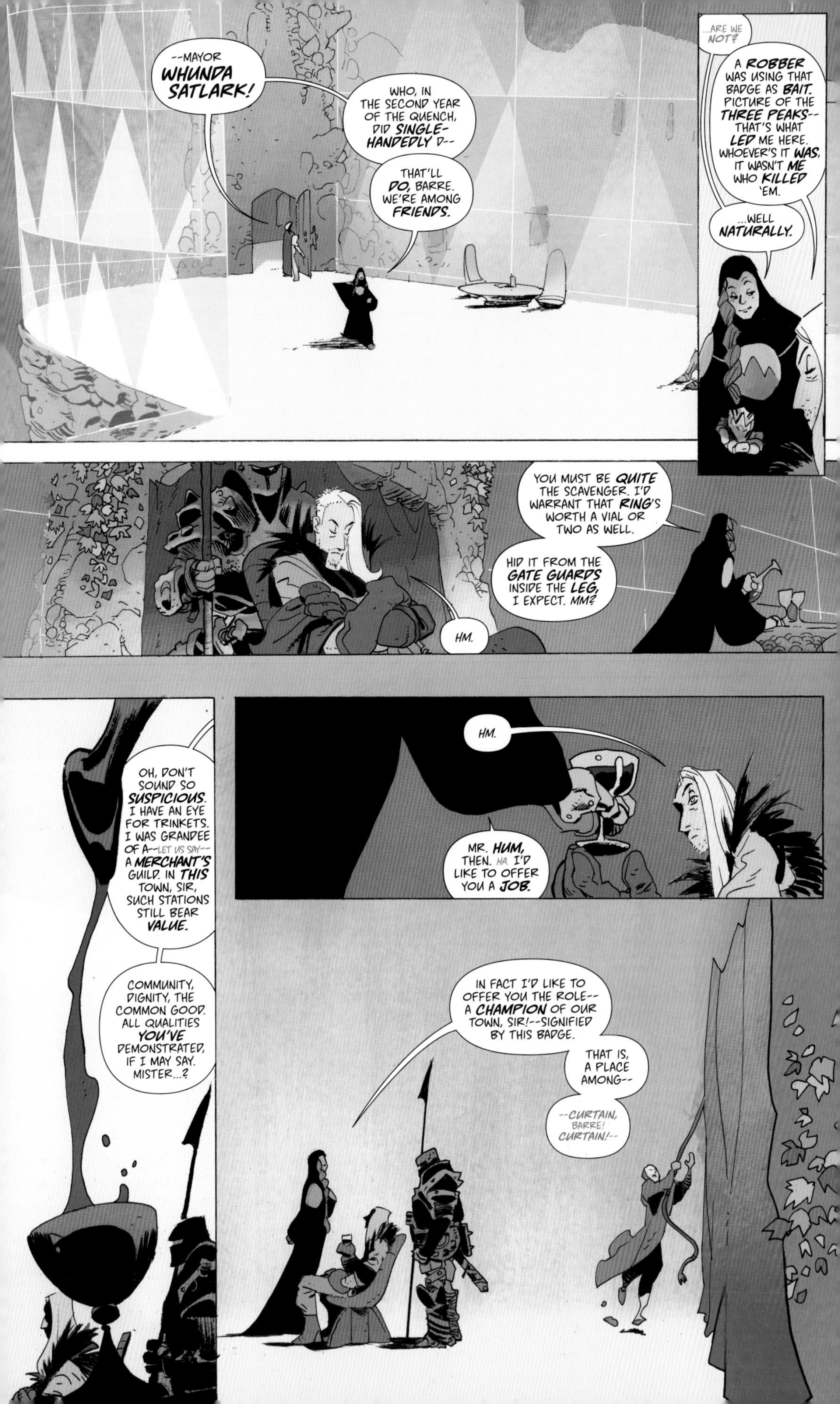

--MAYOR WHUNDA SATLARK!
WHO, IN THE SECOND YEAR OF THE QUENCH, DID SINGLE-HANDEDLY D--
THAT'LL DO, BARRE. WE'RE AMONG FRIENDS.
...ARE WE NOT?
A ROBBER WAS USING THAT BADGE AS BAIT. PICTURE OF THE THREE PEAKS--THAT'S WHAT LED ME HERE. WHOEVER'S IT WAS, IT WASN'T ME WHO KILLED 'EM.
...WELL NATURALLY.
YOU MUST BE QUITE THE SCAVENGER. I'D WARRANT THAT RING'S WORTH A VIAL OR TWO AS WELL.
HID IT FROM THE GATE GUARDS INSIDE THE LEG, I EXPECT. MM?
HM.
OH, DON'T SOUND SO SUSPICIOUS. I HAVE AN EYE FOR TRINKETS. I WAS GRANDEE OF A--LET US SAY--A MERCHANT'S GUILD. IN THIS TOWN, SIR, SUCH STATIONS STILL BEAR VALUE.
COMMUNITY, DIGNITY, THE COMMON GOOD. ALL QUALITIES YOU'VE DEMONSTRATED, IF I MAY SAY. MISTER...?
HM.
MR. HUM, THEN. HA. I'D LIKE TO OFFER YOU A JOB.
IN FACT I'D LIKE TO OFFER YOU THE ROLE--A CHAMPION OF OUR TOWN, SIR!--SIGNIFIED BY THIS BADGE.
THAT IS, A PLACE AMONG--
--CURTAIN, BARRE! CURTAIN!--

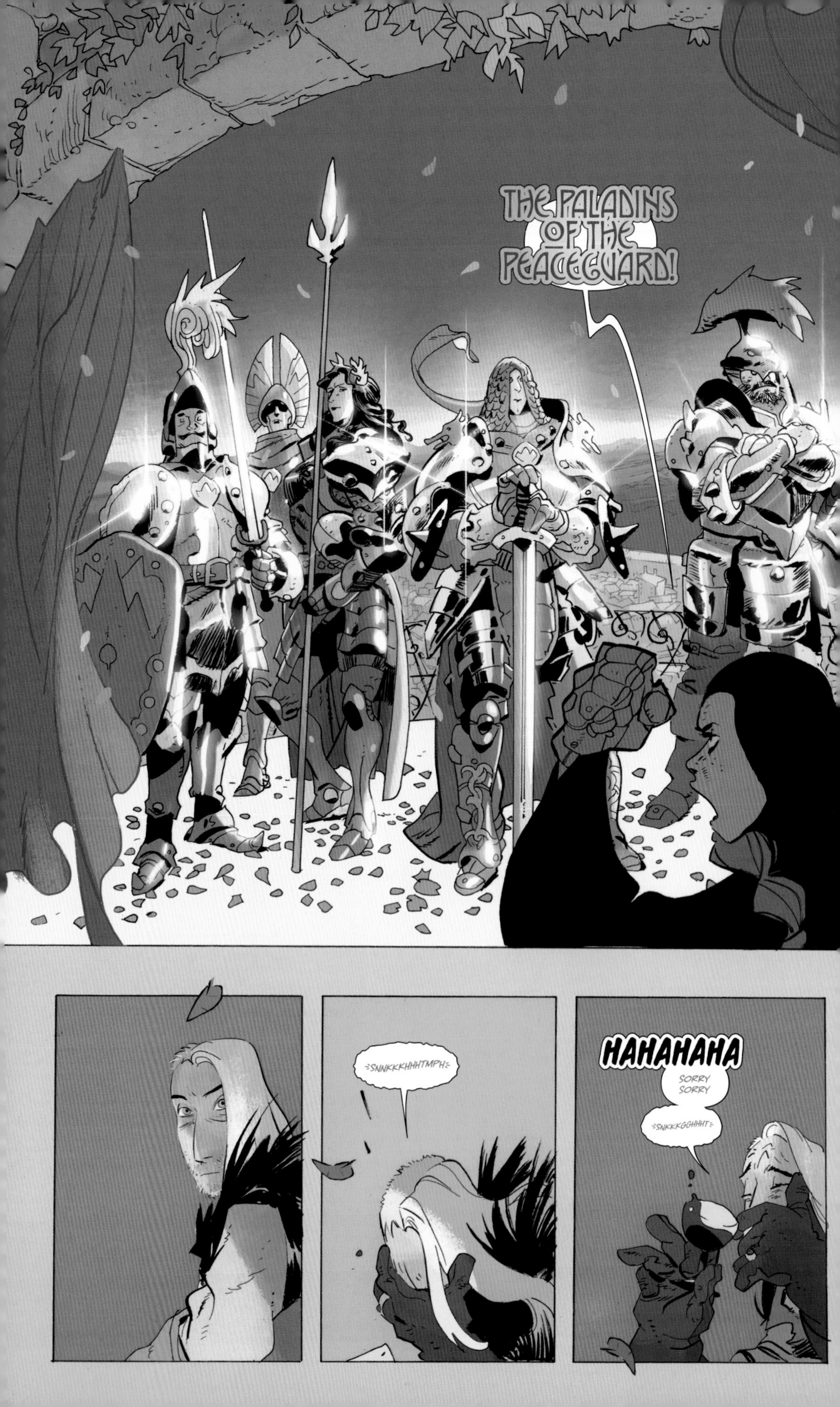
THE PALADINS OF THE PEACEGUARD!
SNNKKKHHHTMPH
HAHAHAHA
SORRY SORRY
SNKKKGGHHHT

SOMETHING **AMUSES**, MR. HUM? **THIS** WAY, PLEASE.

S-SORRY. IT'S JUST... ⸫HRM⸫ **LOOK**--ALL THIS STUFF. GUILDS. CHAMPIONS. **DIGNITY**. AND--

⸫SNNKKHHHT⸫

PALADINS. HAHAH.

SORRY.

I MEAN, IT WAS ALL PRETTY BLOODY STUPID EVEN **BEFORE** THE **QUENCH**. NO OFFENSE, LADS. BUT **NOW**? HEH.

BUT--LISTEN-- IT'S NOT **MY** PLACE TO SAY HOW TO RUN A TOWN. I'VE GOT MY **OWN** TROUBLES.

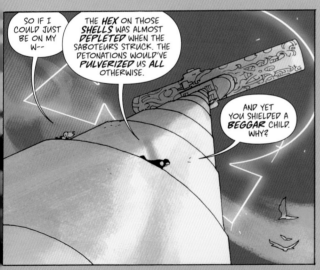

SO IF I COULD JUST BE ON MY **W**--

THE **HEX** ON THOSE **SHELLS** WAS ALMOST **DEPLETED** WHEN THE SABOTEURS STRUCK. THE DETONATIONS WOULD'VE **PULVERIZED** US **ALL** OTHERWISE.

AND YET YOU SHIELDED A **BEGGAR** CHILD. WHY?

HM.

MY EXPERIENCE? IT'S THE **UNDERDOGS** WHO MOST DESERVE THE **BONE**.

ARE WE NOT **ALL** UNDERDOGS, IN THIS WORLD? RIDGETOWN HAS **FEARFUL** ENEMIES, SIR.

BOLLOCKS. YOU GOT A TEAM OF PINHEADS IN **PLATE** AND A BOMB-LOBBER BIG AS A HOUSE. YOU AIN'T **UNDER** ANYONE.

MM. IF YOU **SAY** SO. AT LEAST ENJOY THE **VIEW** WHILE YOU'RE HERE?

I **INSIST**.

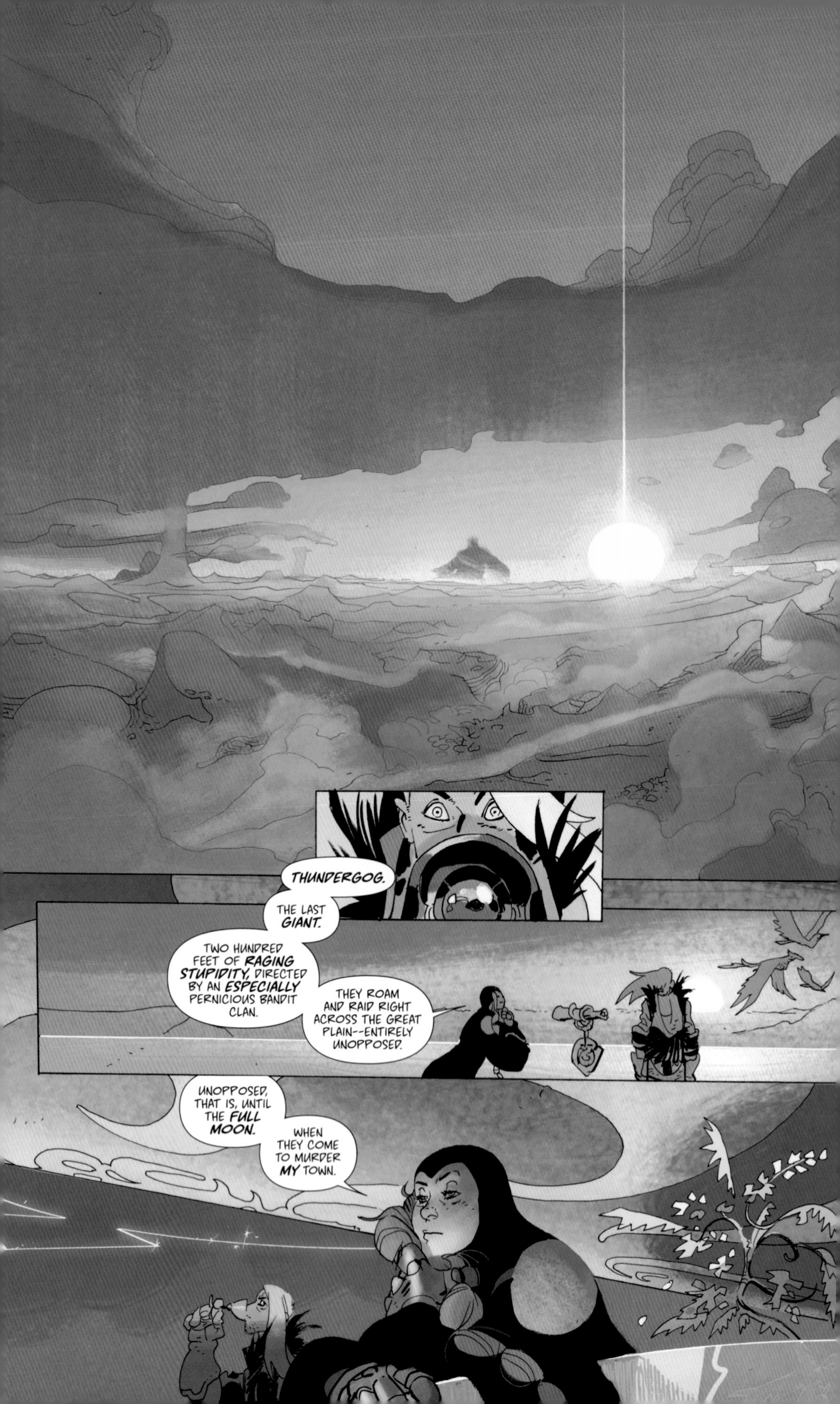
THUNDERGOG.
THE LAST GIANT.
TWO HUNDRED FEET OF RAGING STUPIDITY, DIRECTED BY AN ESPECIALLY PERNICIOUS BANDIT CLAN.
THEY ROAM AND RAID RIGHT ACROSS THE GREAT PLAIN--ENTIRELY UNOPPOSED.
UNOPPOSED, THAT IS, UNTIL THE FULL MOON.
WHEN THEY COME TO MURDER MY TOWN.

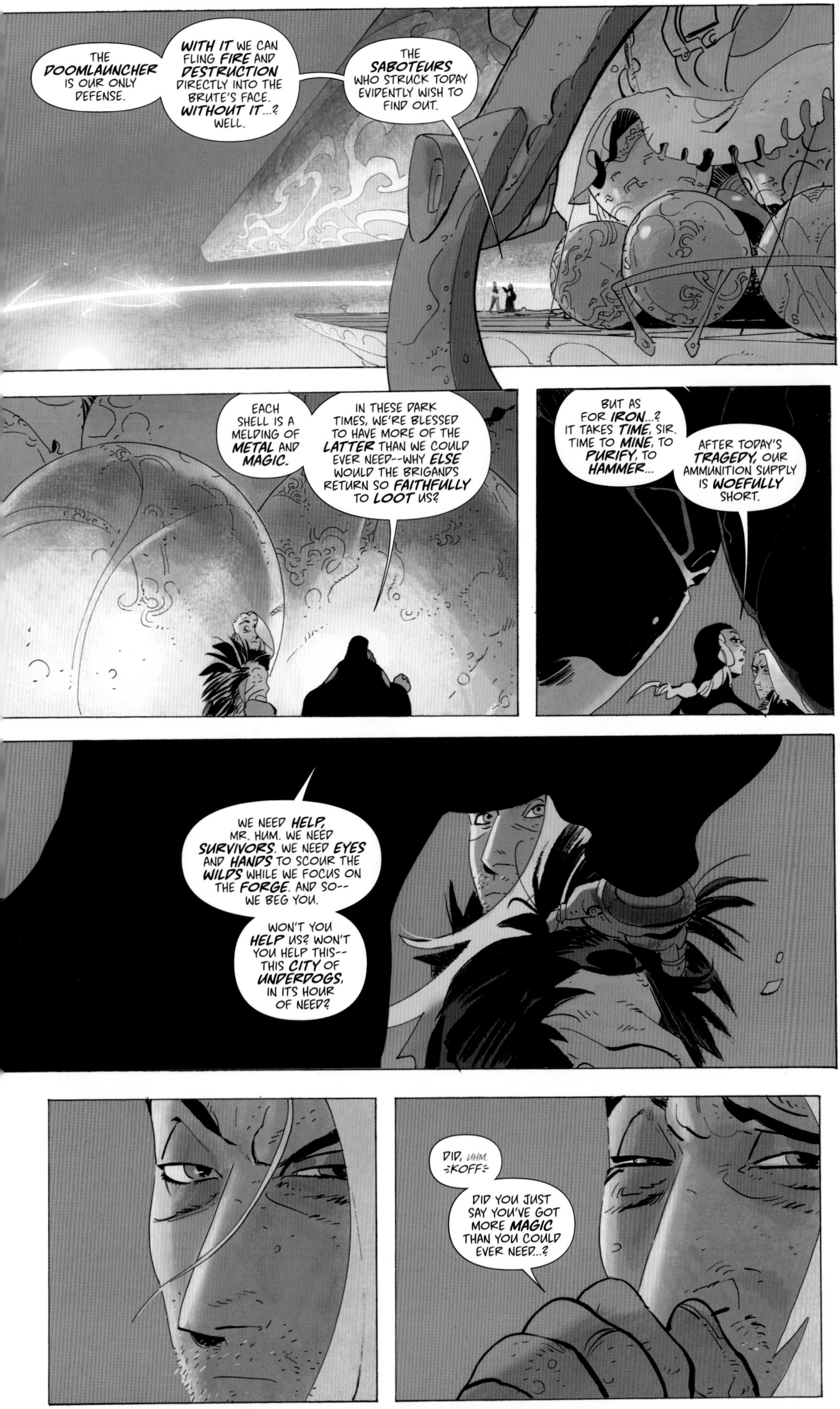

THE DOOMLAUNCHER IS OUR ONLY DEFENSE.
WITH IT WE CAN FLING FIRE AND DESTRUCTION DIRECTLY INTO THE BRUTE'S FACE. WITHOUT IT...? WELL.
THE SABOTEURS WHO STRUCK TODAY EVIDENTLY WISH TO FIND OUT.
EACH SHELL IS A MELDING OF METAL AND MAGIC.
IN THESE DARK TIMES, WE'RE BLESSED TO HAVE MORE OF THE LATTER THAN WE COULD EVER NEED--WHY ELSE WOULD THE BRIGANDS RETURN SO FAITHFULLY TO LOOT US?
BUT AS FOR IRON...? IT TAKES TIME, SIR. TIME TO MINE, TO PURIFY, TO HAMMER...
AFTER TODAY'S TRAGEDY, OUR AMMUNITION SUPPLY IS WOEFULLY SHORT.
WE NEED HELP, MR. HUM. WE NEED SURVIVORS. WE NEED EYES AND HANDS TO SCOUR THE WILDS WHILE WE FOCUS ON THE FORGE. AND SO-- WE BEG YOU.
WON'T YOU HELP US? WON'T YOU HELP THIS-- THIS CITY OF UNDERDOGS, IN ITS HOUR OF NEED?
DID, UHM. =KOFF=
DID YOU JUST SAY YOU'VE GOT MORE MAGIC THAN YOU COULD EVER NEED...?

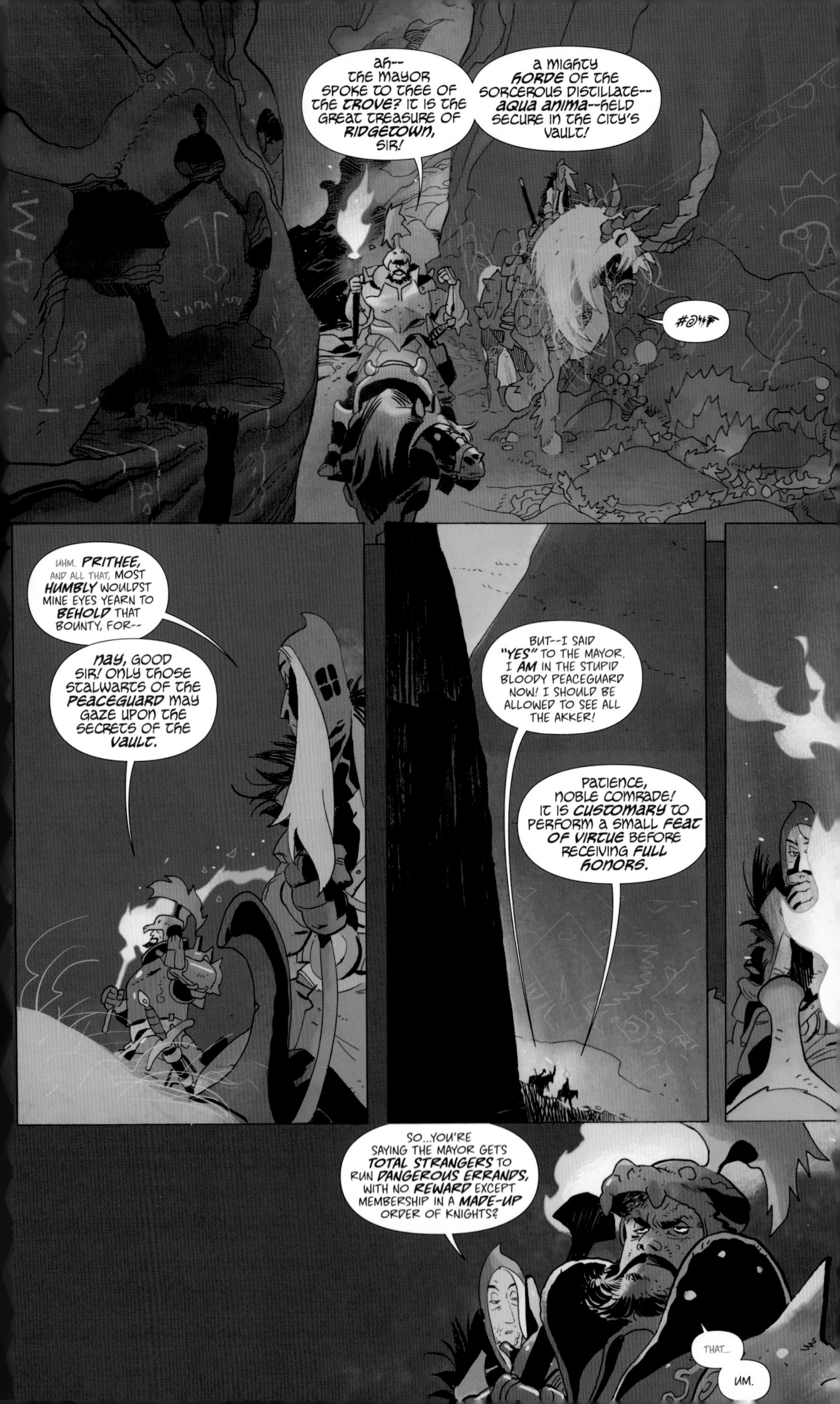
AH-- THE MAYOR SPOKE TO THEE OF THE TROVE? IT IS THE GREAT TREASURE OF RIDGETOWN, SIR!
A MIGHTY HORDE OF THE SORCEROUS DISTILLATE-- AQUA ANIMA--HELD SECURE IN THE CITY'S VAULT!
#@%F
UHM. PRITHEE, AND ALL THAT. MOST HUMBLY WOULDST MINE EYES YEARN TO BEHOLD THAT BOUNTY, FOR--
NAY, GOOD SIR! ONLY THOSE STALWARTS OF THE PEACEGUARD MAY GAZE UPON THE SECRETS OF THE VAULT.
BUT--I SAID "YES" TO THE MAYOR. I AM IN THE STUPID BLOODY PEACEGUARD NOW! I SHOULD BE ALLOWED TO SEE ALL THE AKKER!
PATIENCE, NOBLE COMRADE! IT IS CUSTOMARY TO PERFORM A SMALL FEAT OF VIRTUE BEFORE RECEIVING FULL HONORS.
SO...YOU'RE SAYING THE MAYOR GETS TOTAL STRANGERS TO RUN DANGEROUS ERRANDS, WITH NO REWARD EXCEPT MEMBERSHIP IN A MADE-UP ORDER OF KNIGHTS?
THAT...
UM.

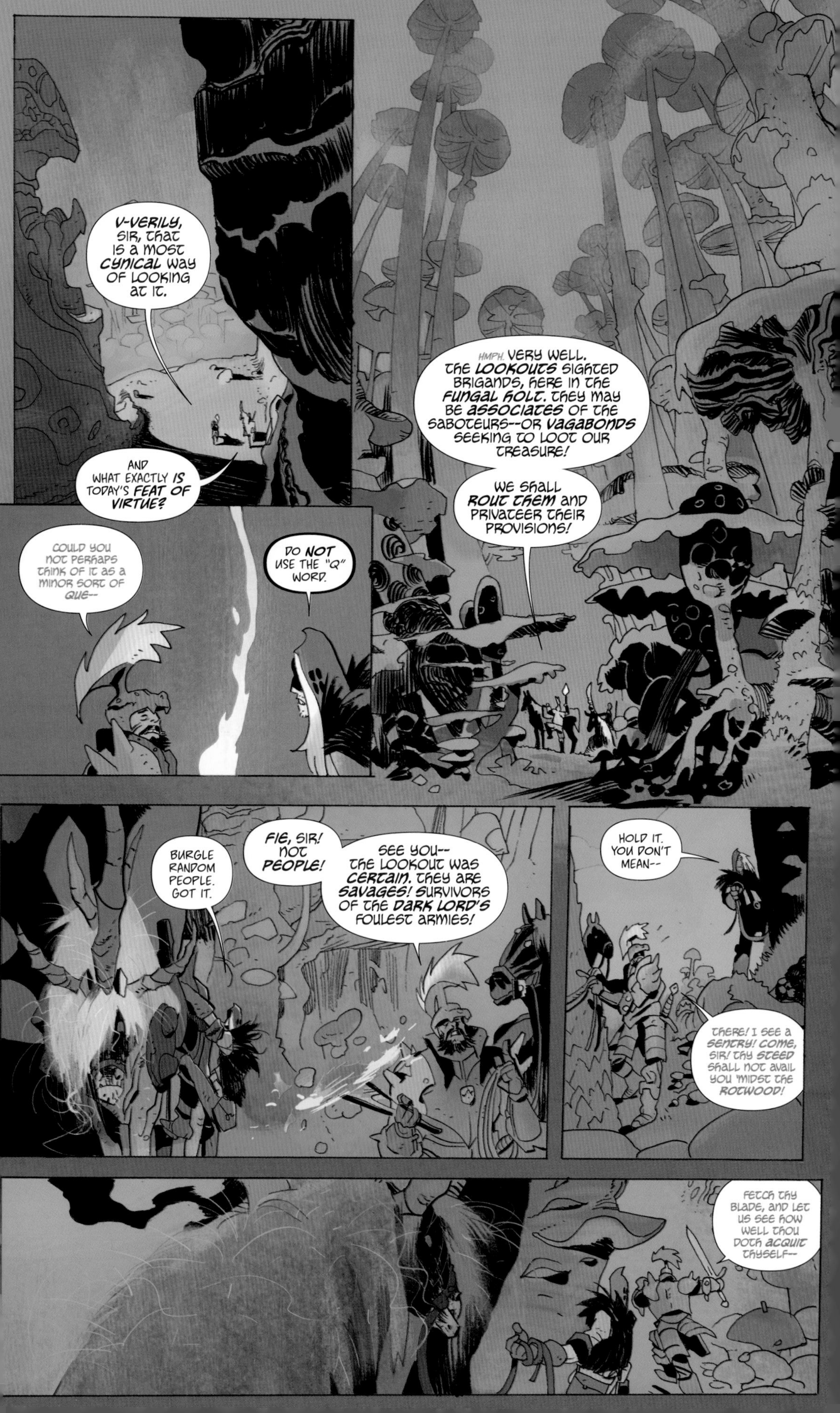

V-VERILY, SIR, THAT IS A MOST CYNICAL WAY OF LOOKING AT IT.
AND WHAT EXACTLY IS TODAY'S FEAT OF VIRTUE?
HMPH. VERY WELL. THE LOOKOUTS SIGHTED BRIGANDS, HERE IN THE FUNGAL HOLT. THEY MAY BE ASSOCIATES OF THE SABOTEURS--OR VAGABONDS SEEKING TO LOOT OUR TREASURE!
WE SHALL ROUT THEM AND PRIVATEER THEIR PROVISIONS!
COULD YOU NOT PERHAPS THINK OF IT AS A MINOR SORT OF QUE--
DO NOT USE THE "Q" WORD.
BURGLE RANDOM PEOPLE. GOT IT.
FIE, SIR! NOT PEOPLE!
SEE YOU-- THE LOOKOUT WAS CERTAIN. THEY ARE SAVAGES! SURVIVORS OF THE DARK LORD'S FOULEST ARMIES!
HOLD IT. YOU DON'T MEAN--
THERE! I SEE A SENTRY! COME, SIR! THY STEED SHALL NOT AVAIL YOU 'MIDST THE ROTWOOD!
FETCH THY BLADE, AND LET US SEE HOW WELL THOU DOTH ACQUIT THYSELF--

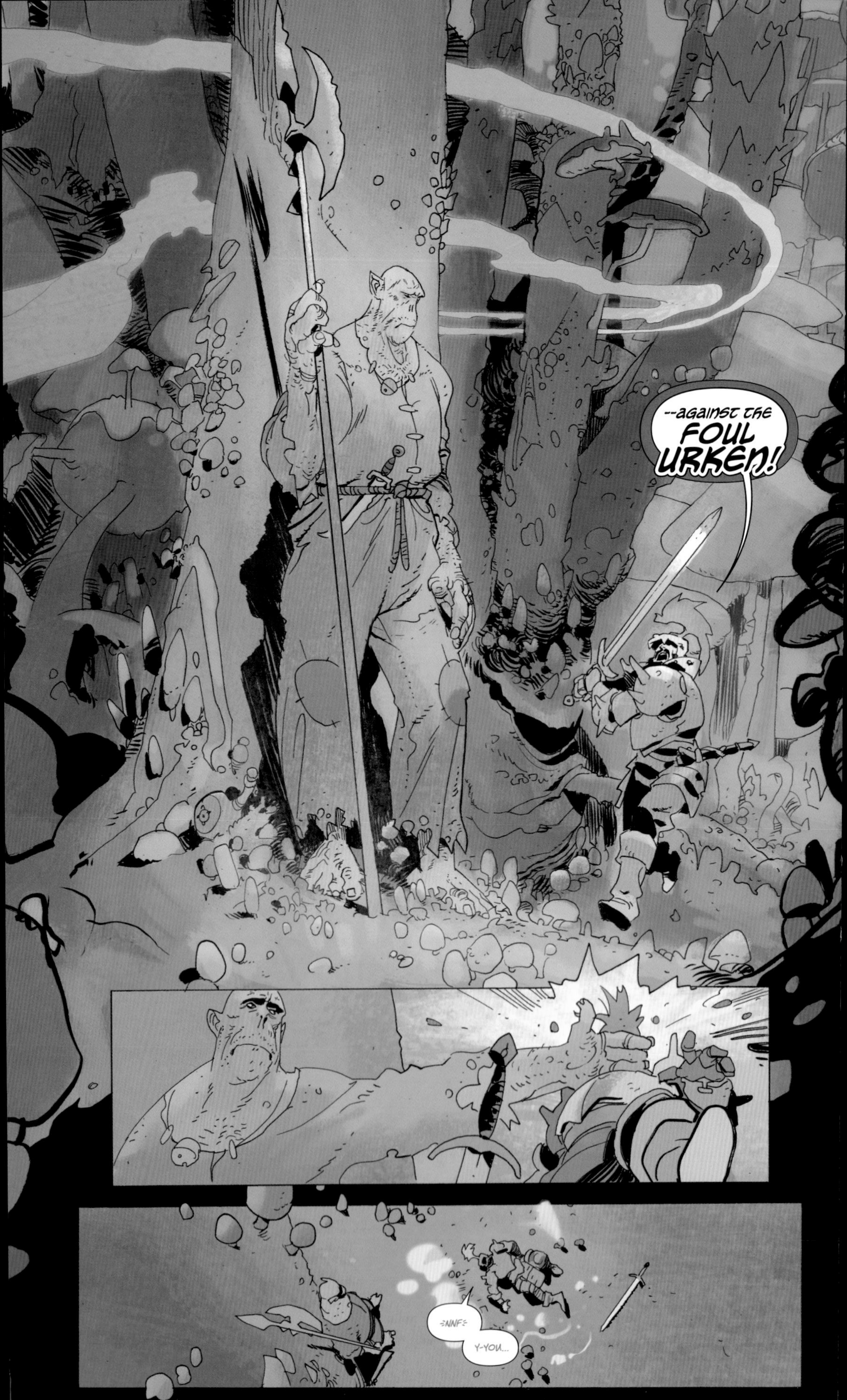
--against the FOUL URKEN!
NNF
Y-YOU...

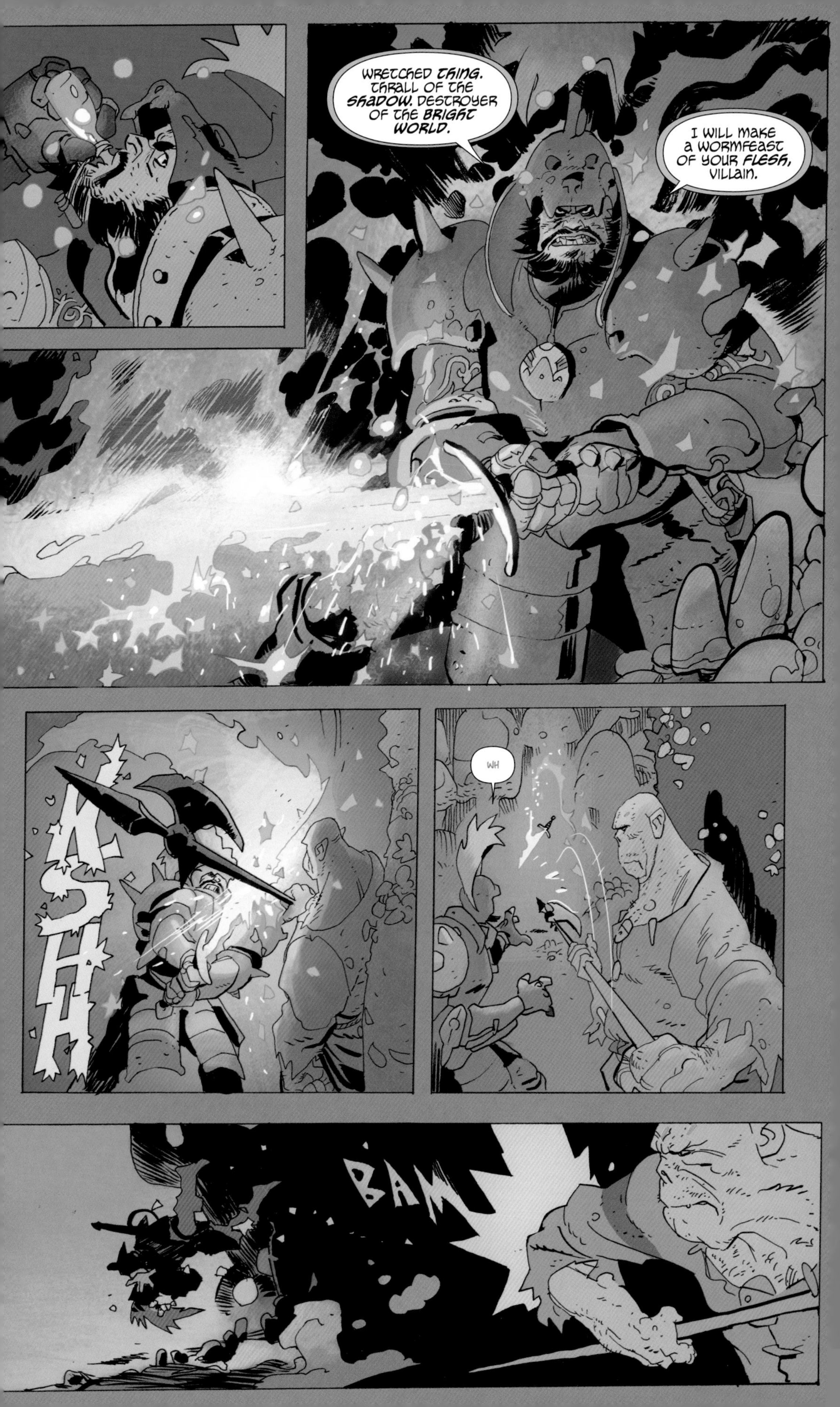
WRETCHED THING. THRALL OF THE SHADOW. DESTROYER OF THE BRIGHT WORLD.
I WILL MAKE A WORMFEAST OF YOUR FLESH, VILLAIN.
WH
BAM

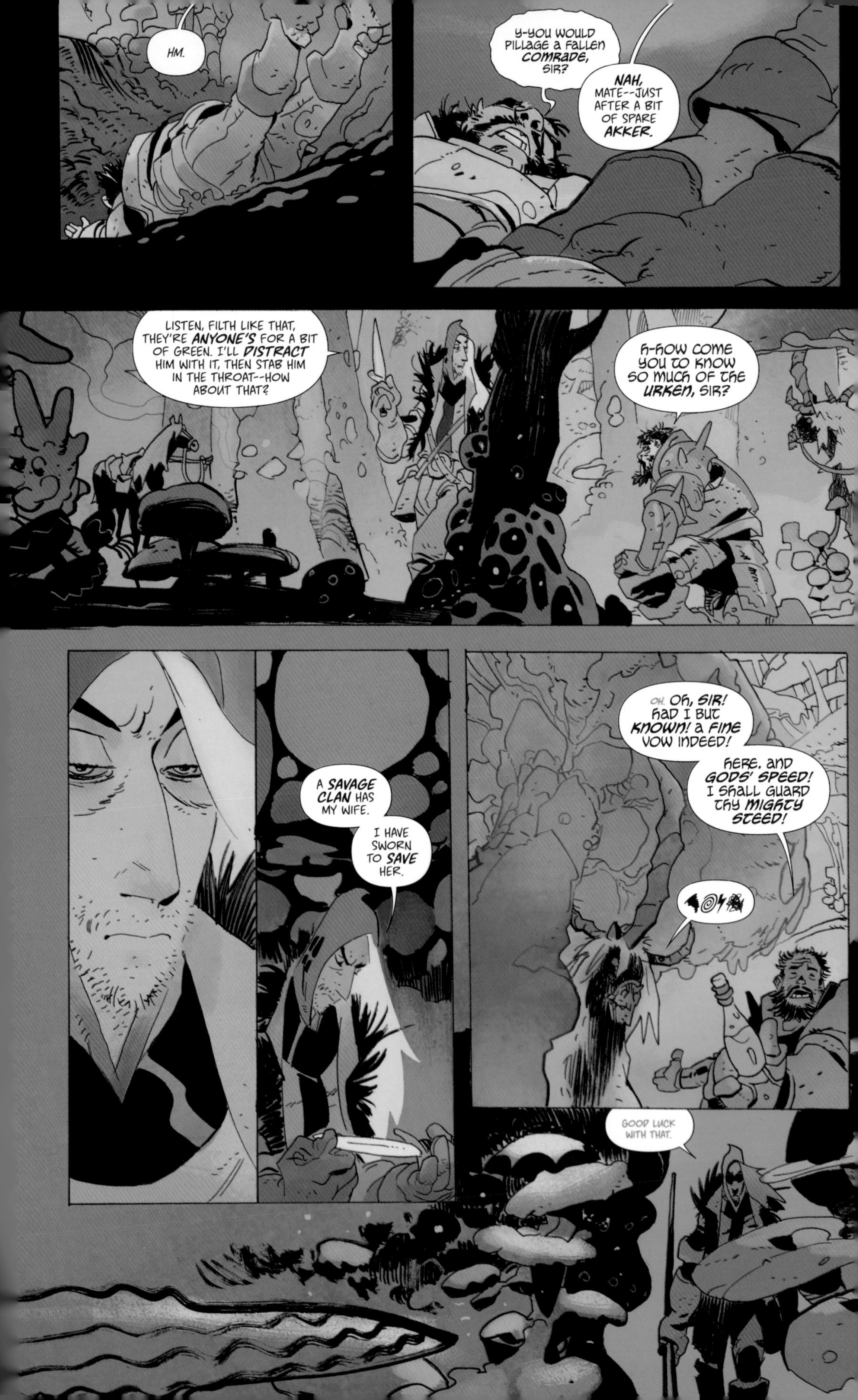
HM.
Y-YOU WOULD PILLAGE A FALLEN COMRADE, SIR?
NAH, MATE--JUST AFTER A BIT OF SPARE AKKER.
LISTEN, FILTH LIKE THAT, THEY'RE ANYONE'S FOR A BIT OF GREEN. I'LL DISTRACT HIM WITH IT, THEN STAB HIM IN THE THROAT--HOW ABOUT THAT?
H-HOW COME YOU TO KNOW SO MUCH OF THE URKEN, SIR?
A SAVAGE CLAN HAS MY WIFE.
I HAVE SWORN TO SAVE HER.
OH. OH, SIR! HAD I BUT KNOWN! A FINE VOW INDEED!
HERE. AND GODS' SPEED! I SHALL GUARD THY MIGHTY STEED!
GOOD LUCK WITH THAT.

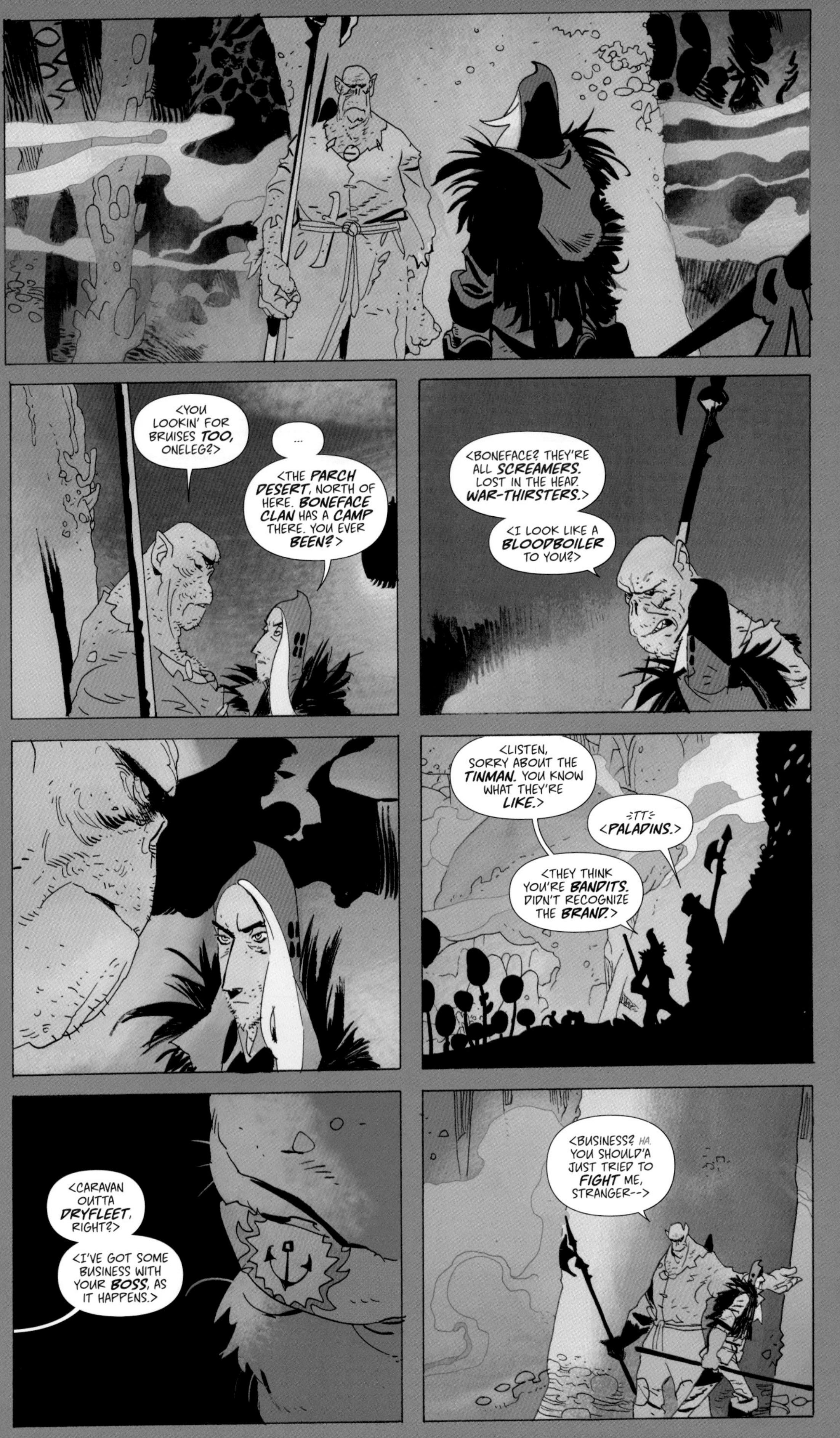
<YOU LOOKIN' FOR BRUISES TOO, ONELEG?>
...
<THE PARCH DESERT, NORTH OF HERE. BONEFACE CLAN HAS A CAMP THERE. YOU EVER BEEN?>
<BONEFACE? THEY'RE ALL SCREAMERS. LOST IN THE HEAD. WAR-THIRSTERS.>
<I LOOK LIKE A BLOODBOILER TO YOU?>
<LISTEN, SORRY ABOUT THE TINMAN. YOU KNOW WHAT THEY'RE LIKE.>
TT
<PALADINS.>
<THEY THINK YOU'RE BANDITS. DIDN'T RECOGNIZE THE BRAND.>
<CARAVAN OUTTA DRYFLEET, RIGHT?>
<I'VE GOT SOME BUSINESS WITH YOUR BOSS, AS IT HAPPENS.>
<BUSINESS? HA. YOU SHOULD'A JUST TRIED TO FIGHT ME, STRANGER-->

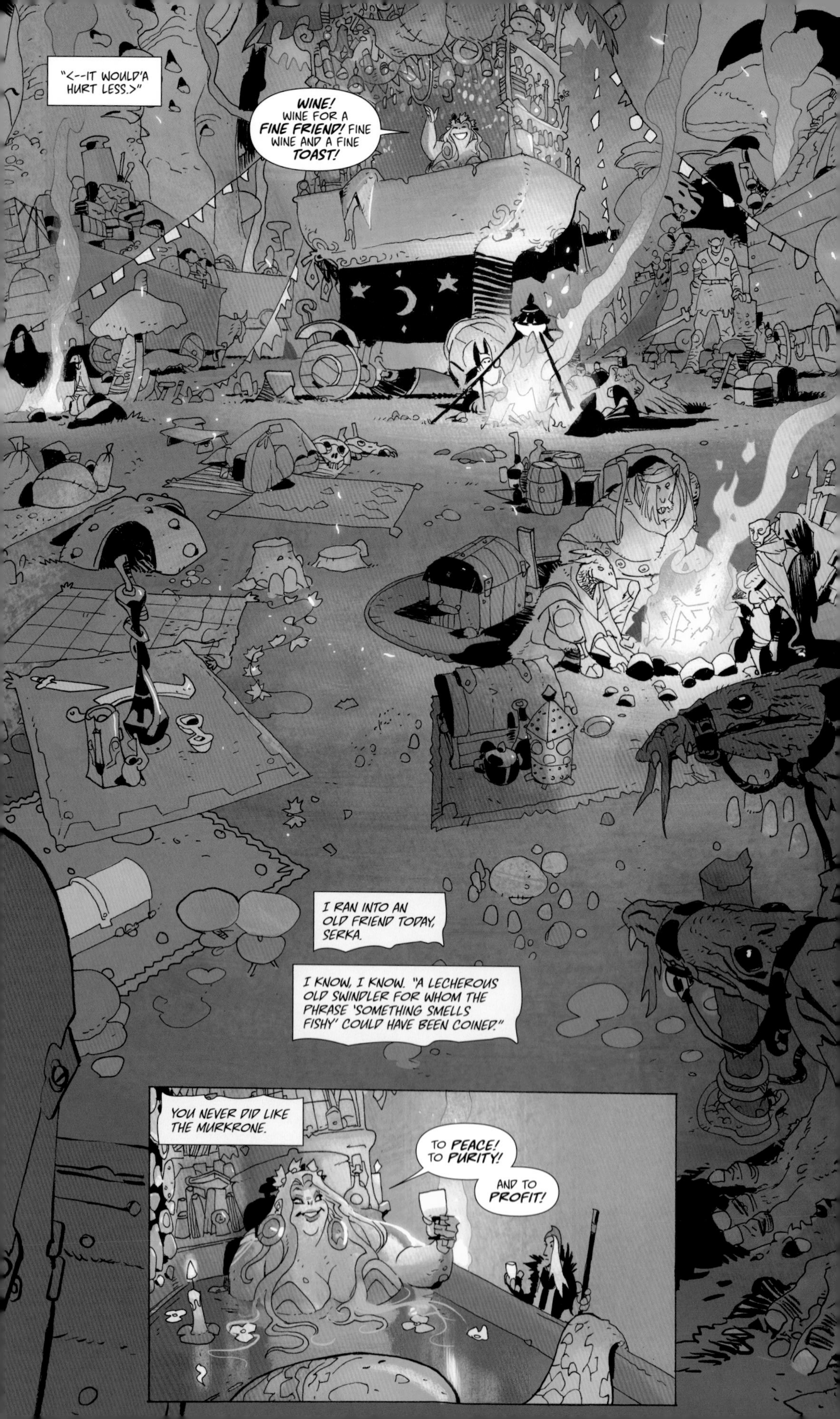

"<--IT WOULD'A HURT LESS.>"
WINE! WINE FOR A FINE FRIEND! FINE WINE AND A FINE TOAST!
I RAN INTO AN OLD FRIEND TODAY, SERKA.
I KNOW, I KNOW. "A LECHEROUS OLD SWINDLER FOR WHOM THE PHRASE 'SOMETHING SMELLS FISHY' COULD HAVE BEEN COINED."
YOU NEVER DID LIKE THE MURKRONE.
TO PEACE! TO PURITY!
AND TO PROFIT!

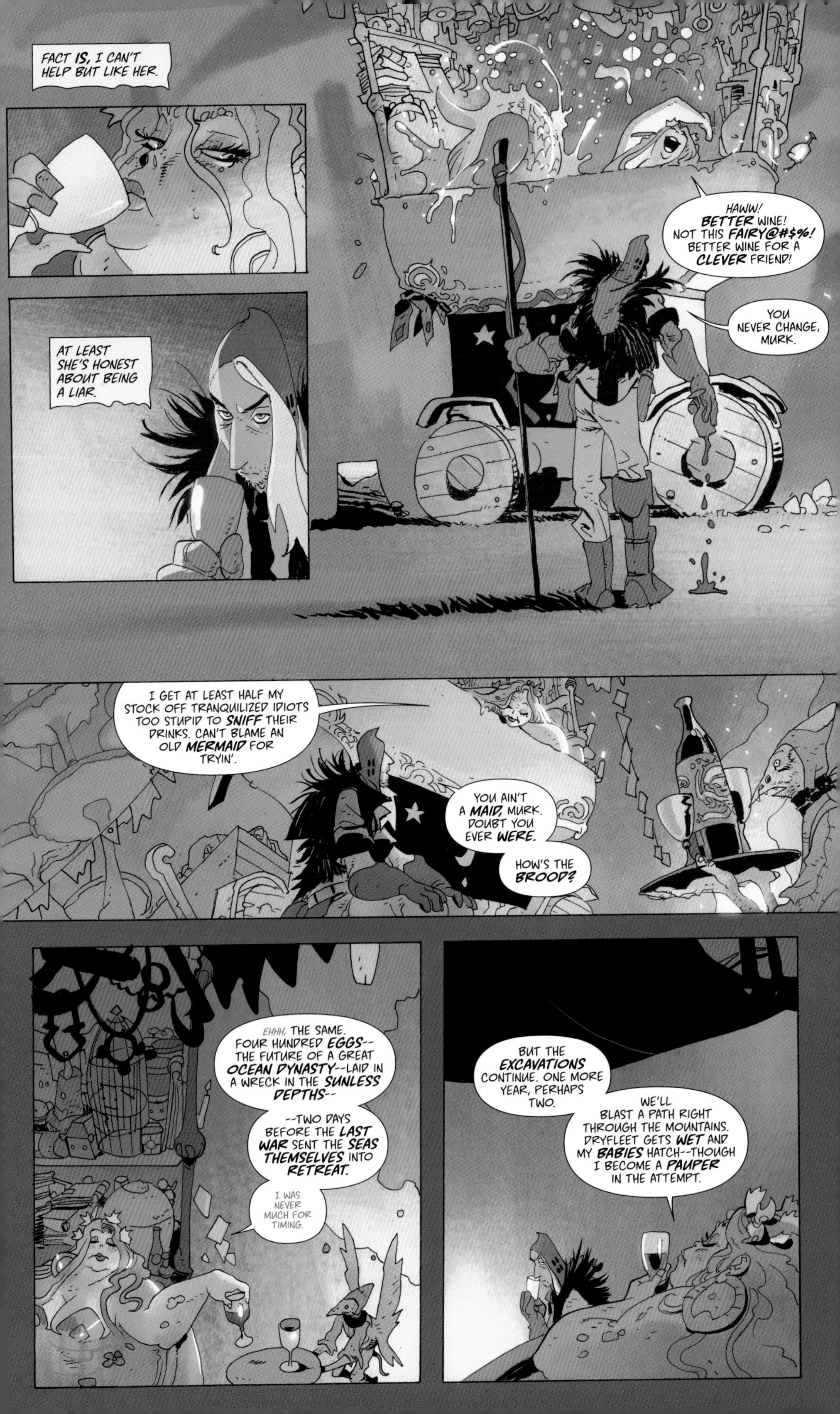

FACT IS, I CAN'T HELP BUT LIKE HER.
AT LEAST SHE'S HONEST ABOUT BEING A LIAR.
HAWW! BETTER WINE! NOT THIS FAIRY@#$%! BETTER WINE FOR A CLEVER FRIEND!
YOU NEVER CHANGE, MURK.
I GET AT LEAST HALF MY STOCK OFF TRANQUILIZED IDIOTS TOO STUPID TO SNIFF THEIR DRINKS. CAN'T BLAME AN OLD MERMAID FOR TRYIN'.
YOU AIN'T A MAID, MURK. DOUBT YOU EVER WERE.
HOW'S THE BROOD?
EHHH, THE SAME. FOUR HUNDRED EGGS--THE FUTURE OF A GREAT OCEAN DYNASTY--LAID IN A WRECK IN THE SUNLESS DEPTHS--
--TWO DAYS BEFORE THE LAST WAR SENT THE SEAS THEMSELVES INTO RETREAT.
I WAS NEVER MUCH FOR TIMING.
BUT THE EXCAVATIONS CONTINUE. ONE MORE YEAR, PERHAPS TWO.
WE'LL BLAST A PATH RIGHT THROUGH THE MOUNTAINS. DRYFLEET GETS WET AND MY BABIES HATCH--THOUGH I BECOME A PAUPER IN THE ATTEMPT.

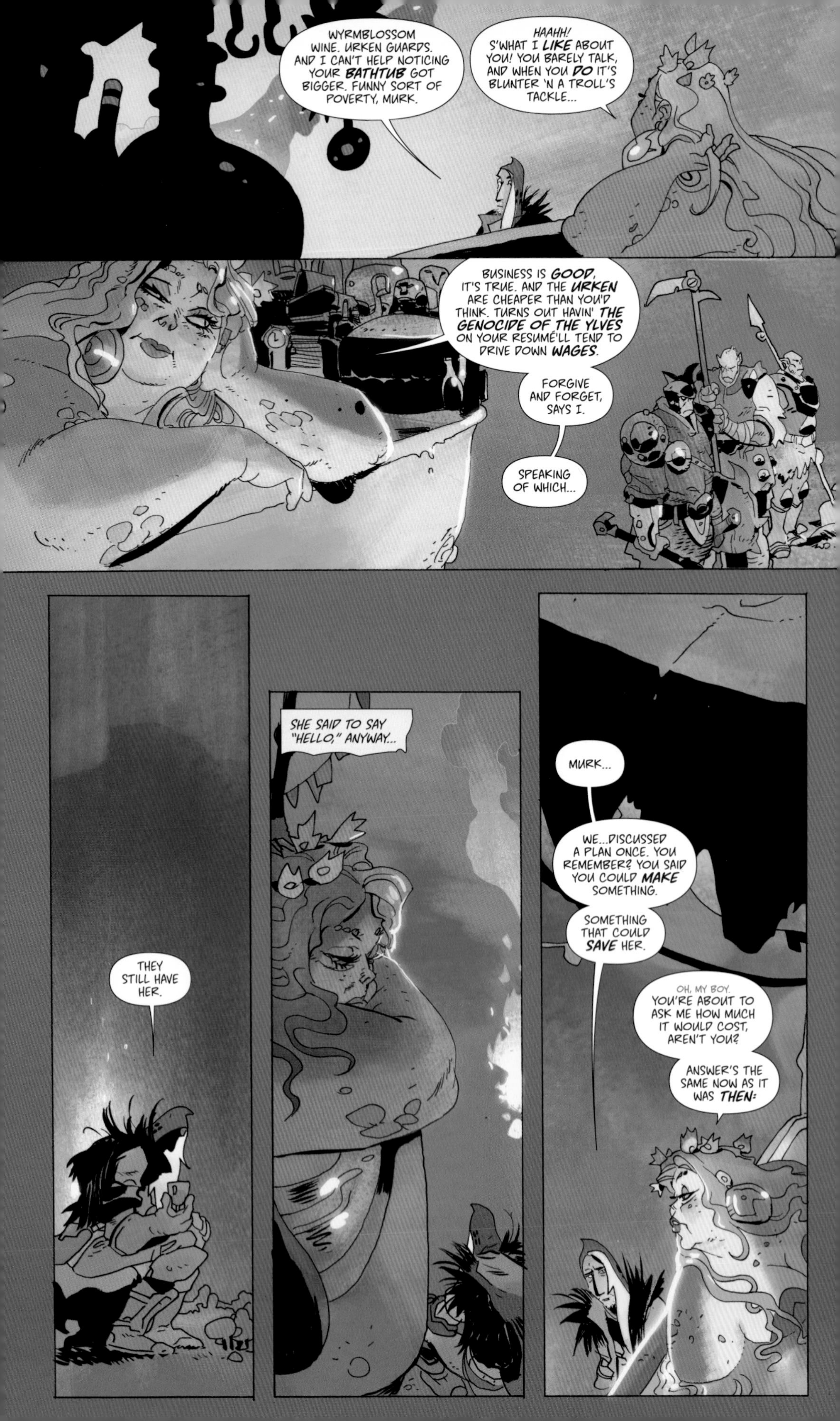
WYRMBLOSSOM WINE. URKEN GUARDS. AND I CAN'T HELP NOTICING YOUR BATHTUB GOT BIGGER. FUNNY SORT OF POVERTY, MURK.
HAAHH! S'WHAT I LIKE ABOUT YOU! YOU BARELY TALK, AND WHEN YOU DO IT'S BLUNTER 'N A TROLL'S TACKLE...
BUSINESS IS GOOD, IT'S TRUE. AND THE URKEN ARE CHEAPER THAN YOU'D THINK. TURNS OUT HAVIN' THE GENOCIDE OF THE YLVES ON YOUR RESUMÉ'LL TEND TO DRIVE DOWN WAGES.
FORGIVE AND FORGET, SAYS I.
SPEAKING OF WHICH...
THEY STILL HAVE HER.
SHE SAID TO SAY "HELLO," ANYWAY...
MURK...
WE...DISCUSSED A PLAN ONCE. YOU REMEMBER? YOU SAID YOU COULD MAKE SOMETHING.
SOMETHING THAT COULD SAVE HER.
OH, MY BOY. YOU'RE ABOUT TO ASK ME HOW MUCH IT WOULD COST, AREN'T YOU?
ANSWER'S THE SAME NOW AS IT WAS THEN:

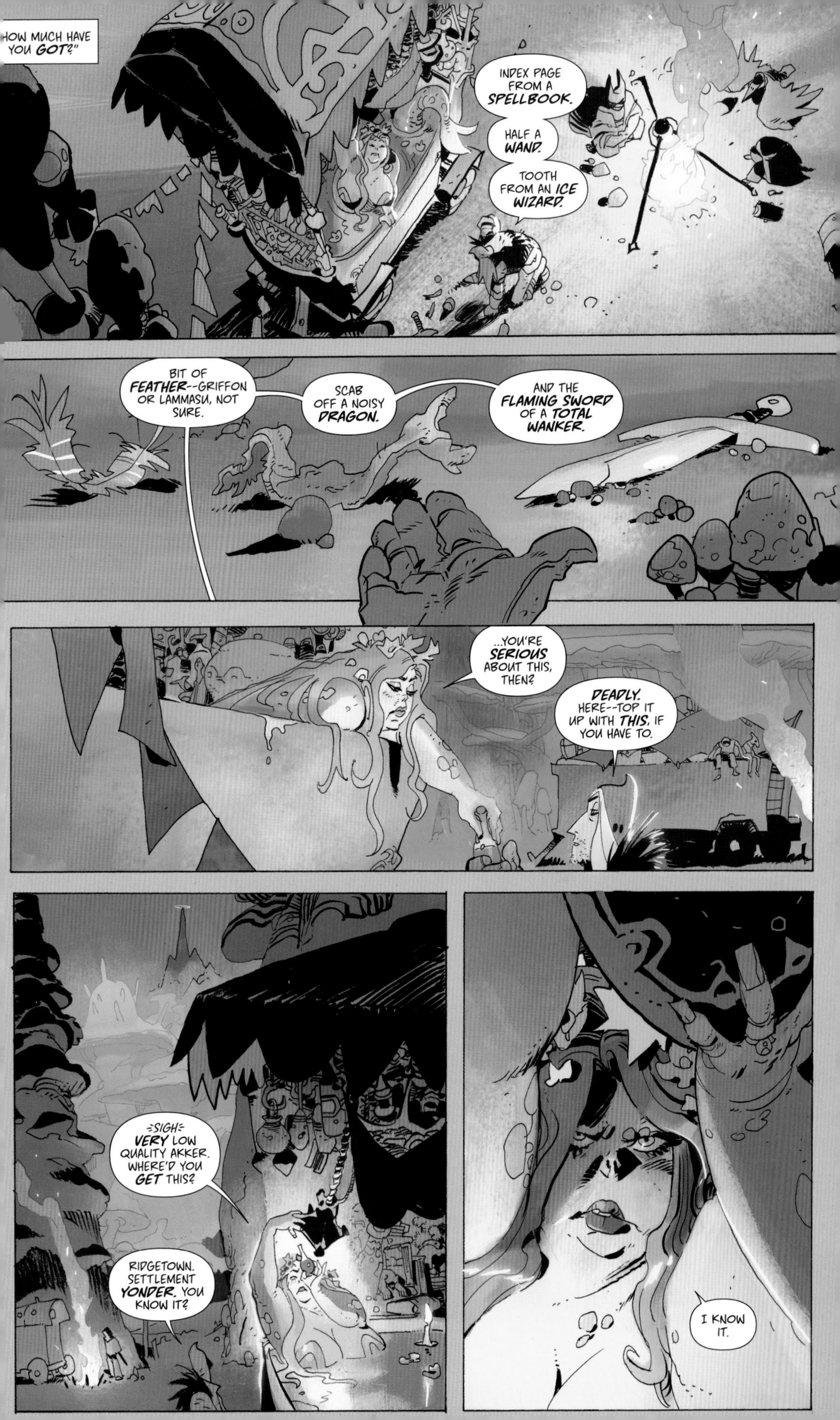

HOW MUCH HAVE YOU GOT?"
INDEX PAGE FROM A SPELLBOOK.
HALF A WAND.
TOOTH FROM AN ICE WIZARD.
BIT OF FEATHER--GRIFFON OR LAMMASU, NOT SURE.
SCAB OFF A NOISY DRAGON.
AND THE FLAMING SWORD OF A TOTAL WANKER.
...YOU'RE SERIOUS ABOUT THIS, THEN?
DEADLY. HERE--TOP IT UP WITH THIS, IF YOU HAVE TO.
=SIGH= VERY LOW QUALITY AKKER. WHERE'D YOU GET THIS?
RIDGETOWN. SETTLEMENT YONDER. YOU KNOW IT?
I KNOW IT.

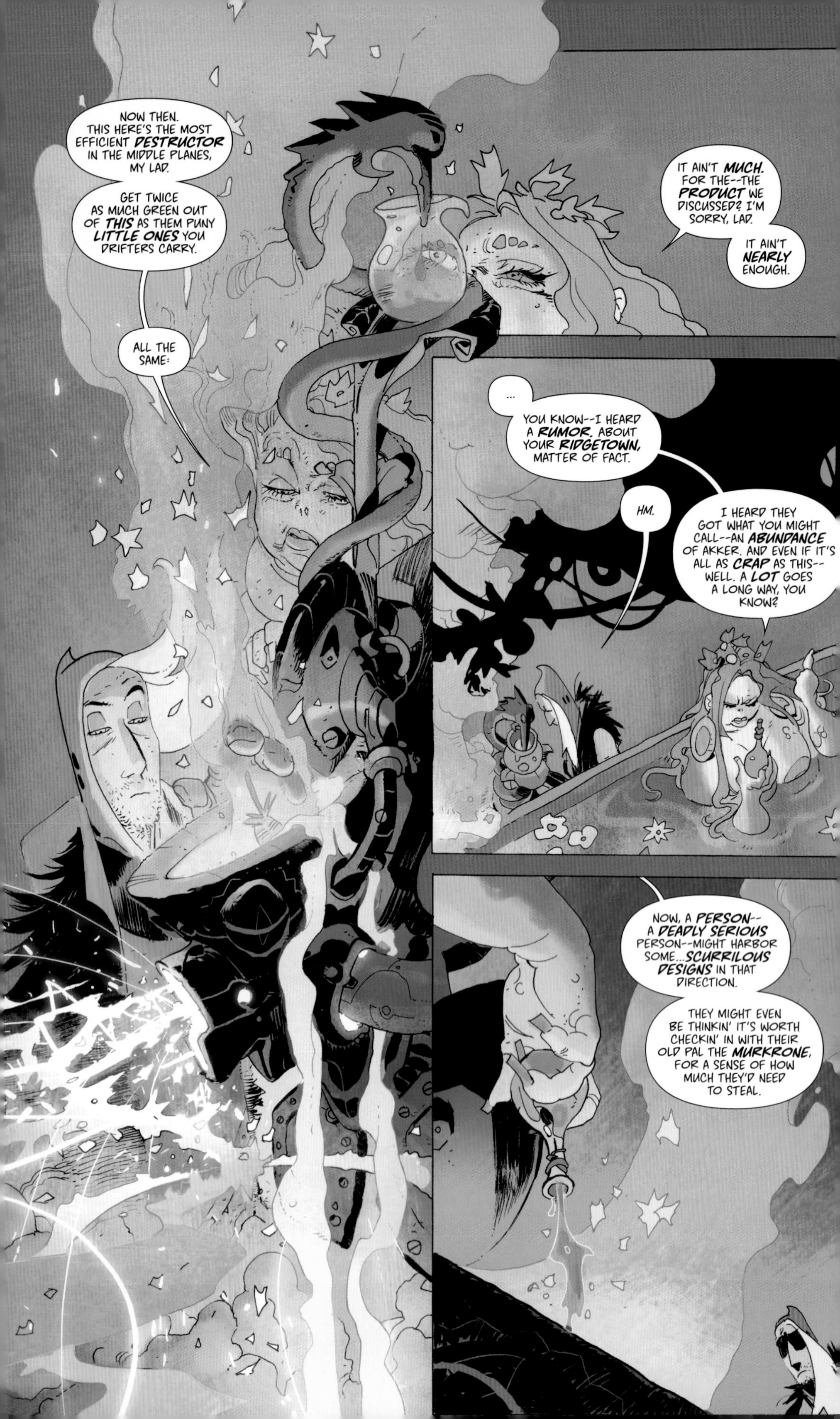

NOW THEN. THIS HERE'S THE MOST EFFICIENT DESTRUCTOR IN THE MIDDLE PLANES, MY LAD.
GET TWICE AS MUCH GREEN OUT OF THIS AS THEM PUNY LITTLE ONES YOU DRIFTERS CARRY.
ALL THE SAME:
IT AIN'T MUCH. FOR THE--THE PRODUCT WE DISCUSSED? I'M SORRY, LAD.
IT AIN'T NEARLY ENOUGH.
...
YOU KNOW--I HEARD A RUMOR. ABOUT YOUR RIDGETOWN, MATTER OF FACT.
HM.
I HEARD THEY GOT WHAT YOU MIGHT CALL--AN ABUNDANCE OF AKKER. AND EVEN IF IT'S ALL AS CRAP AS THIS--WELL. A LOT GOES A LONG WAY, YOU KNOW?
NOW, A PERSON--A DEADLY SERIOUS PERSON--MIGHT HARBOR SOME...SCURRILOUS DESIGNS IN THAT DIRECTION.
THEY MIGHT EVEN BE THINKIN' IT'S WORTH CHECKIN' IN WITH THEIR OLD PAL THE MURKRONE, FOR A SENSE OF HOW MUCH THEY'D NEED TO STEAL.

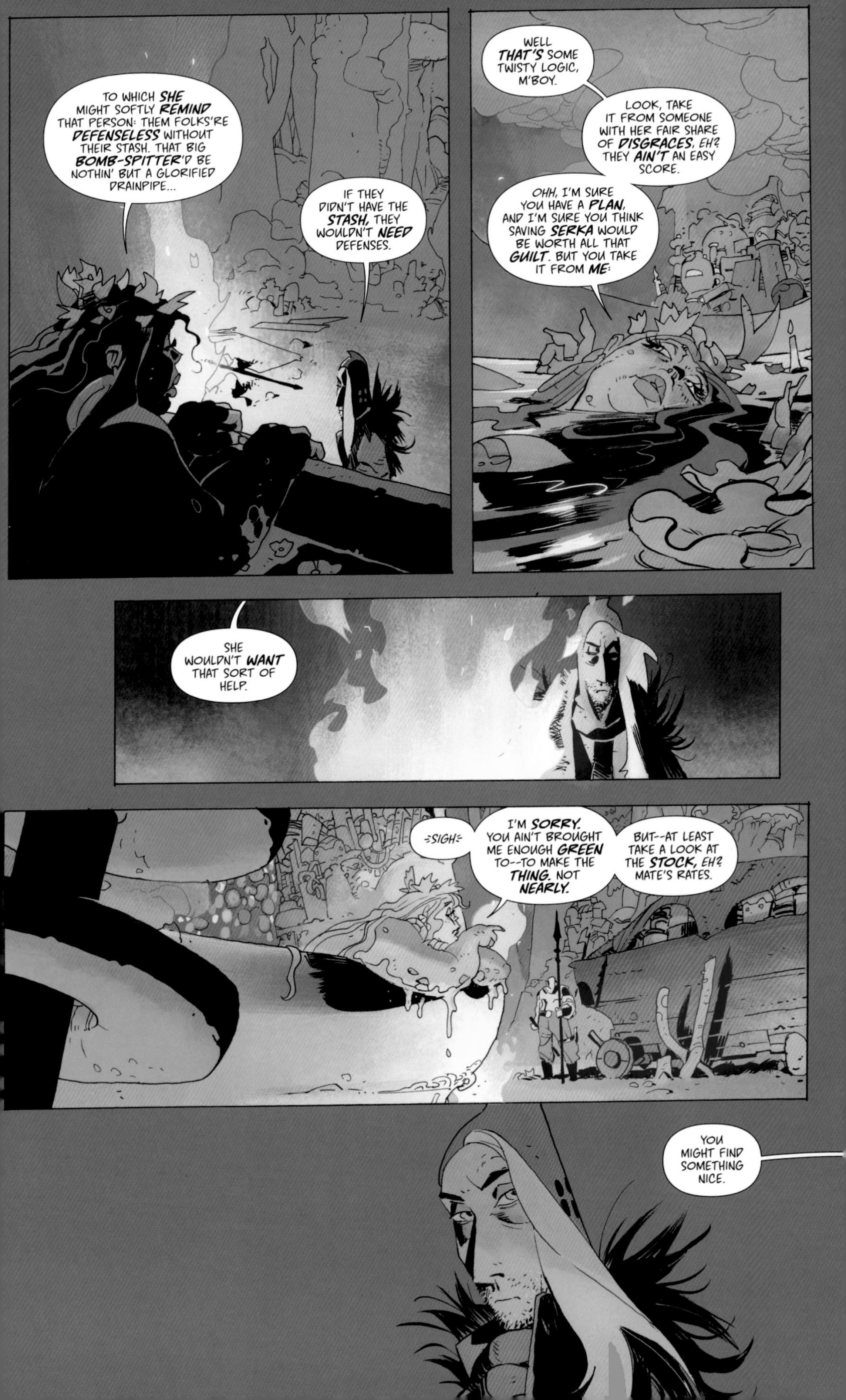
TO WHICH SHE MIGHT SOFTLY REMIND THAT PERSON: THEM FOLKS'RE DEFENSELESS WITHOUT THEIR STASH. THAT BIG BOMB-SPITTER'D BE NOTHIN' BUT A GLORIFIED DRAINPIPE...
IF THEY DIDN'T HAVE THE STASH, THEY WOULDN'T NEED DEFENSES.
WELL THAT'S SOME TWISTY LOGIC, M'BOY.
LOOK, TAKE IT FROM SOMEONE WITH HER FAIR SHARE OF DISGRACES, EH? THEY AIN'T AN EASY SCORE.
OHH, I'M SURE YOU HAVE A PLAN, AND I'M SURE YOU THINK SAVING SERKA WOULD BE WORTH ALL THAT GUILT. BUT YOU TAKE IT FROM ME:
SHE WOULDN'T WANT THAT SORT OF HELP.
=SIGH=
I'M SORRY. YOU AIN'T BROUGHT ME ENOUGH GREEN TO--TO MAKE THE THING. NOT NEARLY.
BUT--AT LEAST TAKE A LOOK AT THE STOCK, EH? MATE'S RATES.
YOU MIGHT FIND SOMETHING NICE.

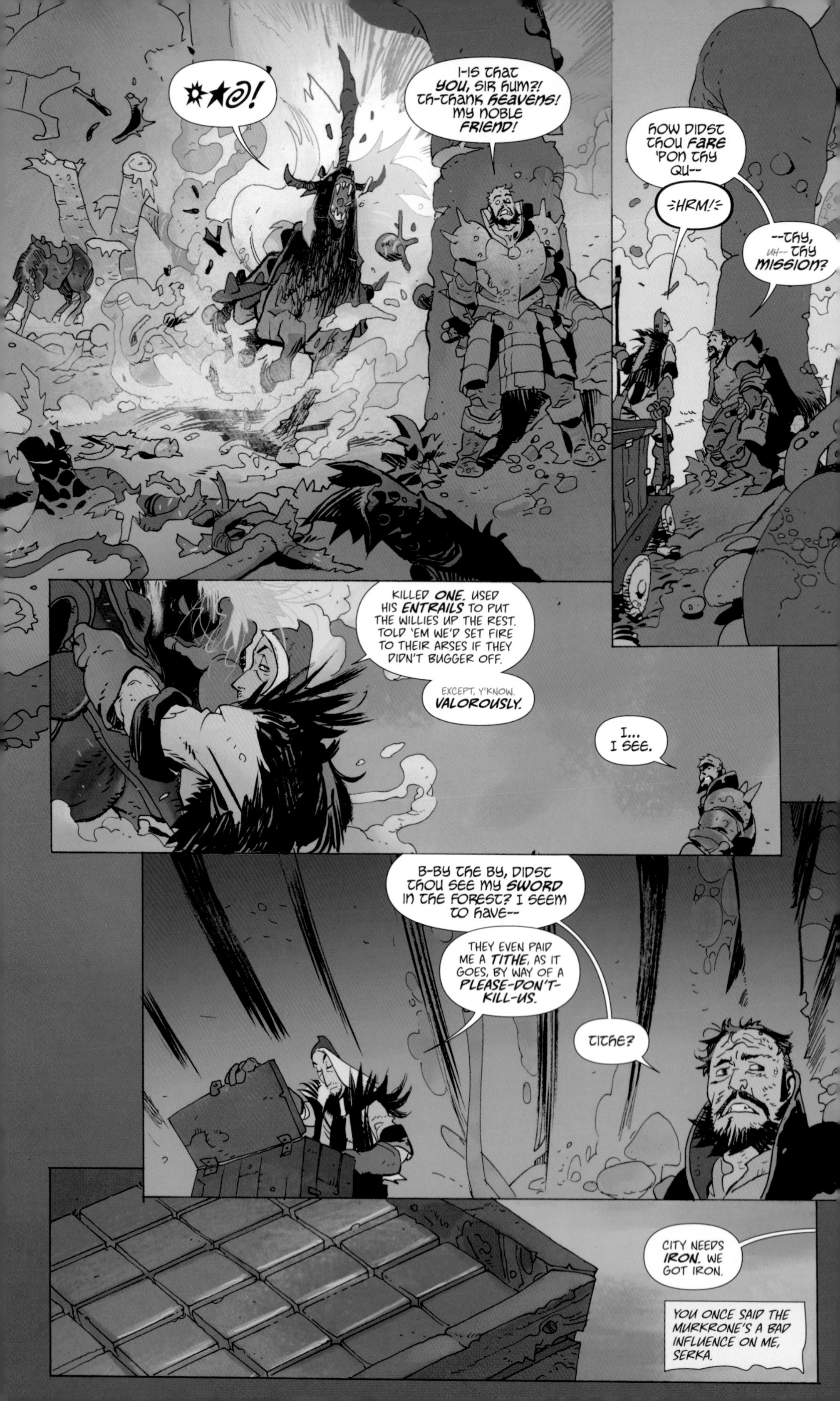

✲★@!
I-IS THAT YOU, SIR HUM?! TH-THANK HEAVENS! MY NOBLE FRIEND!
HOW DIDST THOU FARE 'PON THY QU--
HRM!
--THY, UH-- THY MISSION?
KILLED ONE. USED HIS ENTRAILS TO PUT THE WILLIES UP THE REST. TOLD 'EM WE'D SET FIRE TO THEIR ARSES IF THEY DIDN'T BUGGER OFF.
EXCEPT, Y'KNOW. VALOROUSLY.
I... I SEE.
B-BY THE BY, DIDST THOU SEE MY SWORD IN THE FOREST? I SEEM TO HAVE--
THEY EVEN PAID ME A TITHE, AS IT GOES, BY WAY OF A PLEASE-DON'T-KILL-US.
TITHE?
CITY NEEDS IRON. WE GOT IRON.
YOU ONCE SAID THE MURKRONE'S A BAD INFLUENCE ON ME, SERKA.

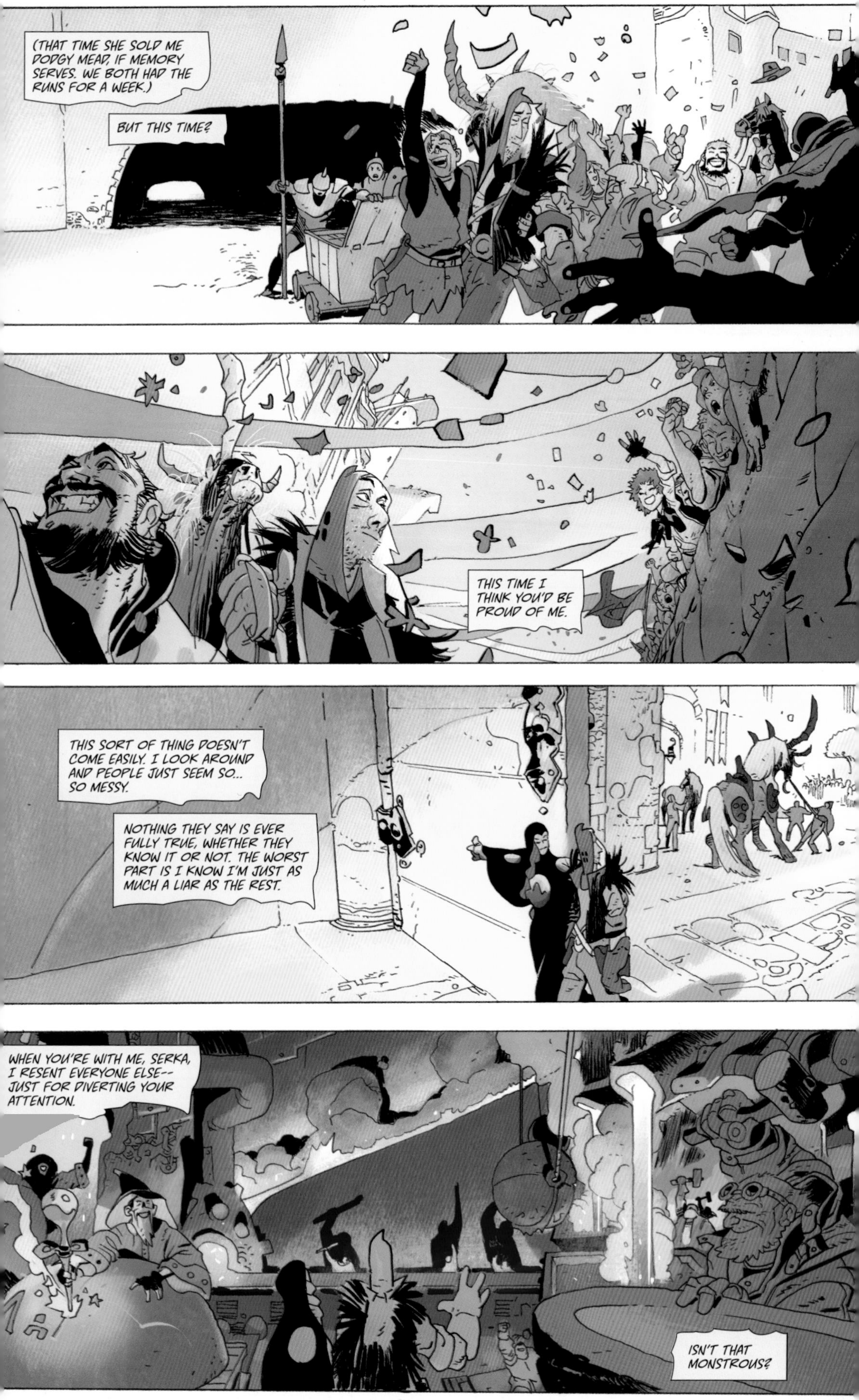

(THAT TIME SHE SOLD ME DODGY MEAD, IF MEMORY SERVES. WE BOTH HAD THE RUNS FOR A WEEK.)
BUT THIS TIME?
THIS TIME I THINK YOU'D BE PROUD OF ME.
THIS SORT OF THING DOESN'T COME EASILY. I LOOK AROUND AND PEOPLE JUST SEEM SO... SO MESSY.
NOTHING THEY SAY IS EVER FULLY TRUE, WHETHER THEY KNOW IT OR NOT. THE WORST PART IS I KNOW I'M JUST AS MUCH A LIAR AS THE REST.
WHEN YOU'RE WITH ME, SERKA, I RESENT EVERYONE ELSE-- JUST FOR DIVERTING YOUR ATTENTION.
ISN'T THAT MONSTROUS?

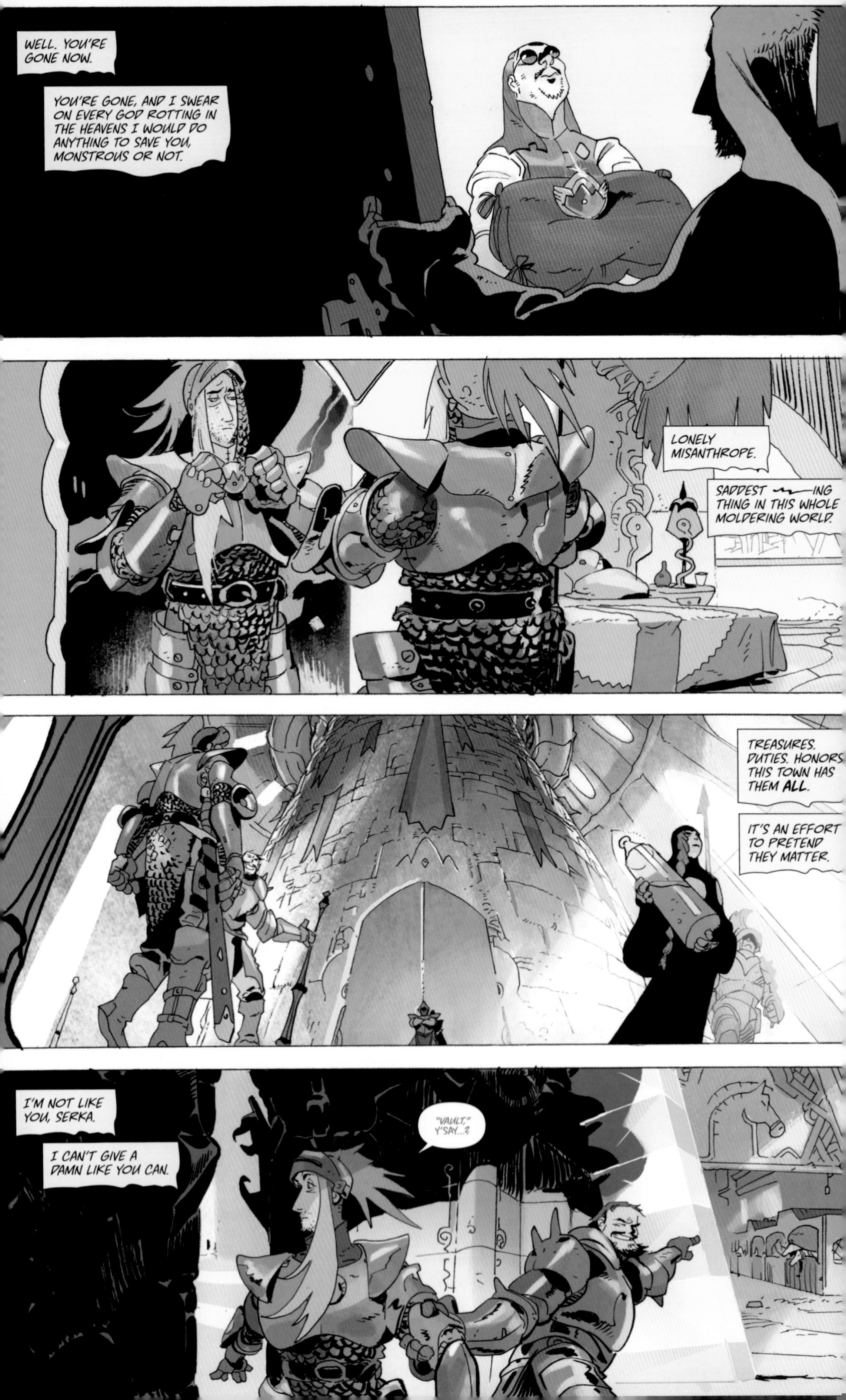
WELL. YOU'RE GONE NOW.
YOU'RE GONE, AND I SWEAR ON EVERY GOD ROTTING IN THE HEAVENS I WOULD DO ANYTHING TO SAVE YOU, MONSTROUS OR NOT.
LONELY MISANTHROPE.
SADDEST —ING THING IN THIS WHOLE MOLDERING WORLD.
TREASURES. DUTIES. HONORS. THIS TOWN HAS THEM ALL.
IT'S AN EFFORT TO PRETEND THEY MATTER.
I'M NOT LIKE YOU, SERKA.
I CAN'T GIVE A DAMN LIKE YOU CAN.
"VAULT," Y'SAY...?

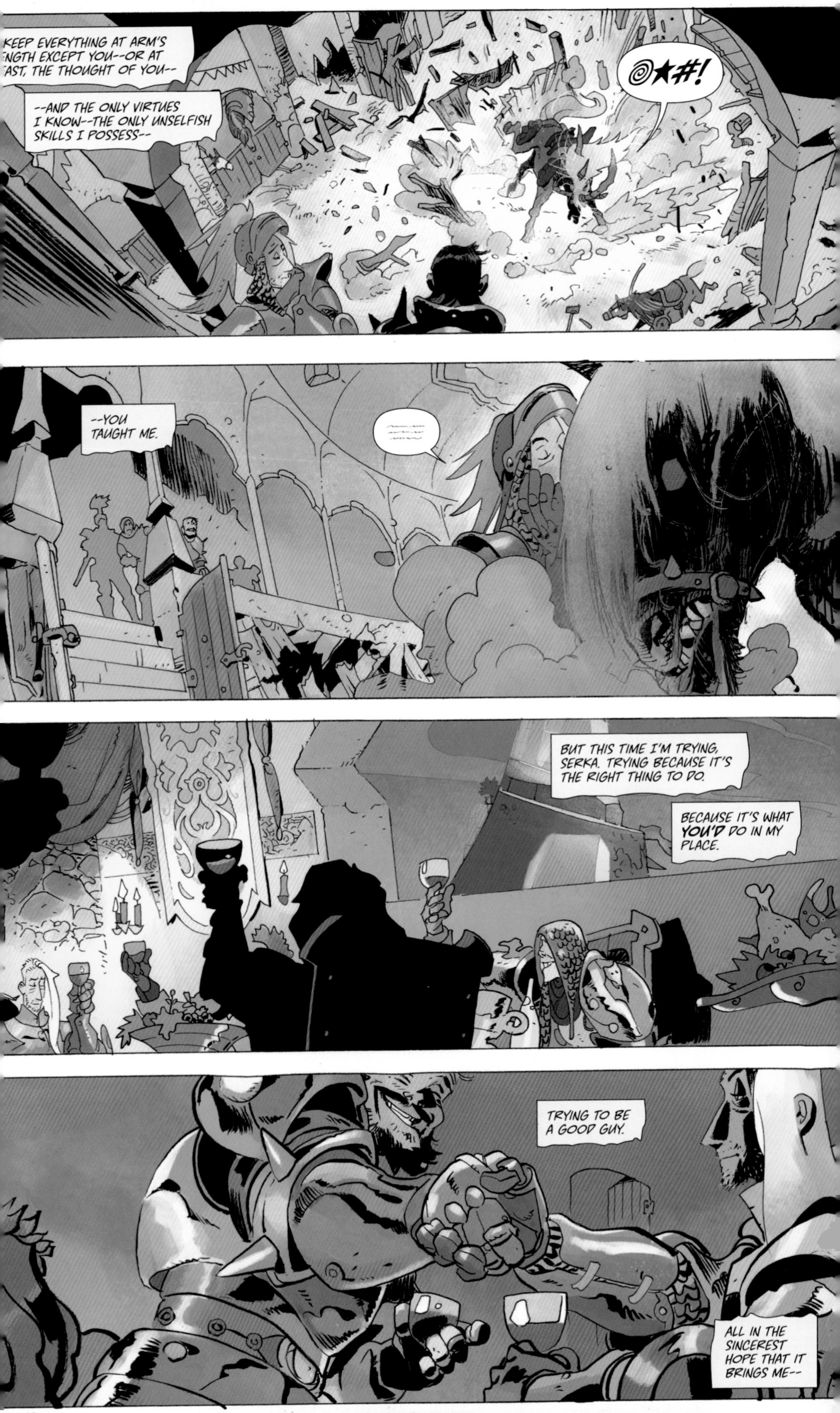
KEEP EVERYTHING AT ARM'S
ENGTH EXCEPT YOU--OR AT
EAST, THE THOUGHT OF YOU--
--AND THE ONLY VIRTUES I KNOW--THE ONLY UNSELFISH SKILLS I POSSESS--
@★#!
--YOU TAUGHT ME.
BUT THIS TIME I'M TRYING, SERKA. TRYING BECAUSE IT'S THE RIGHT THING TO DO.
BECAUSE IT'S WHAT **YOU'D** DO IN MY PLACE.
TRYING TO BE A GOOD GUY.
ALL IN THE SINCEREST HOPE THAT IT BRINGS ME--

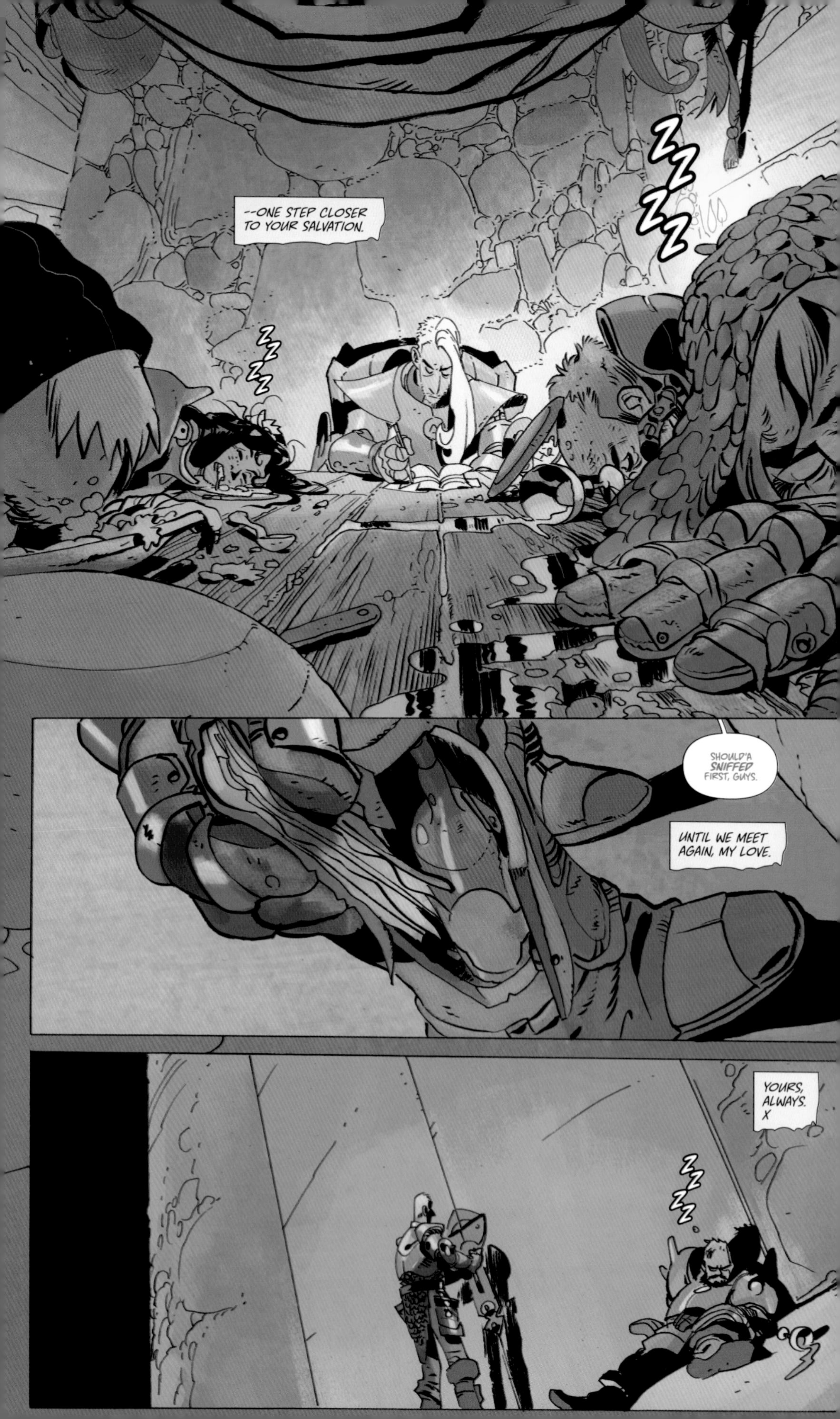
--ONE STEP CLOSER TO YOUR SALVATION.
ZZZZ
ZZZ
SHOULD'A SNIFFED FIRST, GUYS.
UNTIL WE MEET AGAIN, MY LOVE.
YOURS, ALWAYS. X
ZZZ

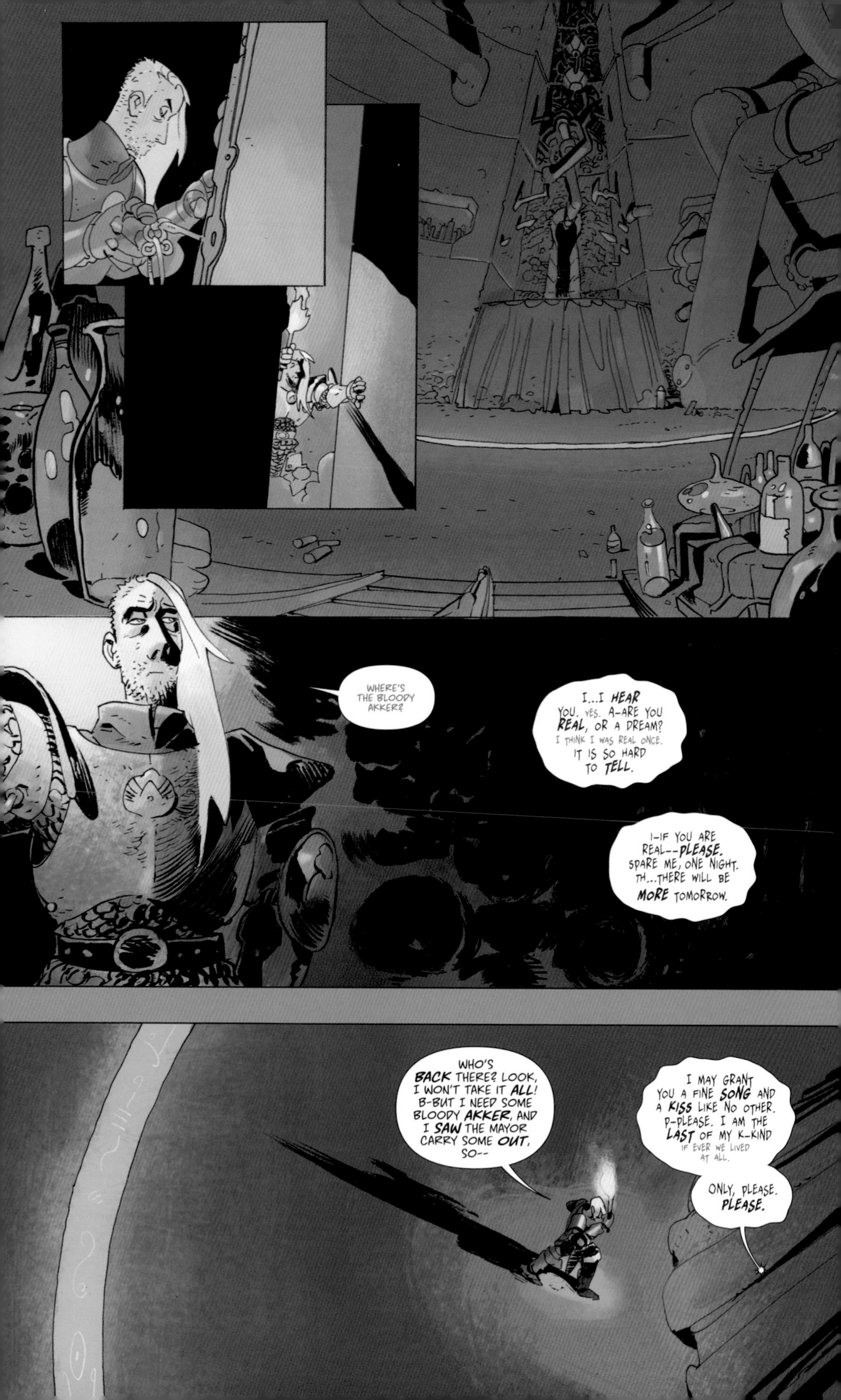
WHERE'S THE BLOODY AKKER?
I...I HEAR YOU. YES. A-ARE YOU REAL, OR A DREAM? I THINK I WAS REAL ONCE. IT IS SO HARD TO TELL.
I-IF YOU ARE REAL--PLEASE. SPARE ME, ONE NIGHT. TH...THERE WILL BE MORE TOMORROW.
WHO'S BACK THERE? LOOK, I WON'T TAKE IT ALL! B-BUT I NEED SOME BLOODY AKKER, AND I SAW THE MAYOR CARRY SOME OUT, SO--
I MAY GRANT YOU A FINE SONG AND A KISS LIKE NO OTHER. P-PLEASE. I AM THE LAST OF MY K-KIND IF EVER WE LIVED AT ALL.
ONLY, PLEASE. PLEASE.

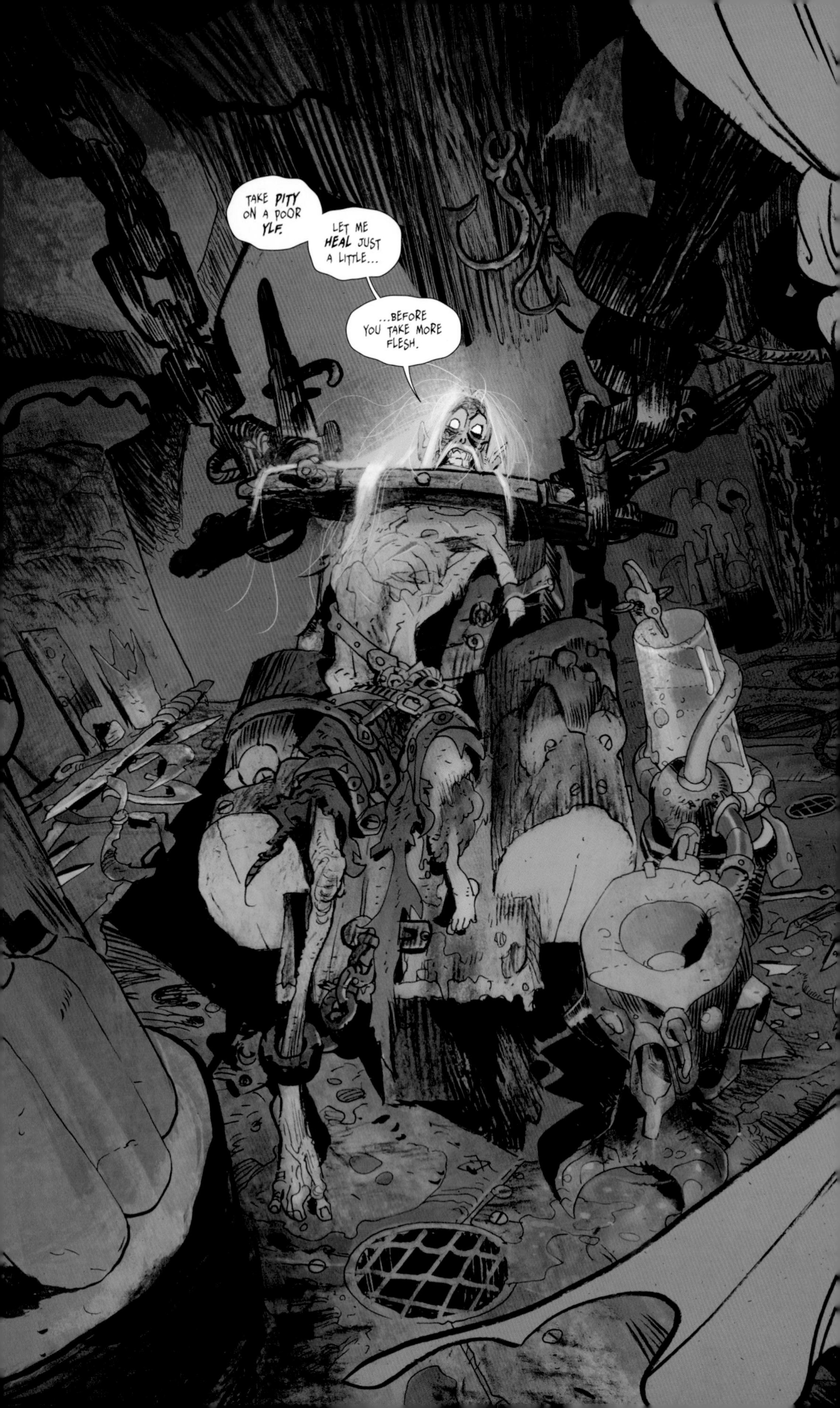
TAKE PITY ON A POOR YLF.
LET ME HEAL JUST A LITTLE...
...BEFORE YOU TAKE MORE FLESH.

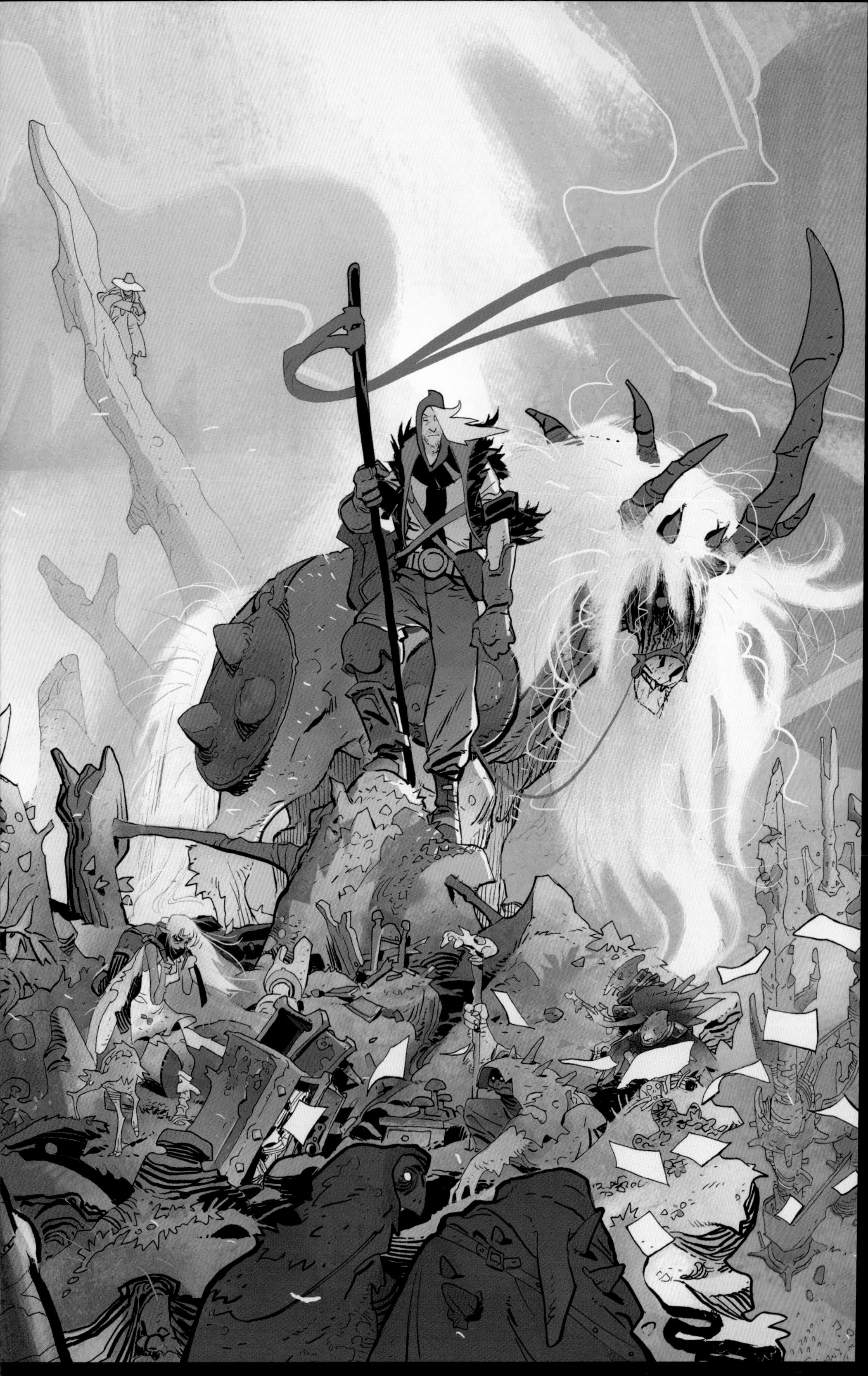

ISSUE ONE COVER BY **MATÍAS BERGARA**

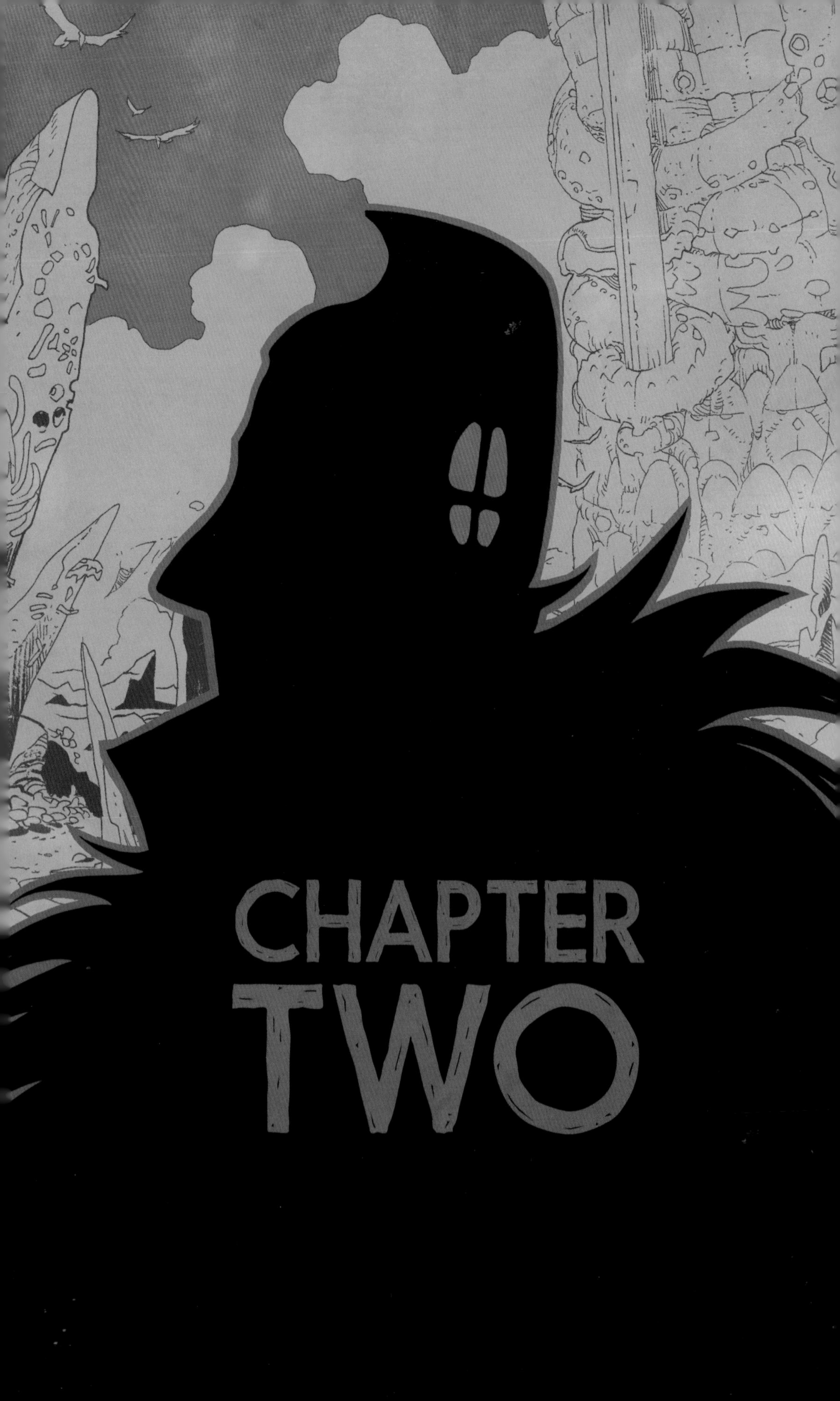
CHAPTER
TWO

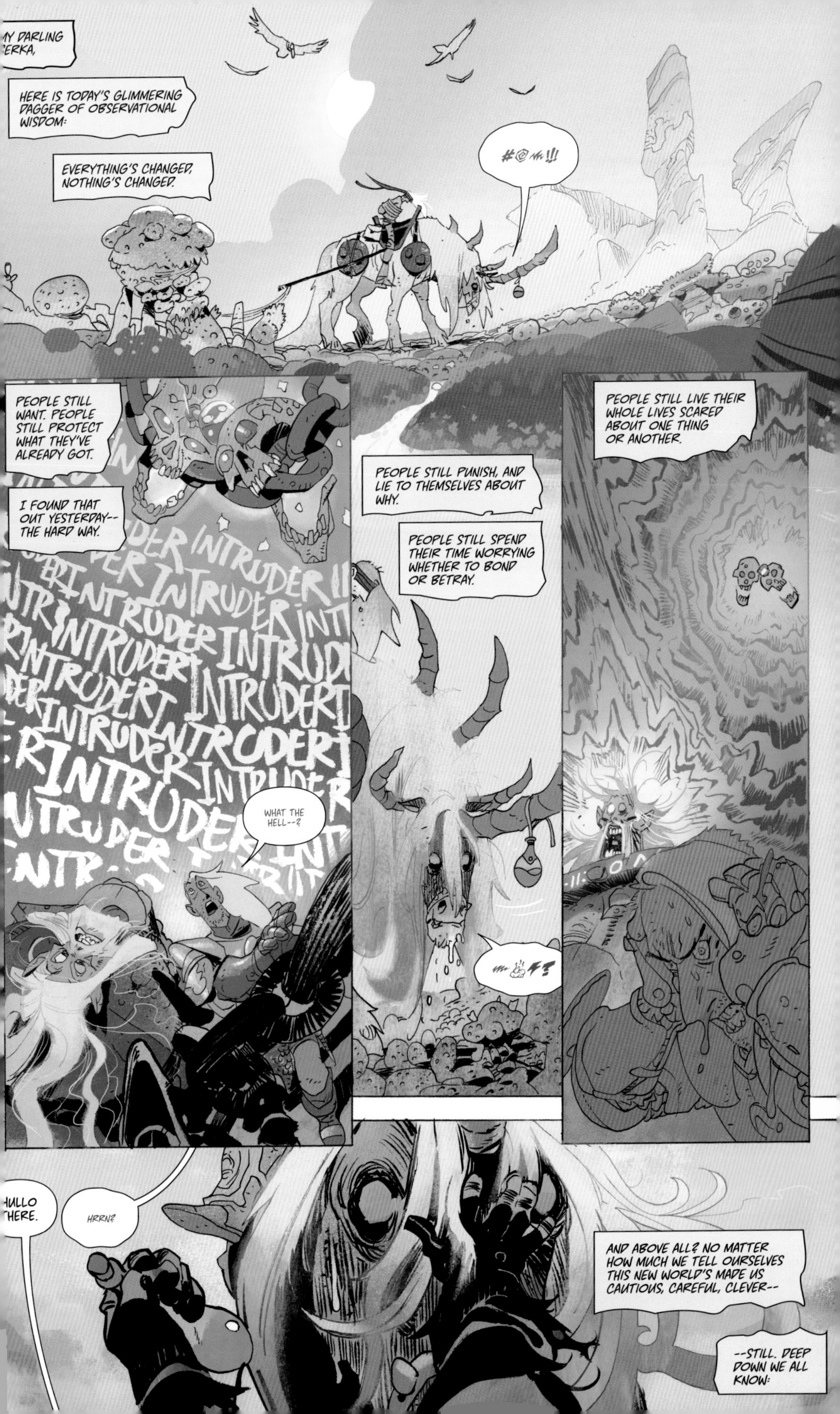

MY DARLING
CERKA,
HERE IS TODAY'S GLIMMERING DAGGER OF OBSERVATIONAL WISDOM:
EVERYTHING'S CHANGED, NOTHING'S CHANGED.
#@!!!
PEOPLE STILL WANT. PEOPLE STILL PROTECT WHAT THEY'VE ALREADY GOT.
I FOUND THAT OUT YESTERDAY-- THE HARD WAY.
INTRUDER INTRUDER INTRUDER INTRUDER INTRUDER INTRUDER INTRUDER
WHAT THE HELL--?
PEOPLE STILL PUNISH, AND LIE TO THEMSELVES ABOUT WHY.
PEOPLE STILL SPEND THEIR TIME WORRYING WHETHER TO BOND OR BETRAY.
PEOPLE STILL LIVE THEIR WHOLE LIVES SCARED ABOUT ONE THING OR ANOTHER.
HULLO THERE.
HRRN?
AND ABOVE ALL? NO MATTER HOW MUCH WE TELL OURSELVES THIS NEW WORLD'S MADE US CAUTIOUS, CAREFUL, CLEVER--
--STILL. DEEP DOWN WE ALL KNOW:

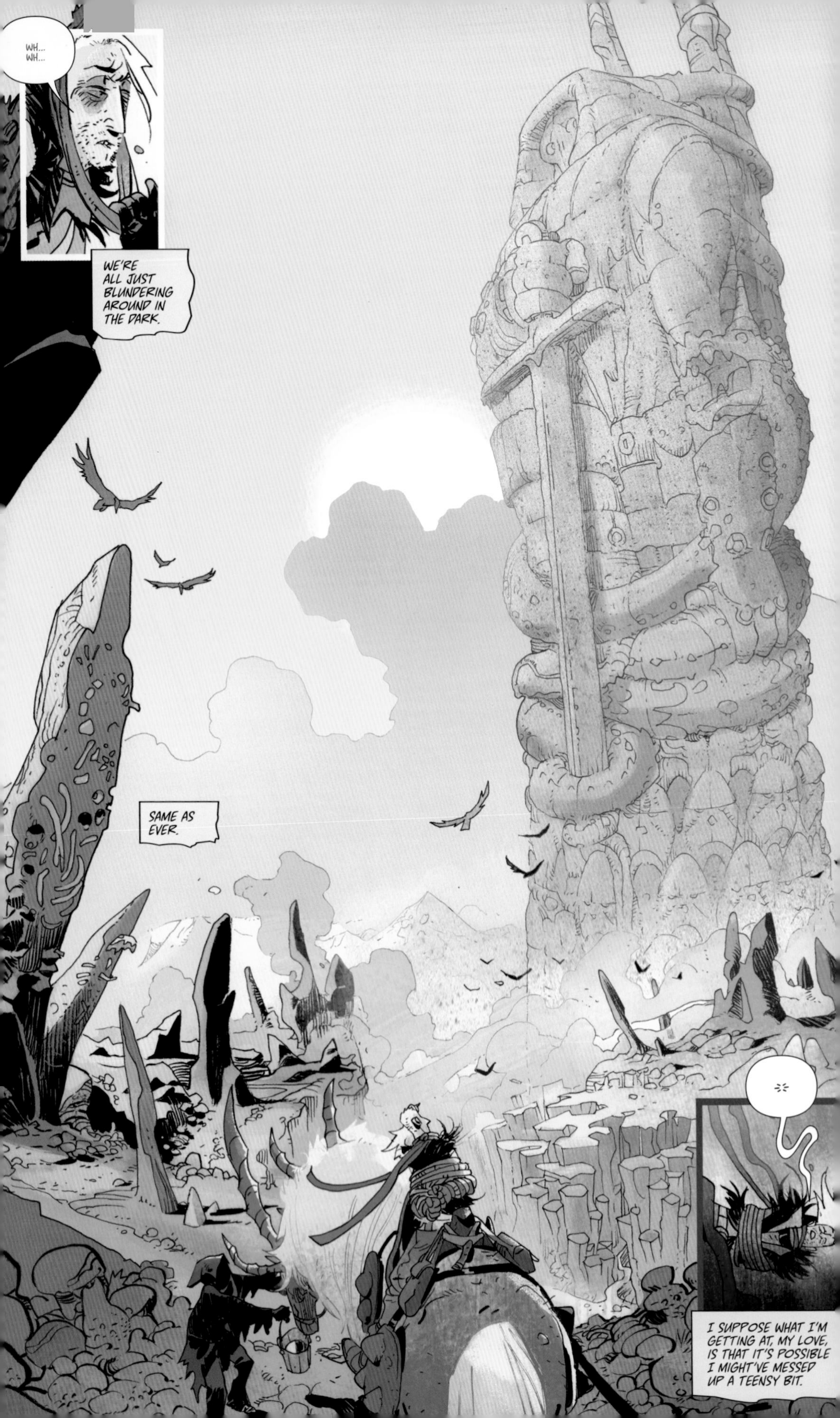
WH...
WH...
WE'RE ALL JUST BLUNDERING AROUND IN THE DARK.
SAME AS EVER.
I SUPPOSE WHAT I'M GETTING AT, MY LOVE, IS THAT IT'S POSSIBLE I MIGHT'VE MESSED UP A TEENSY BIT.

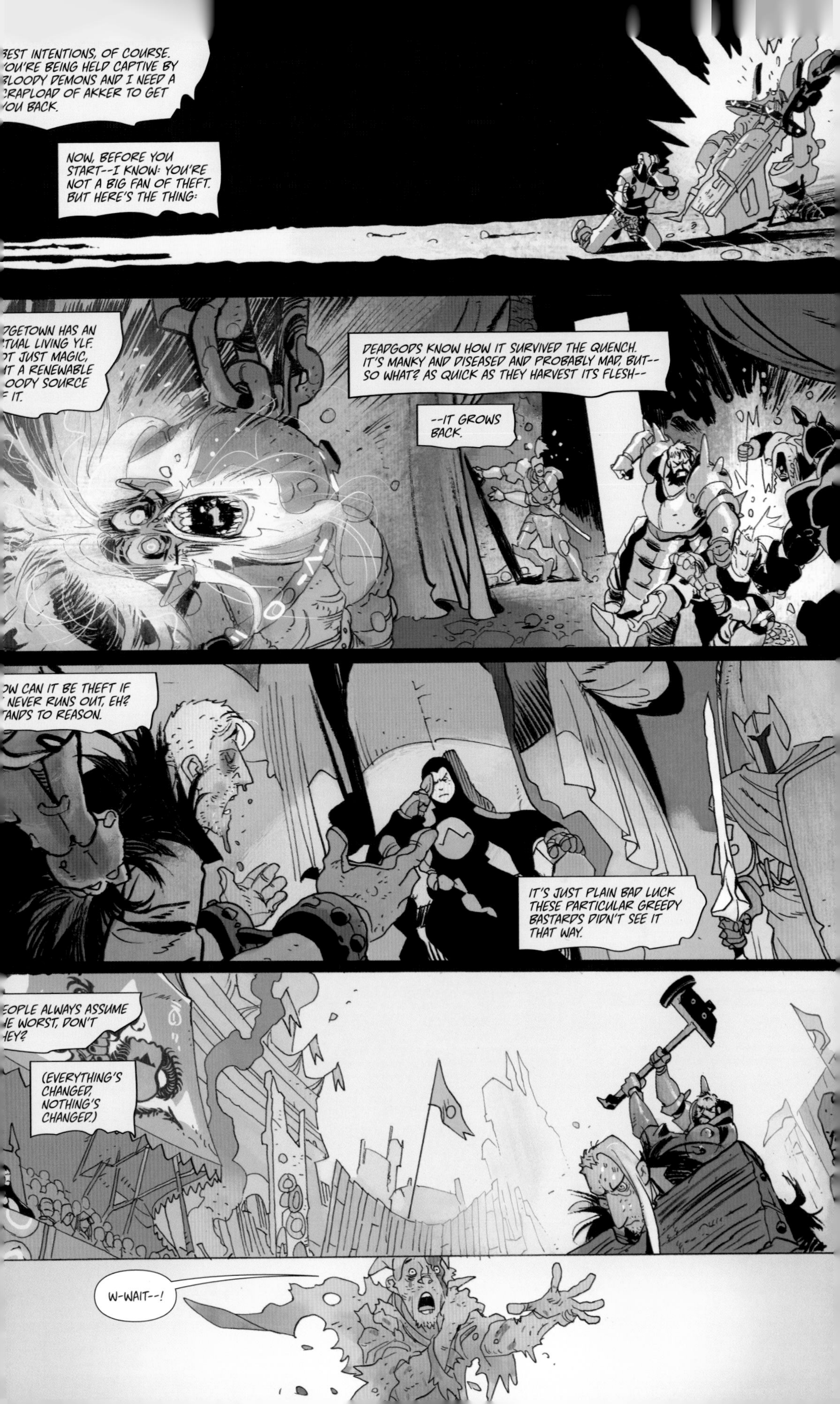

BEST INTENTIONS, OF COURSE. YOU'RE BEING HELD CAPTIVE BY BLOODY DEMONS AND I NEED A CRAPLOAD OF AKKER TO GET YOU BACK.
NOW, BEFORE YOU START--I KNOW: YOU'RE NOT A BIG FAN OF THEFT. BUT HERE'S THE THING:
DGETOWN HAS AN CTUAL LIVING YLF. OT JUST MAGIC, UT A RENEWABLE LOODY SOURCE F IT.
DEADGODS KNOW HOW IT SURVIVED THE QUENCH. IT'S MANKY AND DISEASED AND PROBABLY MAD, BUT--SO WHAT? AS QUICK AS THEY HARVEST ITS FLESH--
--IT GROWS BACK.
OW CAN IT BE THEFT IF NEVER RUNS OUT, EH? TANDS TO REASON.
IT'S JUST PLAIN BAD LUCK THESE PARTICULAR GREEDY BASTARDS DIDN'T SEE IT THAT WAY.
EOPLE ALWAYS ASSUME HE WORST, DON'T HEY?
(EVERYTHING'S CHANGED, NOTHING'S CHANGED.)
W-WAIT--!

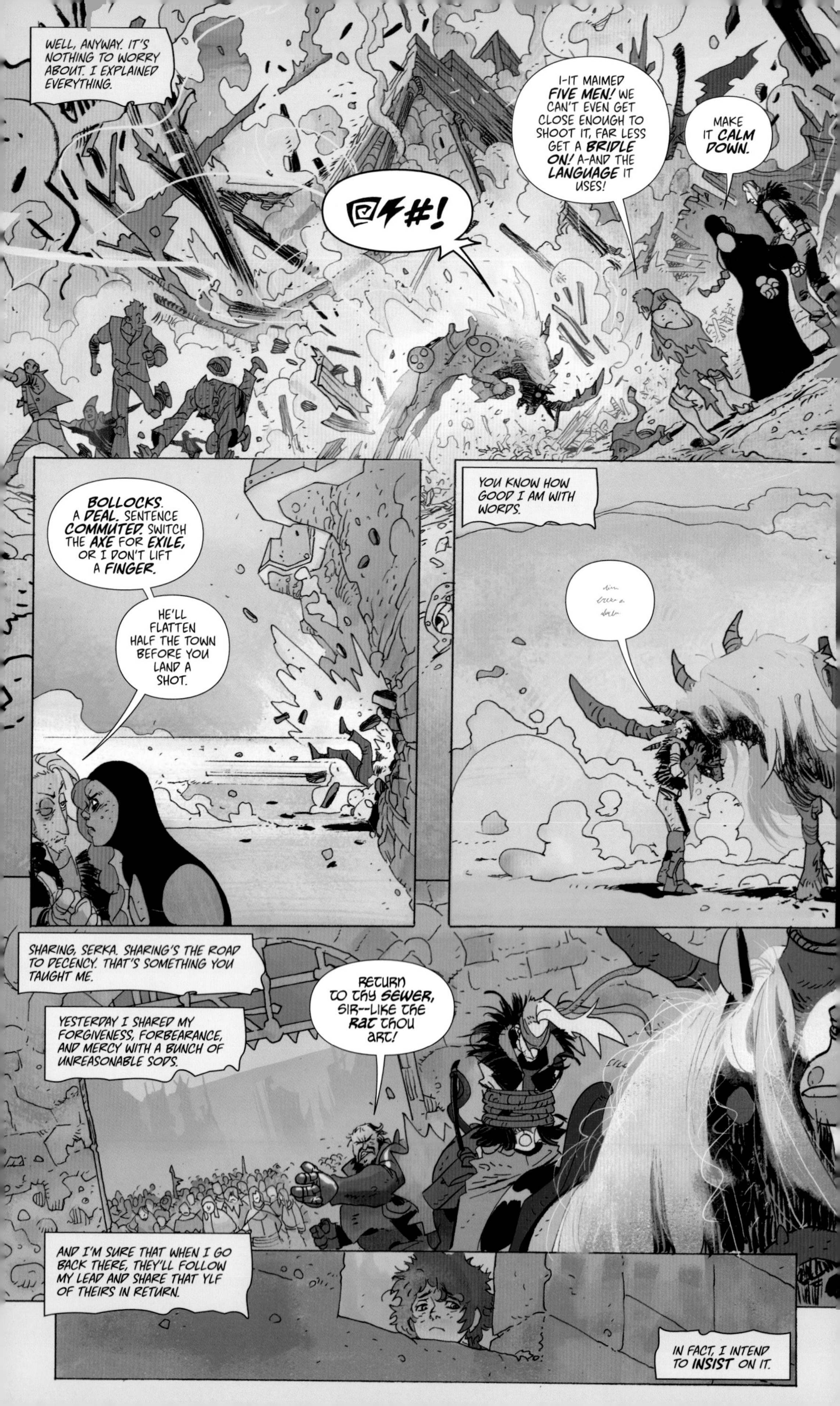
WELL, ANYWAY. IT'S NOTHING TO WORRY ABOUT. I EXPLAINED EVERYTHING.
@⚡#!
I-IT MAIMED FIVE MEN! WE CAN'T EVEN GET CLOSE ENOUGH TO SHOOT IT, FAR LESS GET A BRIDLE ON! A-AND THE LANGUAGE IT USES!
MAKE IT CALM DOWN.
BOLLOCKS. A DEAL. SENTENCE COMMUTED. SWITCH THE AXE FOR EXILE, OR I DON'T LIFT A FINGER.
HE'LL FLATTEN HALF THE TOWN BEFORE YOU LAND A SHOT.
YOU KNOW HOW GOOD I AM WITH WORDS.
SHARING, SERKA. SHARING'S THE ROAD TO DECENCY. THAT'S SOMETHING YOU TAUGHT ME.
YESTERDAY I SHARED MY FORGIVENESS, FORBEARANCE, AND MERCY WITH A BUNCH OF UNREASONABLE SODS.
RETURN TO THY SEWER, SIR--LIKE THE RAT THOU ART!
AND I'M SURE THAT WHEN I GO BACK THERE, THEY'LL FOLLOW MY LEAD AND SHARE THAT YLF OF THEIRS IN RETURN.
IN FACT, I INTEND TO INSIST ON IT.

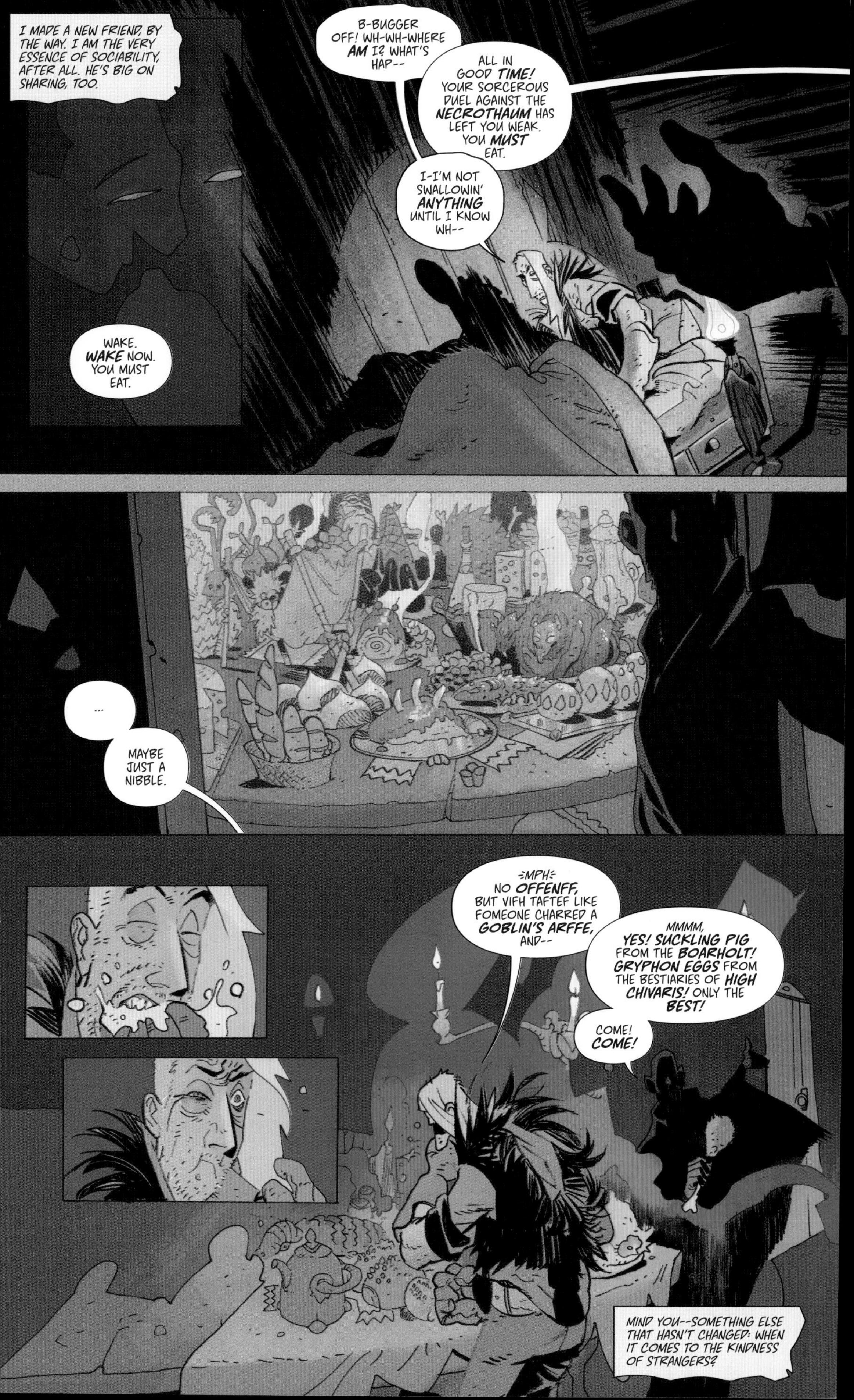
I MADE A NEW FRIEND, BY THE WAY. I AM THE VERY ESSENCE OF SOCIABILITY, AFTER ALL. HE'S BIG ON SHARING, TOO.
WAKE. WAKE NOW. YOU MUST EAT.
B-BUGGER OFF! WH-WH-WHERE AM I? WHAT'S HAP--
ALL IN GOOD TIME! YOUR SORCEROUS DUEL AGAINST THE NECROTHAUM HAS LEFT YOU WEAK. YOU MUST EAT.
I-I'M NOT SWALLOWIN' ANYTHING UNTIL I KNOW WH--
...
MAYBE JUST A NIBBLE.
=MPH= NO OFFENFF, BUT VIFH TAFTEF LIKE FOMEONE CHARRED A GOBLIN'S ARFFE, AND--
MMMM, YES! SUCKLING PIG FROM THE BOARHOLT! GRYPHON EGGS FROM THE BESTIARIES OF HIGH CHIVARIS! ONLY THE BEST!
COME! COME!
MIND YOU--SOMETHING ELSE THAT HASN'T CHANGED: WHEN IT COMES TO THE KINDNESS OF STRANGERS?

THE EMPHASIS IS USUALLY ON "STRANGE."

YOU ARE **MOST WELCOME,** LUNAR MAGUS! AND I **THANK YOU** FOR THE **MANUSCRIPTS** FROM THE MOON LIBRIUM!

"NO NEW MAGIC." THAT'S THE THING, ISN'T IT? THE NEW WORLD ORDER.

PING

HM.

EAT, FRIEND! DRINK! I MUST STUDY!

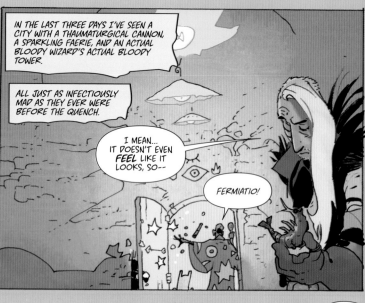

IN THE LAST THREE DAYS I'VE SEEN A CITY WITH A THAUMATURGICAL CANNON, A SPARKLING FAERIE, AND AN ACTUAL BLOODY WIZARD'S ACTUAL BLOODY TOWER.

ALL JUST AS INFECTIOUSLY MAD AS THEY EVER WERE BEFORE THE QUENCH.

I MEAN... IT DOESN'T EVEN **FEEL** LIKE IT LOOKS, SO--

FERMIATIO!

SLAM

=SIGH=

YOU KNOW WHAT THINK?

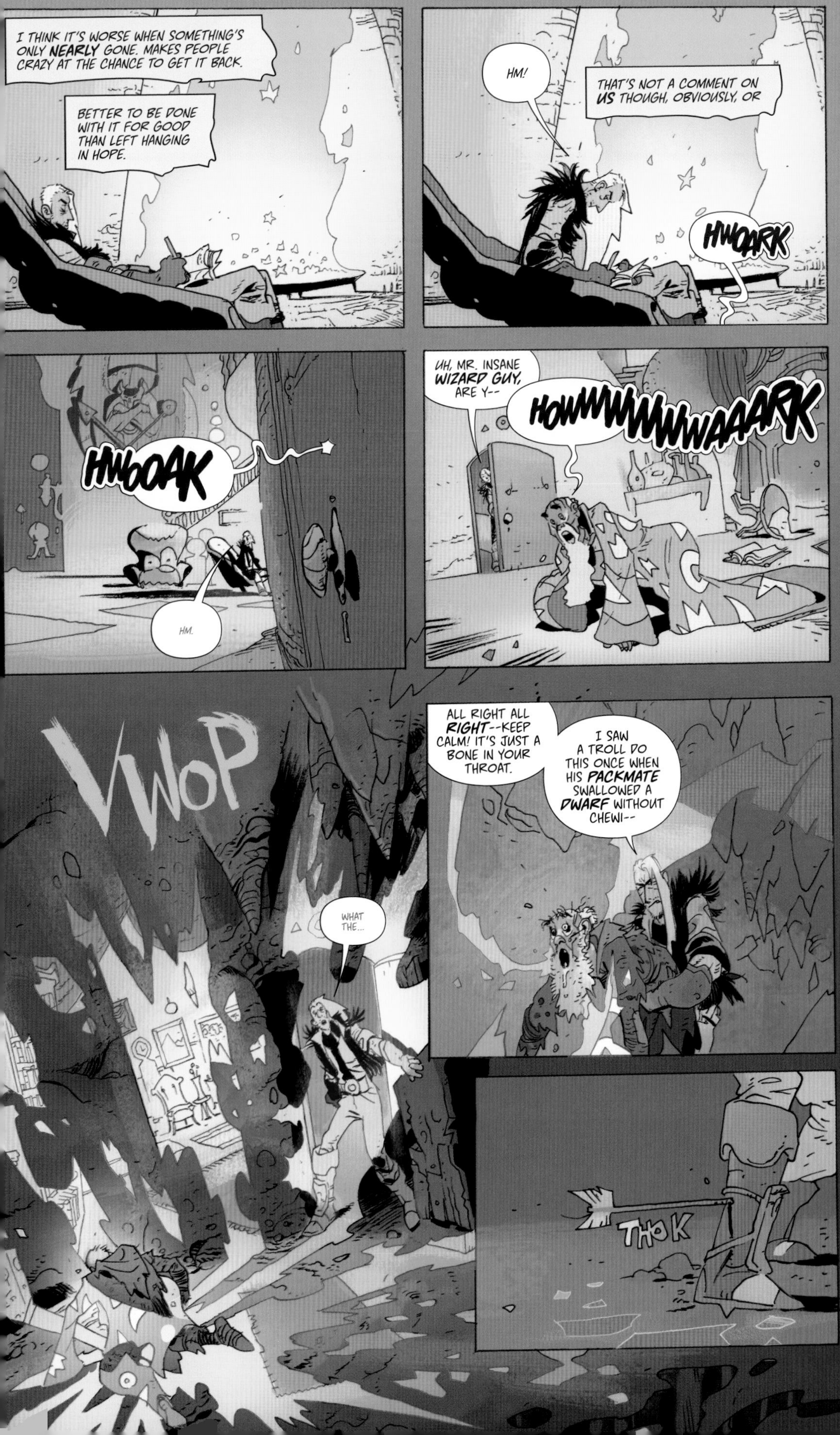

I THINK IT'S WORSE WHEN SOMETHING'S ONLY NEARLY GONE. MAKES PEOPLE CRAZY AT THE CHANCE TO GET IT BACK.
BETTER TO BE DONE WITH IT FOR GOOD THAN LEFT HANGING IN HOPE.
HM!
THAT'S NOT A COMMENT ON US THOUGH, OBVIOUSLY, OR
HWOARK
HWOOAK
HM.
UH, MR. INSANE WIZARD GUY, ARE Y--
HOWWWWWWWAAARK
VWOP
WHAT THE...
ALL RIGHT ALL RIGHT--KEEP CALM! IT'S JUST A BONE IN YOUR THROAT.
I SAW A TROLL DO THIS ONCE WHEN HIS PACKMATE SWALLOWED A DWARF WITHOUT CHEWI--
THOK

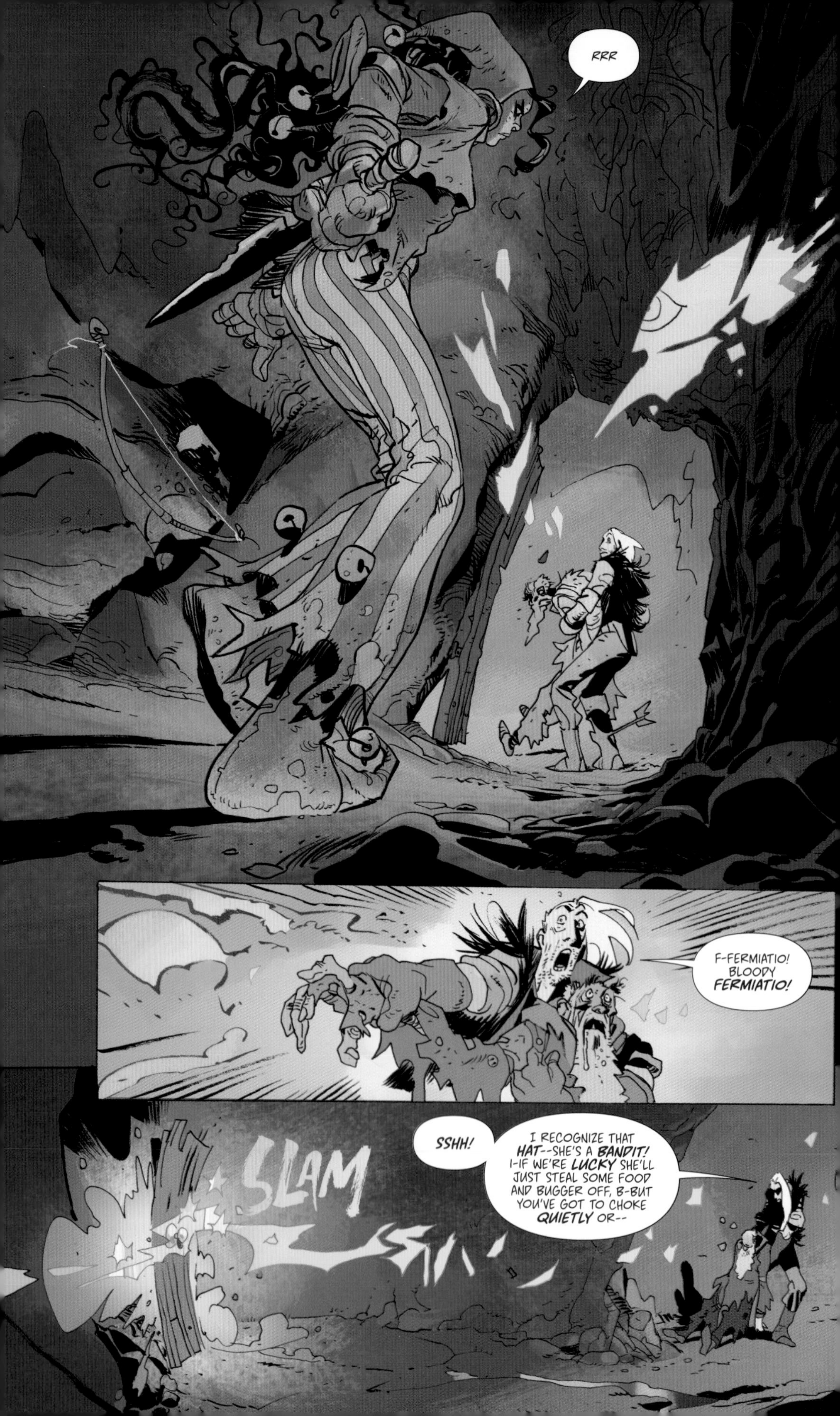
RRR
F-FERMIATIO! BLOODY FERMIATIO!
SSHH!
I RECOGNIZE THAT HAT--SHE'S A BANDIT! I-IF WE'RE LUCKY SHE'LL JUST STEAL SOME FOOD AND BUGGER OFF, B-BUT YOU'VE GOT TO CHOKE QUIETLY OR--
SLAM

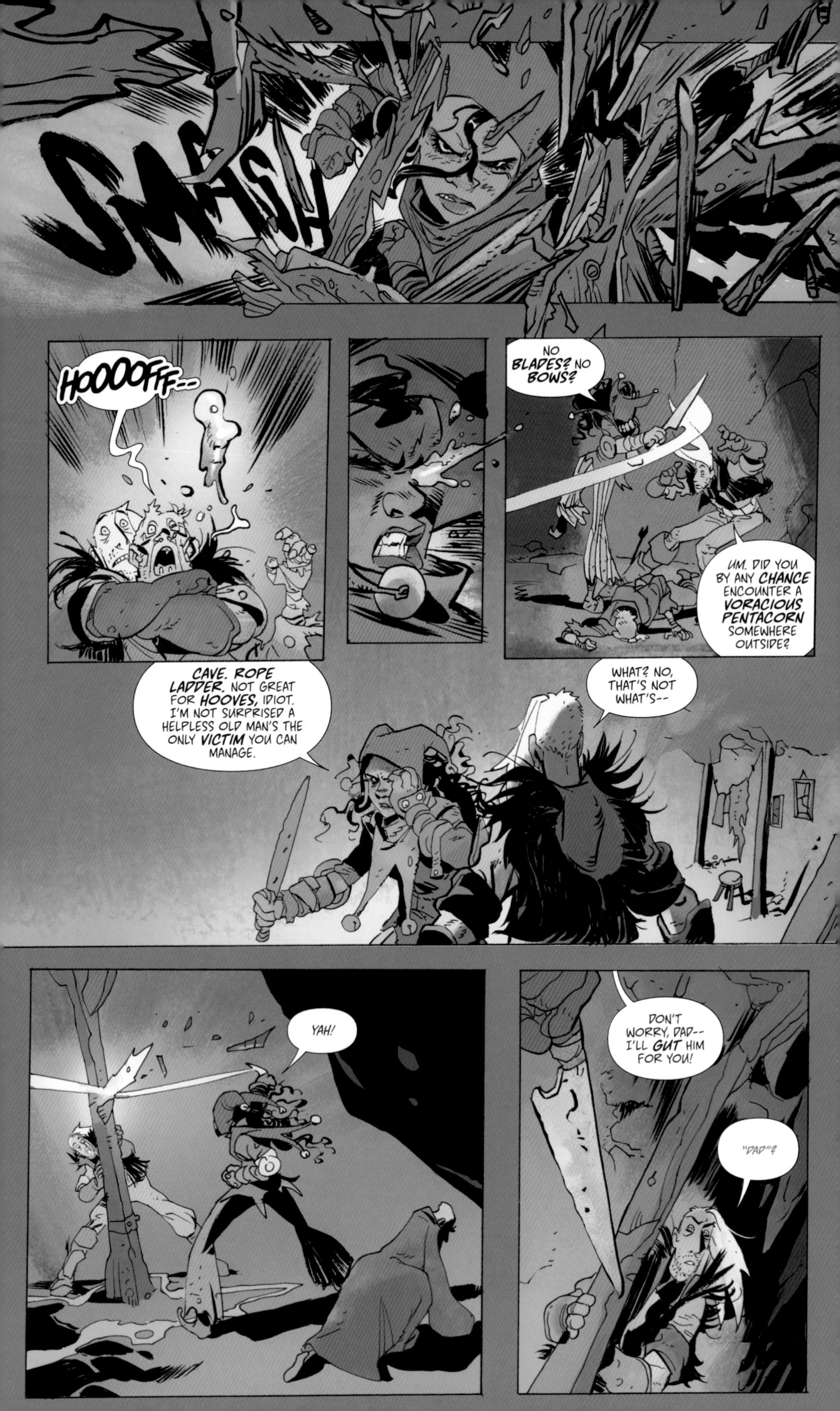
SMASH
HOOOOFFF--
NO BLADES? NO BOWS?
UM. DID YOU BY ANY CHANCE ENCOUNTER A VORACIOUS PENTACORN SOMEWHERE OUTSIDE?
CAVE. ROPE LADDER. NOT GREAT FOR HOOVES, IDIOT. I'M NOT SURPRISED A HELPLESS OLD MAN'S THE ONLY VICTIM YOU CAN MANAGE.
WHAT? NO, THAT'S NOT WHAT'S--
YAH!
DON'T WORRY, DAD-- I'LL GUT HIM FOR YOU!
"DAD"?

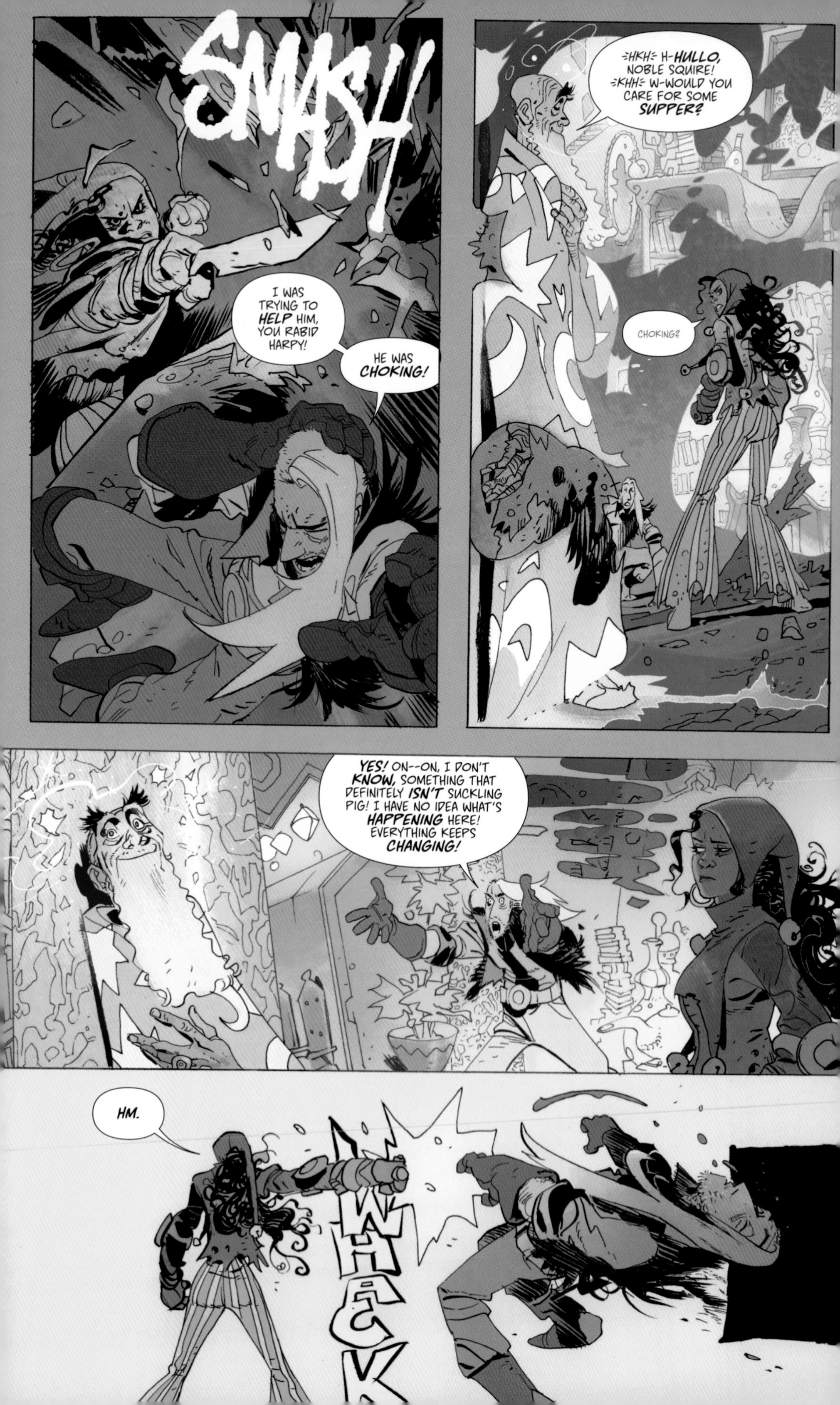
SMASH!
I WAS TRYING TO HELP HIM, YOU RABID HARPY!
HE WAS CHOKING!
=HKH= H-HULLO, NOBLE SQUIRE! =KHH= W-WOULD YOU CARE FOR SOME SUPPER?
CHOKING?
YES! ON--ON, I DON'T KNOW, SOMETHING THAT DEFINITELY ISN'T SUCKLING PIG! I HAVE NO IDEA WHAT'S HAPPENING HERE! EVERYTHING KEEPS CHANGING!
HM.
WHACK

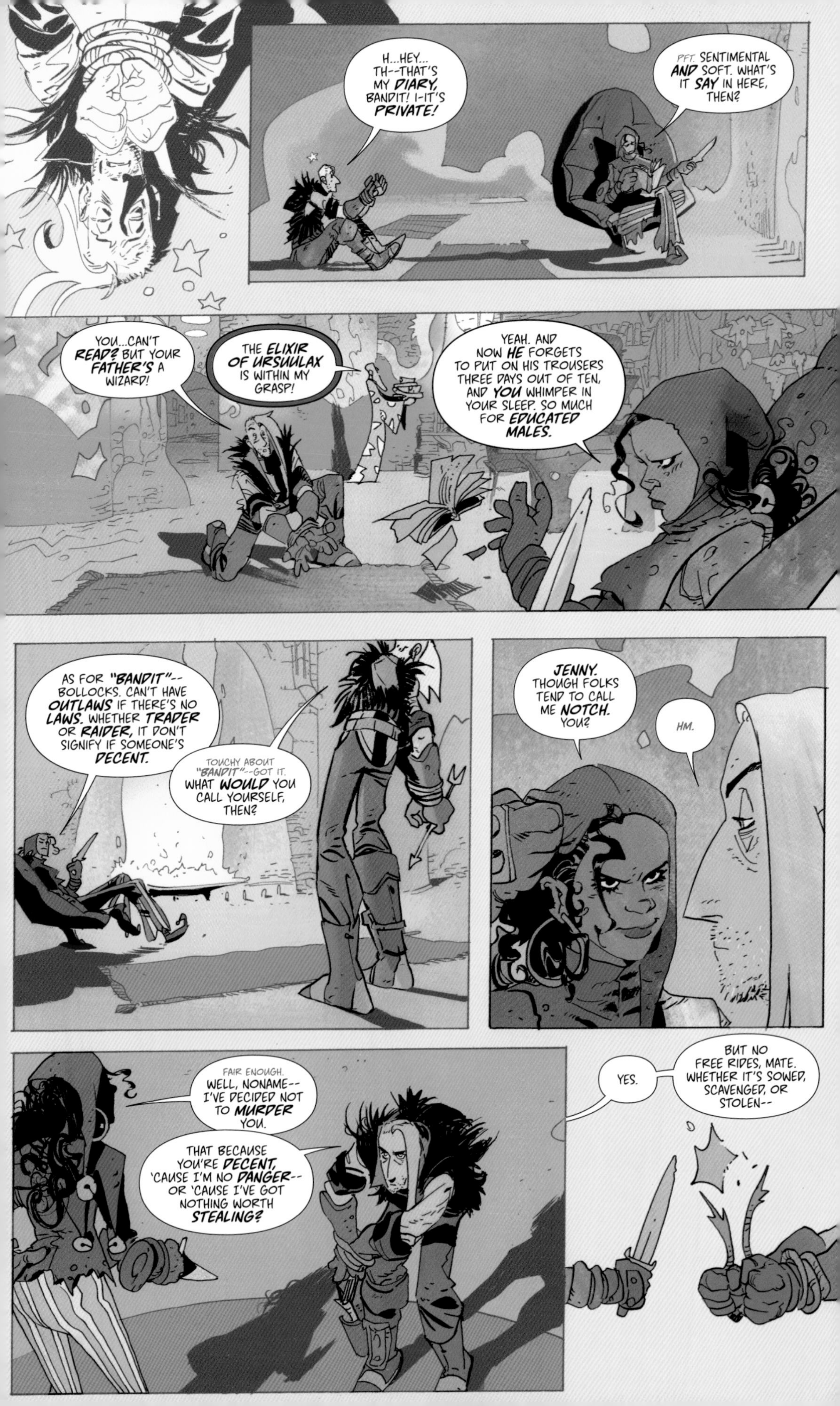
H...HEY... TH--THAT'S MY DIARY, BANDIT! I-IT'S PRIVATE!
PFT. SENTIMENTAL AND SOFT. WHAT'S IT SAY IN HERE, THEN?
YOU...CAN'T READ? BUT YOUR FATHER'S A WIZARD!
THE ELIXIR OF URSUULAX IS WITHIN MY GRASP!
YEAH. AND NOW HE FORGETS TO PUT ON HIS TROUSERS THREE DAYS OUT OF TEN, AND YOU WHIMPER IN YOUR SLEEP. SO MUCH FOR EDUCATED MALES.
AS FOR "BANDIT"-- BOLLOCKS. CAN'T HAVE OUTLAWS IF THERE'S NO LAWS. WHETHER TRADER OR RAIDER, IT DON'T SIGNIFY IF SOMEONE'S DECENT.
TOUCHY ABOUT "BANDIT"--GOT IT. WHAT WOULD YOU CALL YOURSELF, THEN?
JENNY. THOUGH FOLKS TEND TO CALL ME NOTCH. YOU?
HM.
FAIR ENOUGH. WELL, NONAME-- I'VE DECIDED NOT TO MURDER YOU.
THAT BECAUSE YOU'RE DECENT, 'CAUSE I'M NO DANGER-- OR 'CAUSE I'VE GOT NOTHING WORTH STEALING?
YES.
BUT NO FREE RIDES, MATE. WHETHER IT'S SOWED, SCAVENGED, OR STOLEN--

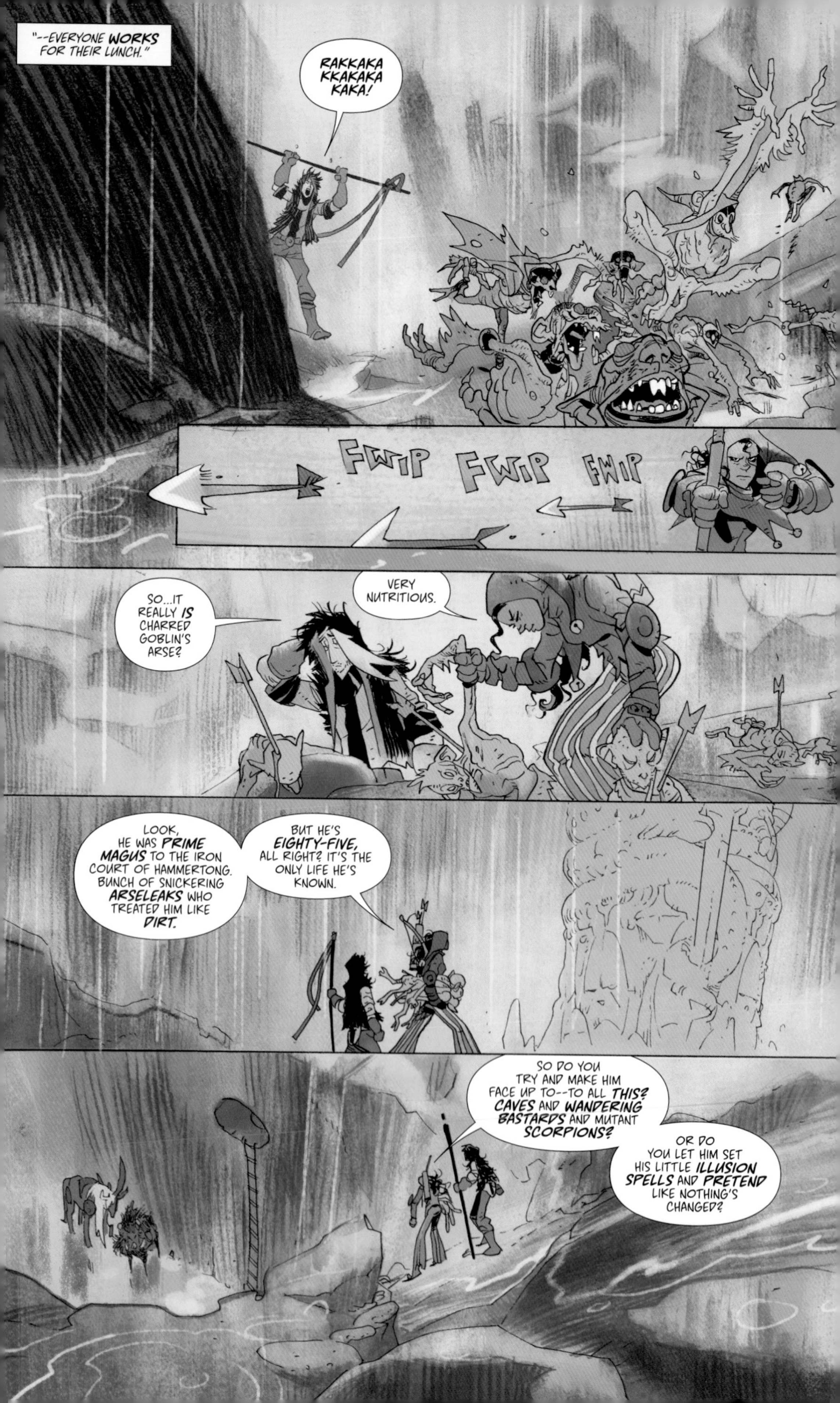
"--EVERYONE WORKS FOR THEIR LUNCH."
RAKKAKA KKAKAKA KAKA!
FWIP FWIP FWIP
SO...IT REALLY IS CHARRED GOBLIN'S ARSE?
VERY NUTRITIOUS.
LOOK, HE WAS PRIME MAGUS TO THE IRON COURT OF HAMMERTONG. BUNCH OF SNICKERING ARSELEAKS WHO TREATED HIM LIKE DIRT.
BUT HE'S EIGHTY-FIVE, ALL RIGHT? IT'S THE ONLY LIFE HE'S KNOWN.
SO DO YOU TRY AND MAKE HIM FACE UP TO--TO ALL THIS? CAVES AND WANDERING BASTARDS AND MUTANT SCORPIONS?
OR DO YOU LET HIM SET HIS LITTLE ILLUSION SPELLS AND PRETEND LIKE NOTHING'S CHANGED?

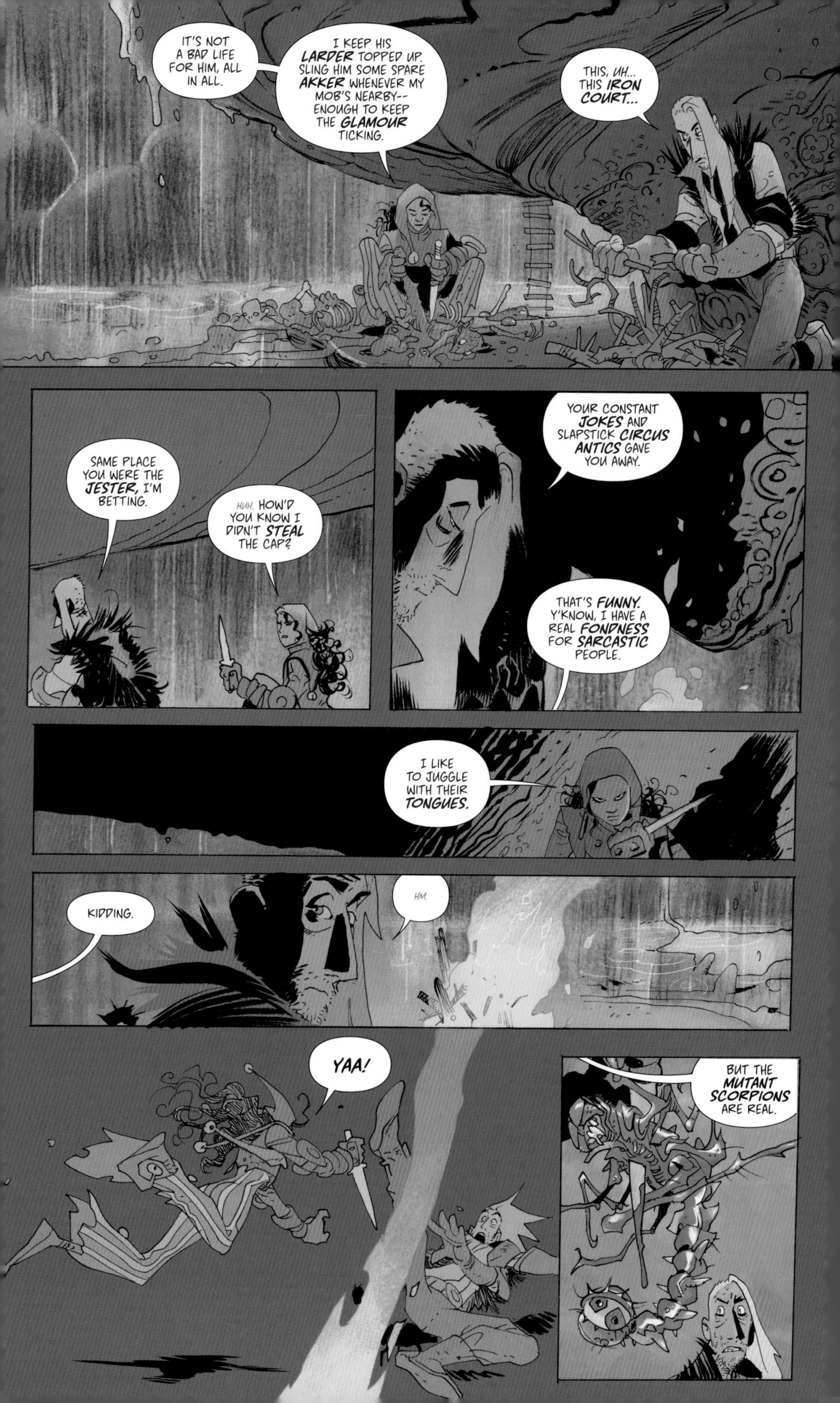

IT'S NOT A BAD LIFE FOR HIM, ALL IN ALL.
I KEEP HIS LARDER TOPPED UP. SLING HIM SOME SPARE AKKER WHENEVER MY MOB'S NEARBY-- ENOUGH TO KEEP THE GLAMOUR TICKING.
THIS, UH... THIS IRON COURT...
SAME PLACE YOU WERE THE JESTER, I'M BETTING.
HUH. HOW'D YOU KNOW I DIDN'T STEAL THE CAP?
YOUR CONSTANT JOKES AND SLAPSTICK CIRCUS ANTICS GAVE YOU AWAY.
THAT'S FUNNY. Y'KNOW, I HAVE A REAL FONDNESS FOR SARCASTIC PEOPLE.
I LIKE TO JUGGLE WITH THEIR TONGUES.
KIDDING.
HM.
YAA!
BUT THE MUTANT SCORPIONS ARE REAL.

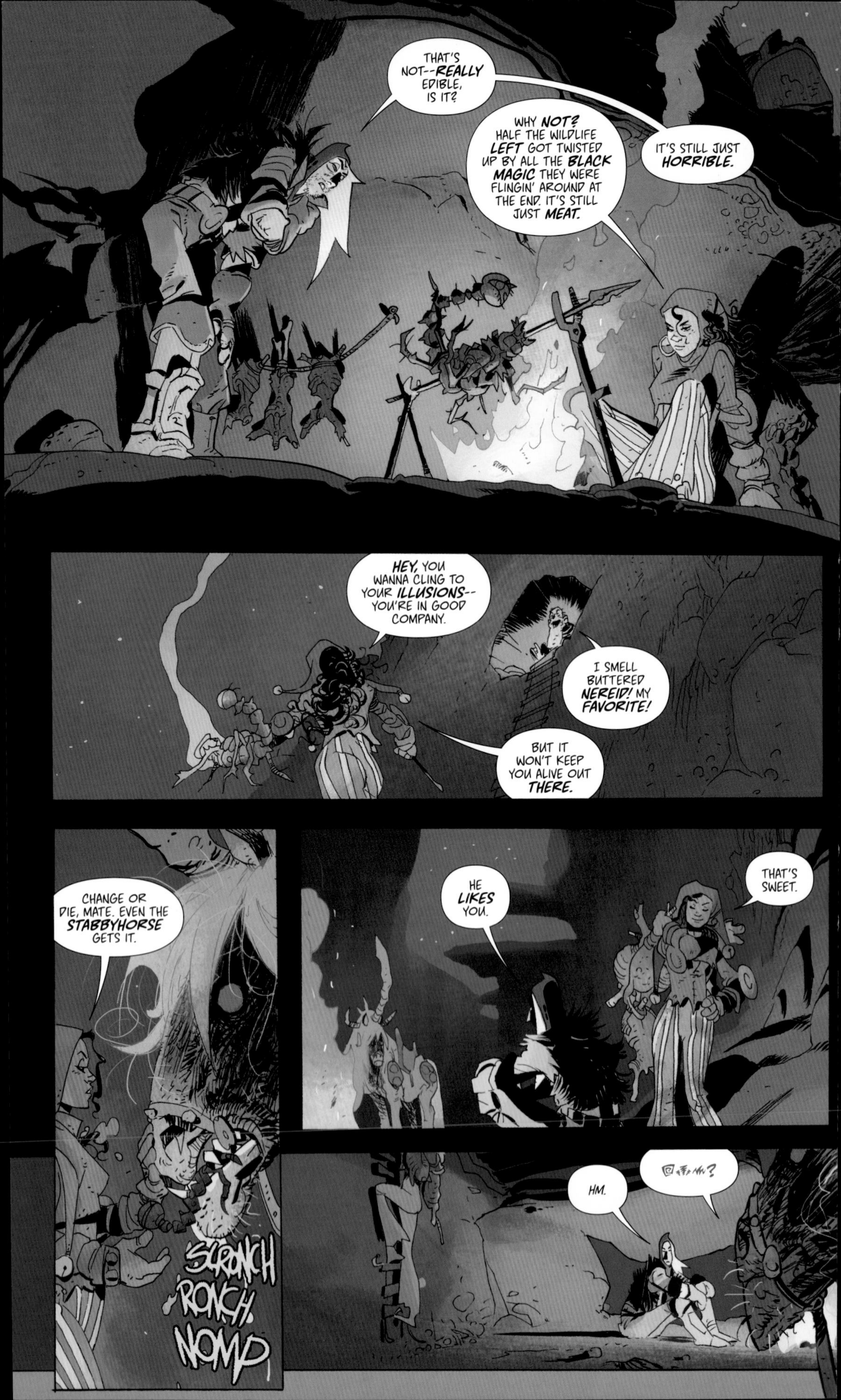
THAT'S NOT--REALLY EDIBLE, IS IT?
WHY NOT? HALF THE WILDLIFE LEFT GOT TWISTED UP BY ALL THE BLACK MAGIC THEY WERE FLINGIN' AROUND AT THE END. IT'S STILL JUST MEAT.
IT'S STILL JUST HORRIBLE.
HEY, YOU WANNA CLING TO YOUR ILLUSIONS-- YOU'RE IN GOOD COMPANY.
I SMELL BUTTERED NEREID! MY FAVORITE!
BUT IT WON'T KEEP YOU ALIVE OUT THERE.
CHANGE OR DIE, MATE. EVEN THE STABBYHORSE GETS IT.
SCRONCH
RONCH
NOMP
HE LIKES YOU.
THAT'S SWEET.
HM.

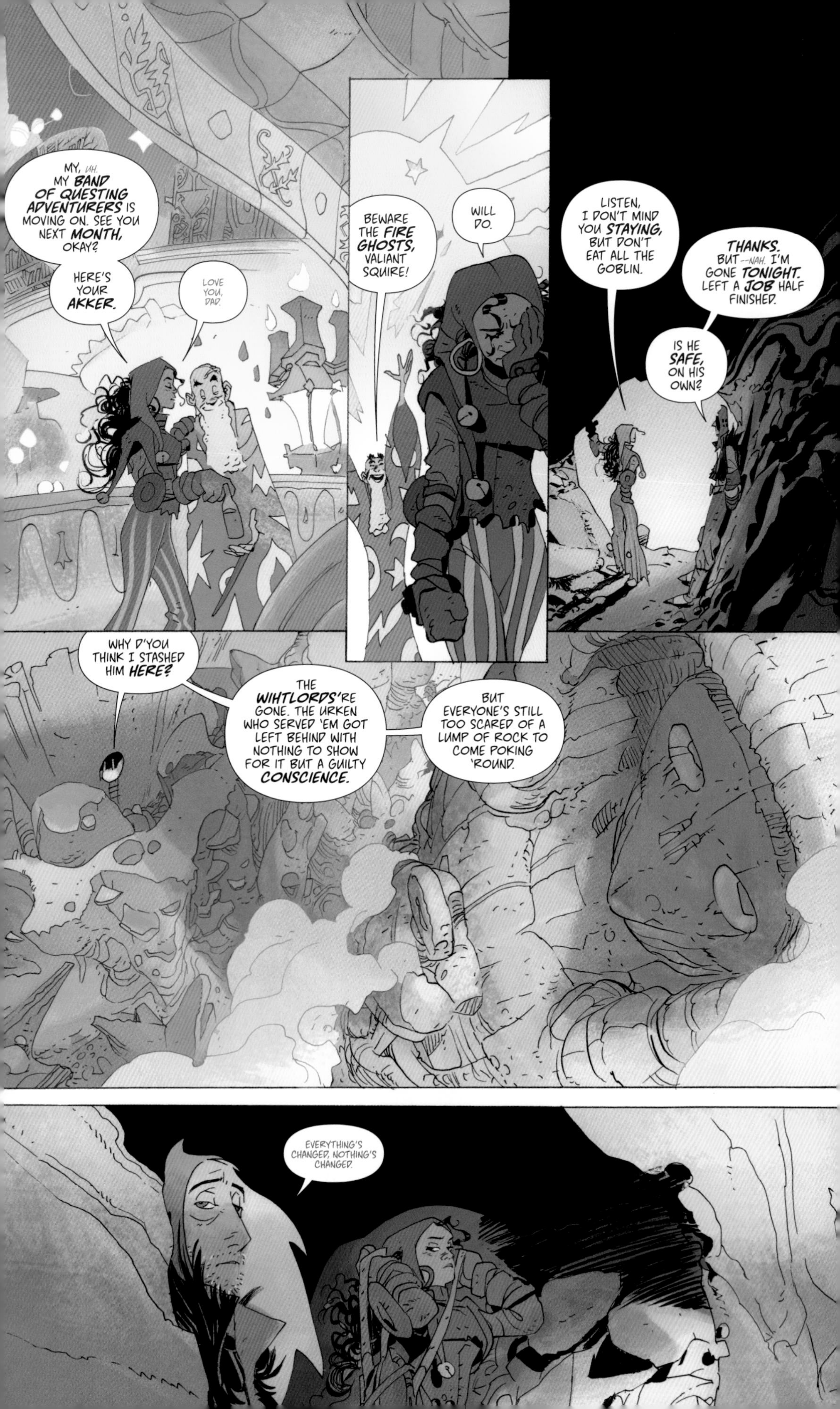

MY, UH. MY BAND OF QUESTING ADVENTURERS IS MOVING ON. SEE YOU NEXT MONTH, OKAY?
HERE'S YOUR AKKER.
LOVE YOU, DAD.
BEWARE THE FIRE GHOSTS, VALIANT SQUIRE!
WILL DO.
LISTEN, I DON'T MIND YOU STAYING, BUT DON'T EAT ALL THE GOBLIN.
THANKS. BUT--NAH. I'M GONE TONIGHT. LEFT A JOB HALF FINISHED.
IS HE SAFE, ON HIS OWN?
WHY D'YOU THINK I STASHED HIM HERE?
THE WIHTLORDS'RE GONE. THE URKEN WHO SERVED 'EM GOT LEFT BEHIND WITH NOTHING TO SHOW FOR IT BUT A GUILTY CONSCIENCE.
BUT EVERYONE'S STILL TOO SCARED OF A LUMP OF ROCK TO COME POKING 'ROUND.
EVERYTHING'S CHANGED, NOTHING'S CHANGED.

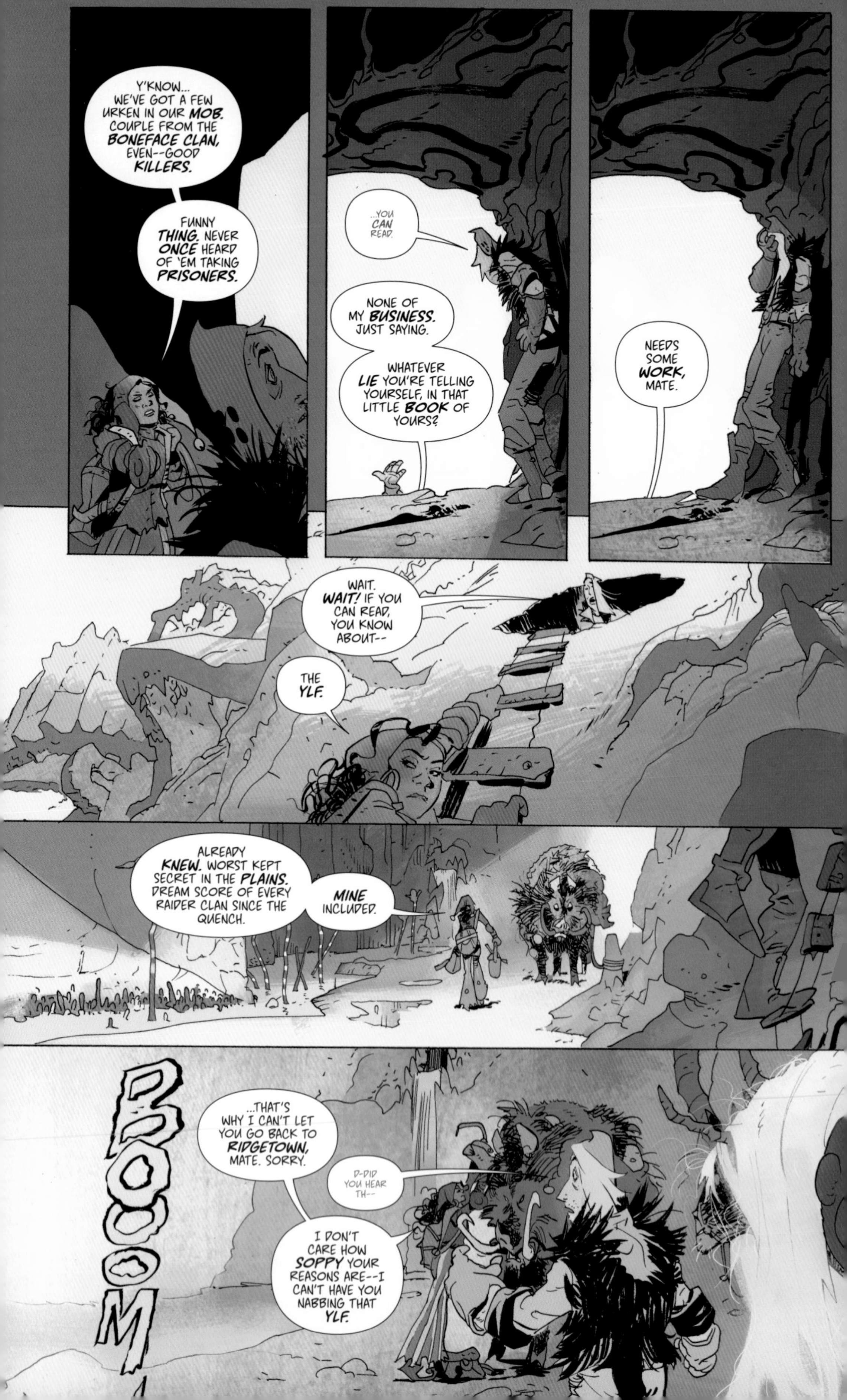
Y'KNOW... WE'VE GOT A FEW URKEN IN OUR MOB. COUPLE FROM THE BONEFACE CLAN, EVEN--GOOD KILLERS.
FUNNY THING. NEVER ONCE HEARD OF 'EM TAKING PRISONERS.
...YOU CAN READ.
NONE OF MY BUSINESS. JUST SAYING.
WHATEVER LIE YOU'RE TELLING YOURSELF, IN THAT LITTLE BOOK OF YOURS?
NEEDS SOME WORK, MATE.
WAIT. WAIT! IF YOU CAN READ, YOU KNOW ABOUT--
THE YLF.
ALREADY KNEW. WORST KEPT SECRET IN THE PLAINS. DREAM SCORE OF EVERY RAIDER CLAN SINCE THE QUENCH.
MINE INCLUDED.
BOOOM
...THAT'S WHY I CAN'T LET YOU GO BACK TO RIDGETOWN, MATE. SORRY.
D-DID YOU HEAR TH--
I DON'T CARE HOW SOPPY YOUR REASONS ARE--I CAN'T HAVE YOU NABBING THAT YLF.

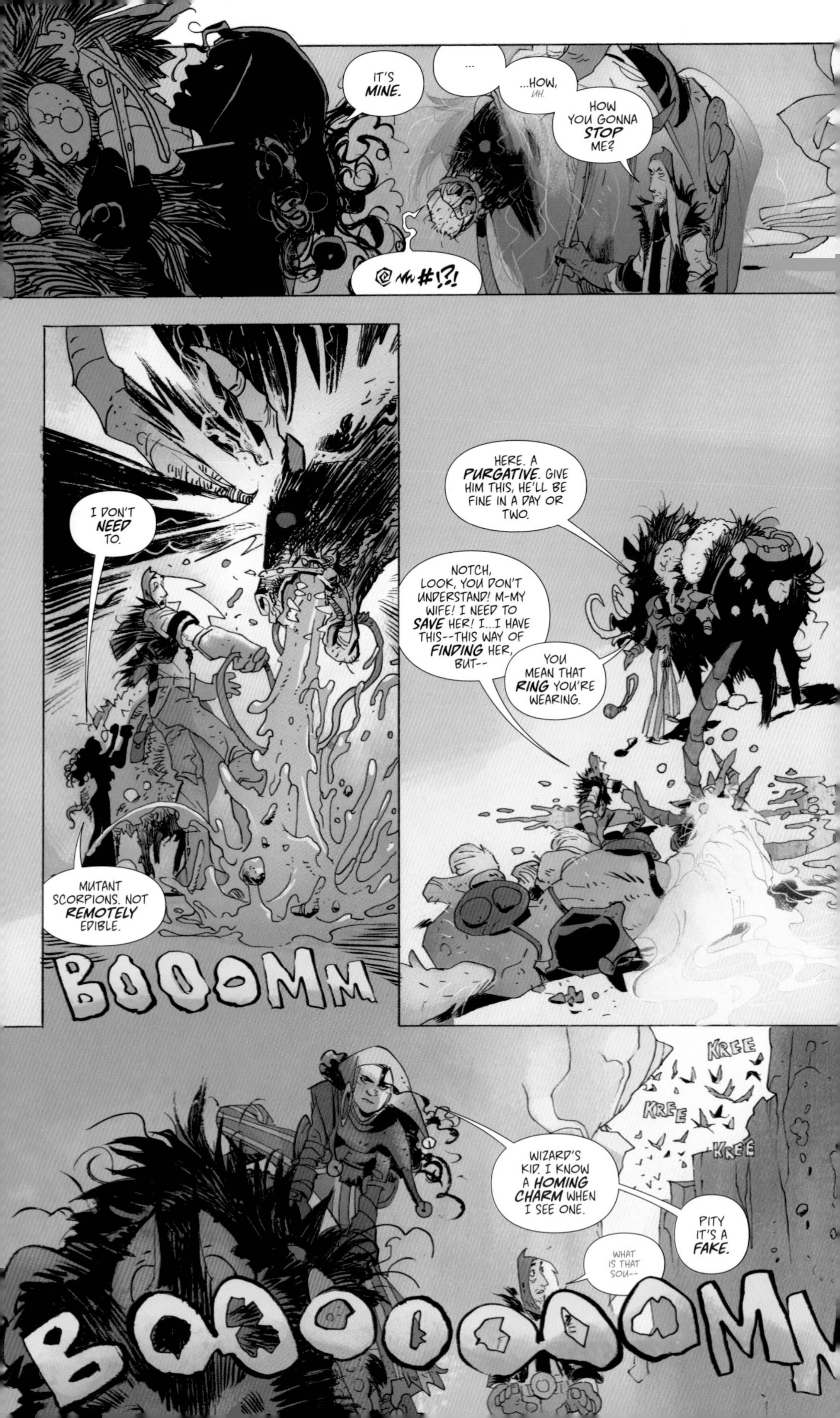
IT'S MINE.
...
...HOW, UH.
HOW YOU GONNA STOP ME?
@#!?!
I DON'T NEED TO.
MUTANT SCORPIONS. NOT REMOTELY EDIBLE.
BOOOMM
HERE. A PURGATIVE. GIVE HIM THIS, HE'LL BE FINE IN A DAY OR TWO.
NOTCH, LOOK, YOU DON'T UNDERSTAND! M-MY WIFE! I NEED TO SAVE HER! I...I HAVE THIS--THIS WAY OF FINDING HER, BUT--
YOU MEAN THAT RING YOU'RE WEARING.
KREE
KREE
KREE
WIZARD'S KID. I KNOW A HOMING CHARM WHEN I SEE ONE.
PITY IT'S A FAKE.
WHAT IS THAT SOU--
BOOOOOOMM

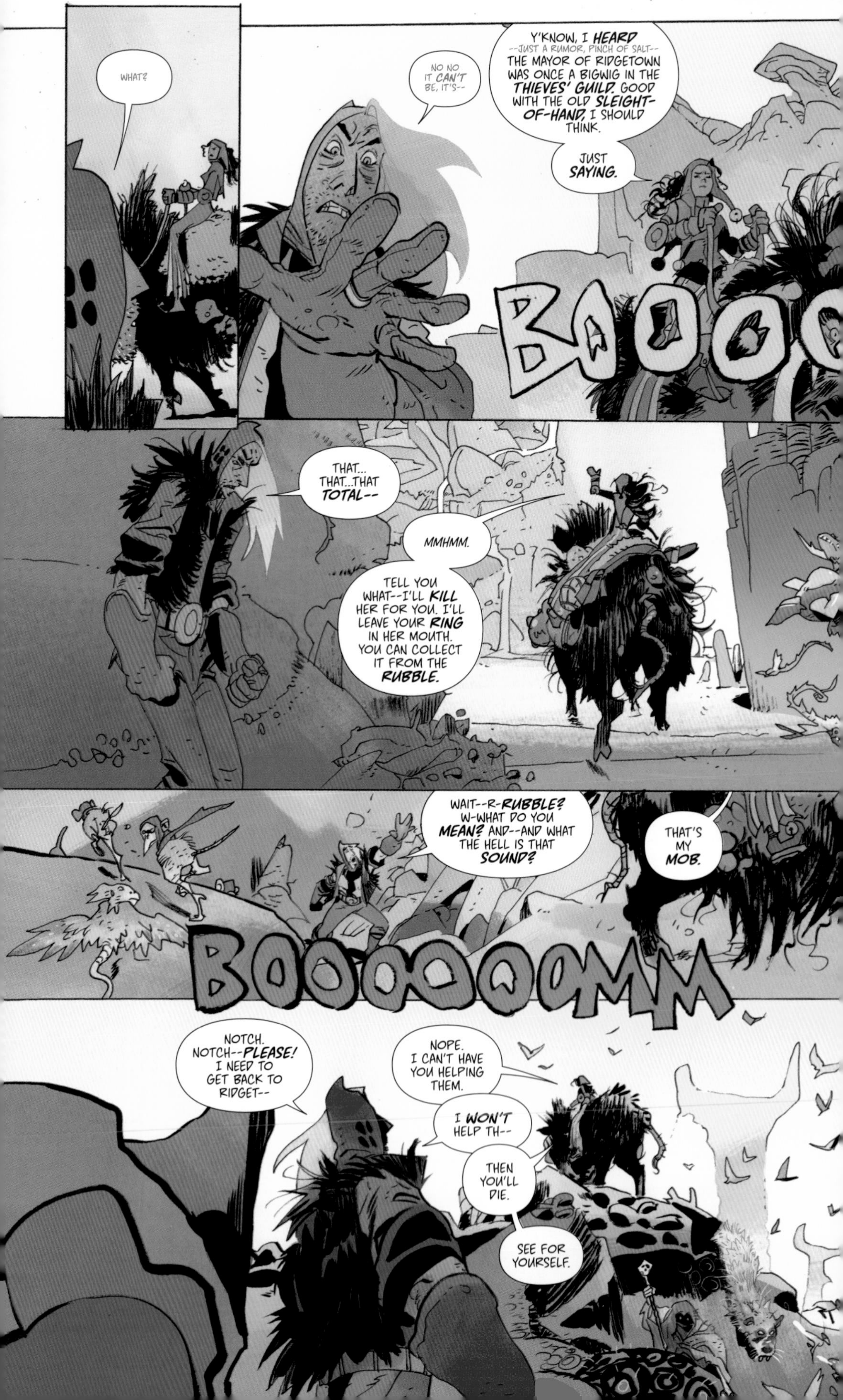
WHAT?
NO NO IT CAN'T BE, IT'S--
Y'KNOW, I HEARD --JUST A RUMOR, PINCH OF SALT-- THE MAYOR OF RIDGETOWN WAS ONCE A BIGWIG IN THE THIEVES' GUILD. GOOD WITH THE OLD SLEIGHT-OF-HAND, I SHOULD THINK.
JUST SAYING.
BOOO
THAT... THAT...THAT TOTAL--
MMHMM.
TELL YOU WHAT--I'LL KILL HER FOR YOU. I'LL LEAVE YOUR RING IN HER MOUTH. YOU CAN COLLECT IT FROM THE RUBBLE.
WAIT--R-RUBBLE? W-WHAT DO YOU MEAN? AND--AND WHAT THE HELL IS THAT SOUND?
THAT'S MY MOB.
BOOOOOMM
NOTCH. NOTCH--PLEASE! I NEED TO GET BACK TO RIDGET--
NOPE. I CAN'T HAVE YOU HELPING THEM.
I WON'T HELP TH--
THEN YOU'LL DIE.
SEE FOR YOURSELF.

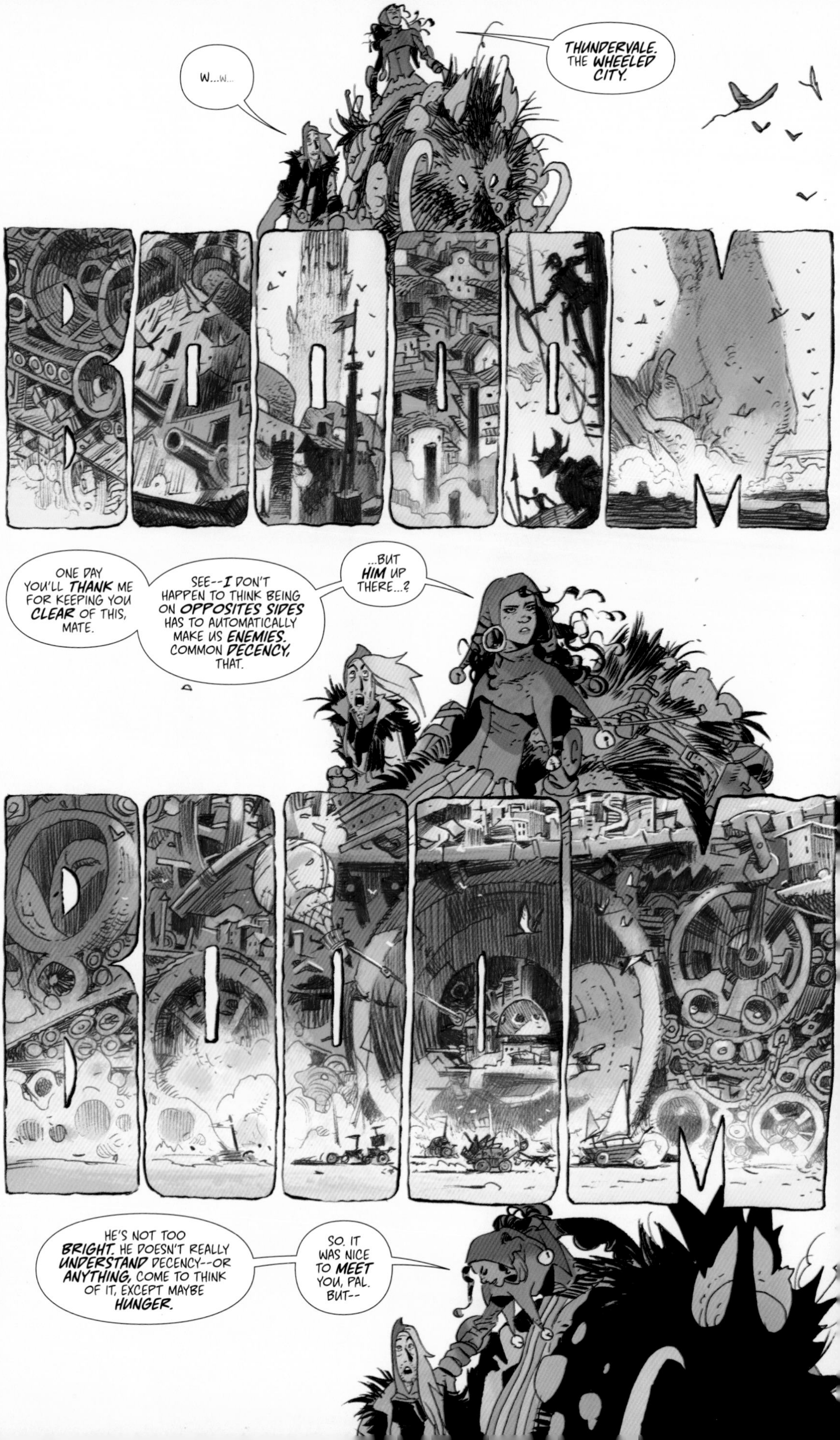

THUNDERVALE. THE WHEELED CITY.
W...W...
BOOOOM
...BUT HIM UP THERE...?
SEE--I DON'T HAPPEN TO THINK BEING ON OPPOSITES SIDES HAS TO AUTOMATICALLY MAKE US ENEMIES. COMMON DECENCY, THAT.
ONE DAY YOU'LL THANK ME FOR KEEPING YOU CLEAR OF THIS, MATE.
BOOOM
SO. IT WAS NICE TO MEET YOU, PAL. BUT--
HE'S NOT TOO BRIGHT. HE DOESN'T REALLY UNDERSTAND DECENCY--OR ANYTHING, COME TO THINK OF IT, EXCEPT MAYBE HUNGER.

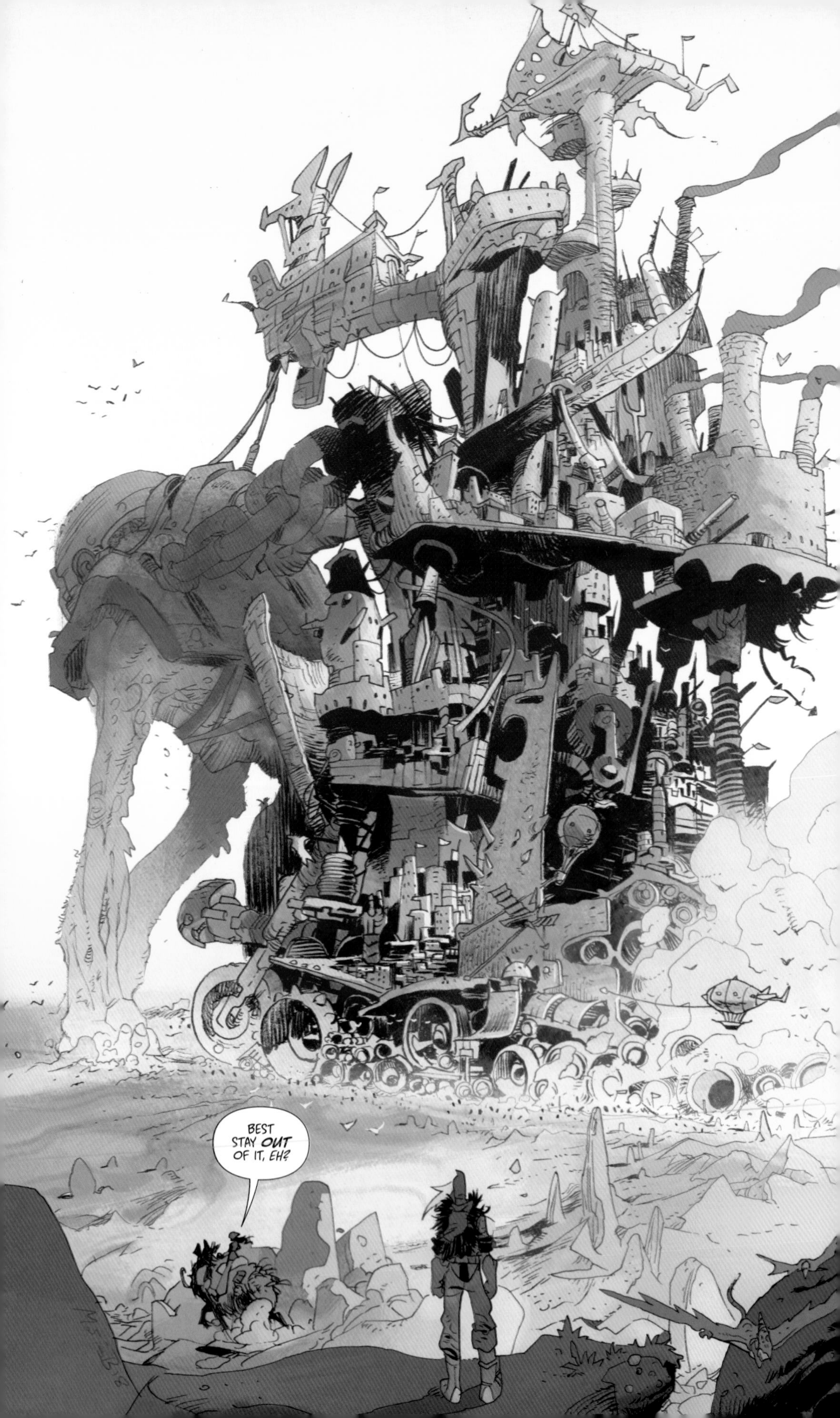
BEST STAY OUT OF IT, EH?

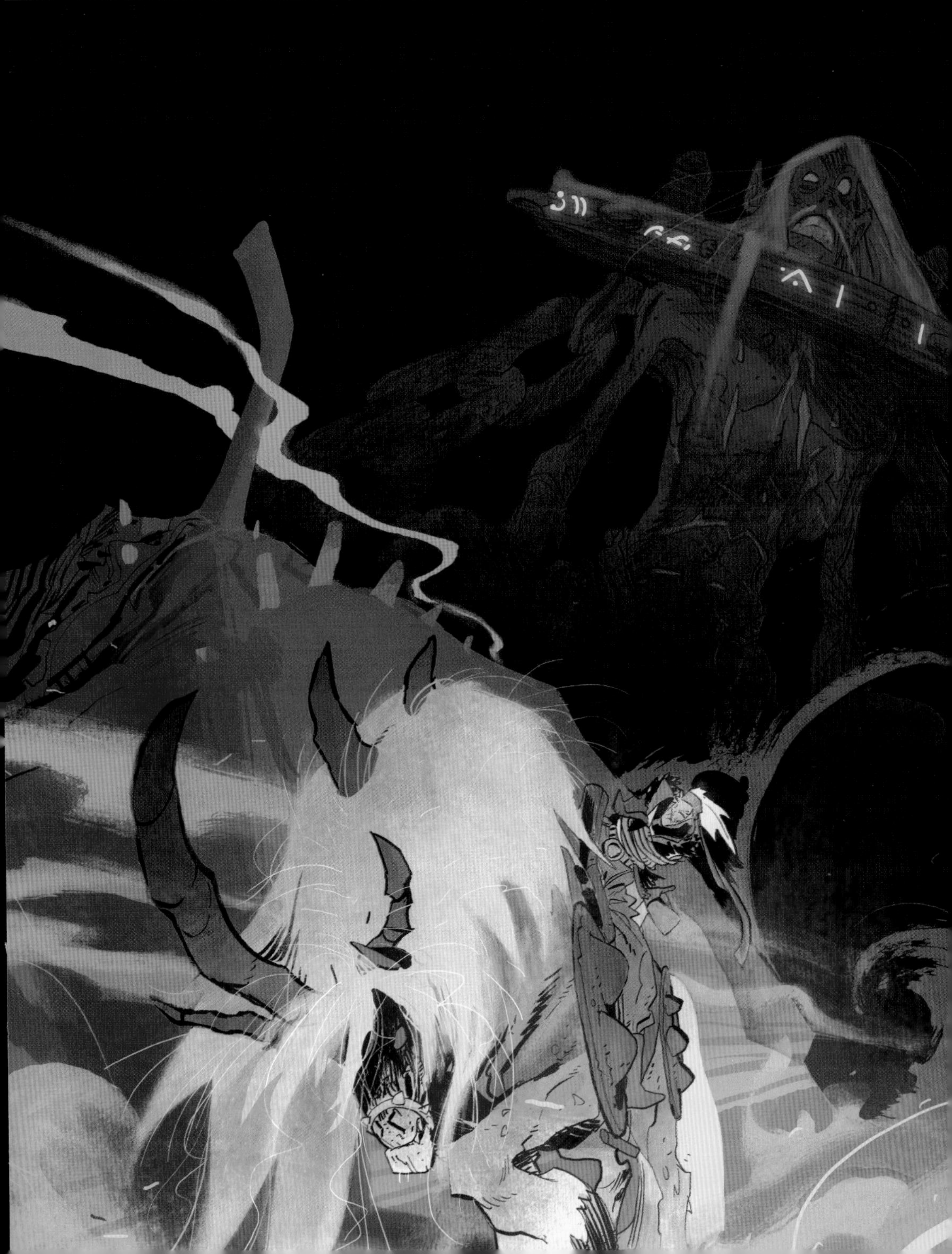

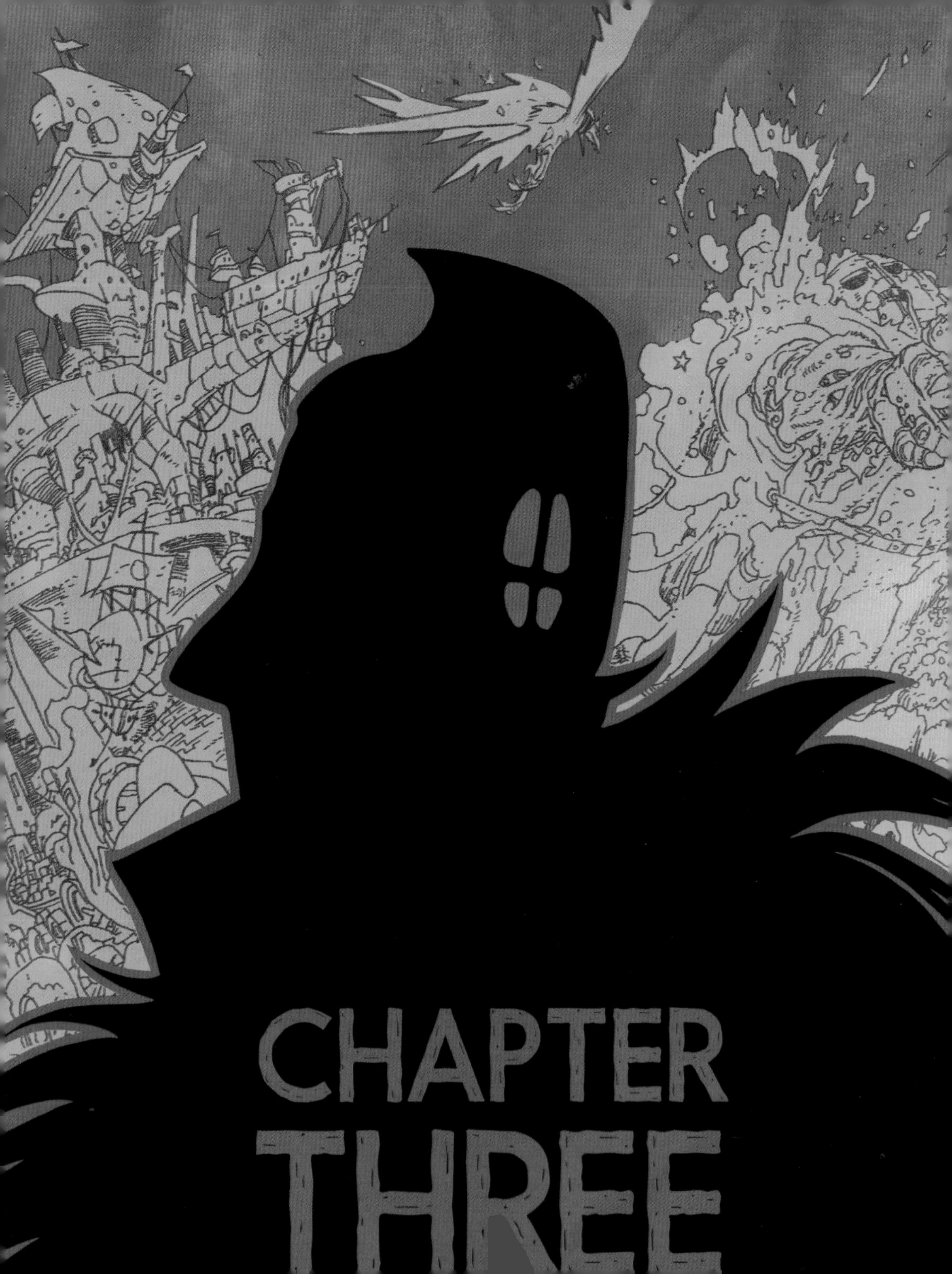
CHAPTER
THREE

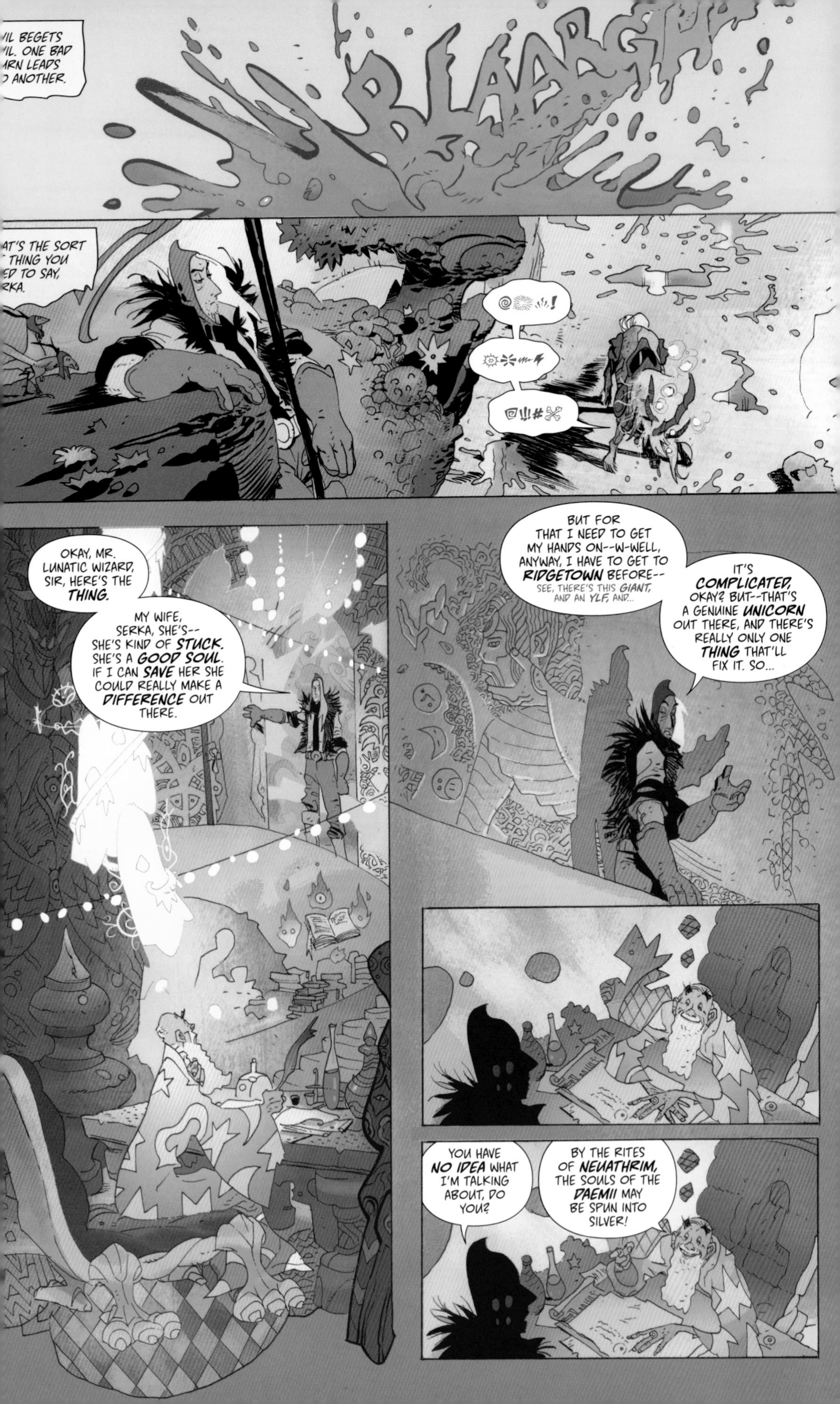

VIL BEGETS
VIL. ONE BAD
URN LEADS
O ANOTHER.
BLAARGH
AT'S THE SORT
THING YOU
ED TO SAY,
RKA.
OKAY, MR. LUNATIC WIZARD, SIR, HERE'S THE THING.
MY WIFE, SERKA, SHE'S-- SHE'S KIND OF STUCK. SHE'S A GOOD SOUL. IF I CAN SAVE HER SHE COULD REALLY MAKE A DIFFERENCE OUT THERE.
BUT FOR THAT I NEED TO GET MY HANDS ON--W-WELL, ANYWAY, I HAVE TO GET TO RIDGETOWN BEFORE-- SEE, THERE'S THIS GIANT, AND AN YLF, AND...
IT'S COMPLICATED, OKAY? BUT--THAT'S A GENUINE UNICORN OUT THERE, AND THERE'S REALLY ONLY ONE THING THAT'LL FIX IT. SO...
YOU HAVE NO IDEA WHAT I'M TALKING ABOUT, DO YOU?
BY THE RITES OF NEUATHRIM, THE SOULS OF THE DAEMII MAY BE SPUN INTO SILVER!

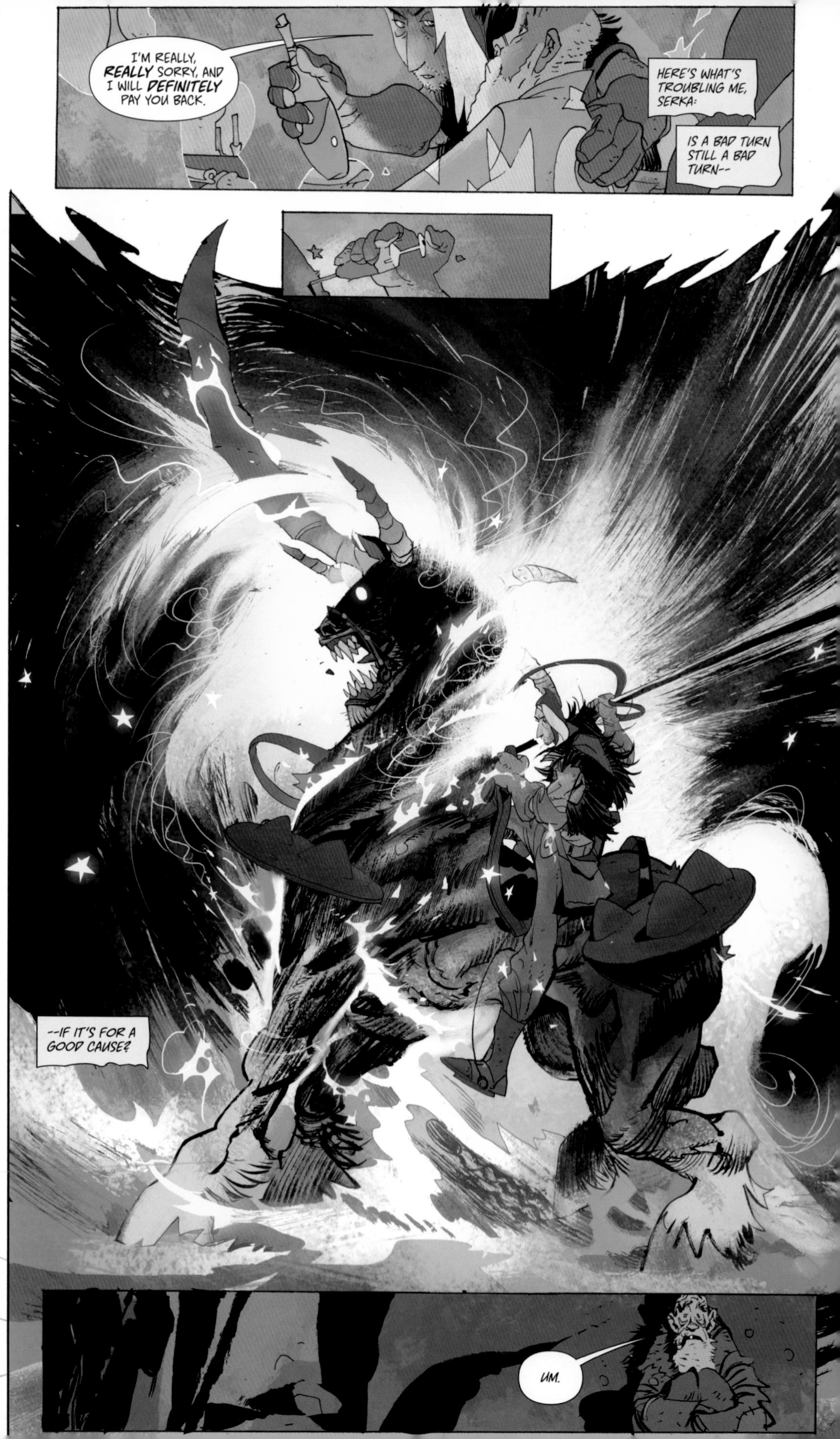
I'M REALLY, **REALLY** SORRY, AND I WILL **DEFINITELY** PAY YOU BACK.
HERE'S WHAT'S TROUBLING ME, SERKA:
IS A BAD TURN STILL A BAD TURN--
--IF IT'S FOR A GOOD CAUSE?
UM.

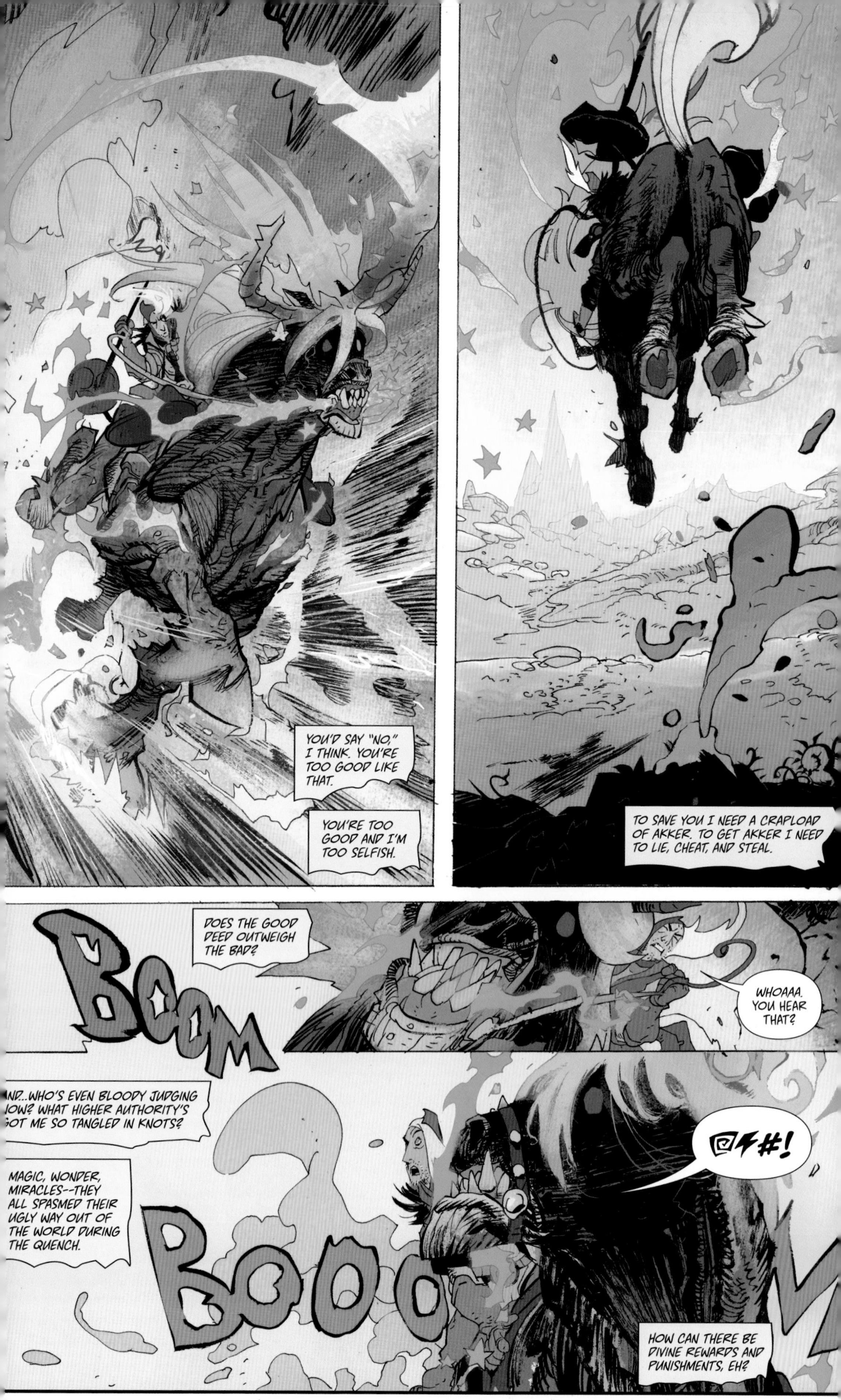

YOU'D SAY "NO," I THINK. YOU'RE TOO GOOD LIKE THAT.
YOU'RE TOO GOOD AND I'M TOO SELFISH.
TO SAVE YOU I NEED A CRAPLOAD OF AKKER. TO GET AKKER I NEED TO LIE, CHEAT, AND STEAL.
BOOM
DOES THE GOOD DEED OUTWEIGH THE BAD?
WHOAAA. YOU HEAR THAT?
ND...WHO'S EVEN BLOODY JUDGING OW? WHAT HIGHER AUTHORITY'S OT ME SO TANGLED IN KNOTS?
MAGIC, WONDER, MIRACLES--THEY ALL SPASMED THEIR UGLY WAY OUT OF THE WORLD DURING THE QUENCH.
BOOO
#!
HOW CAN THERE BE DIVINE REWARDS AND PUNISHMENTS, EH?

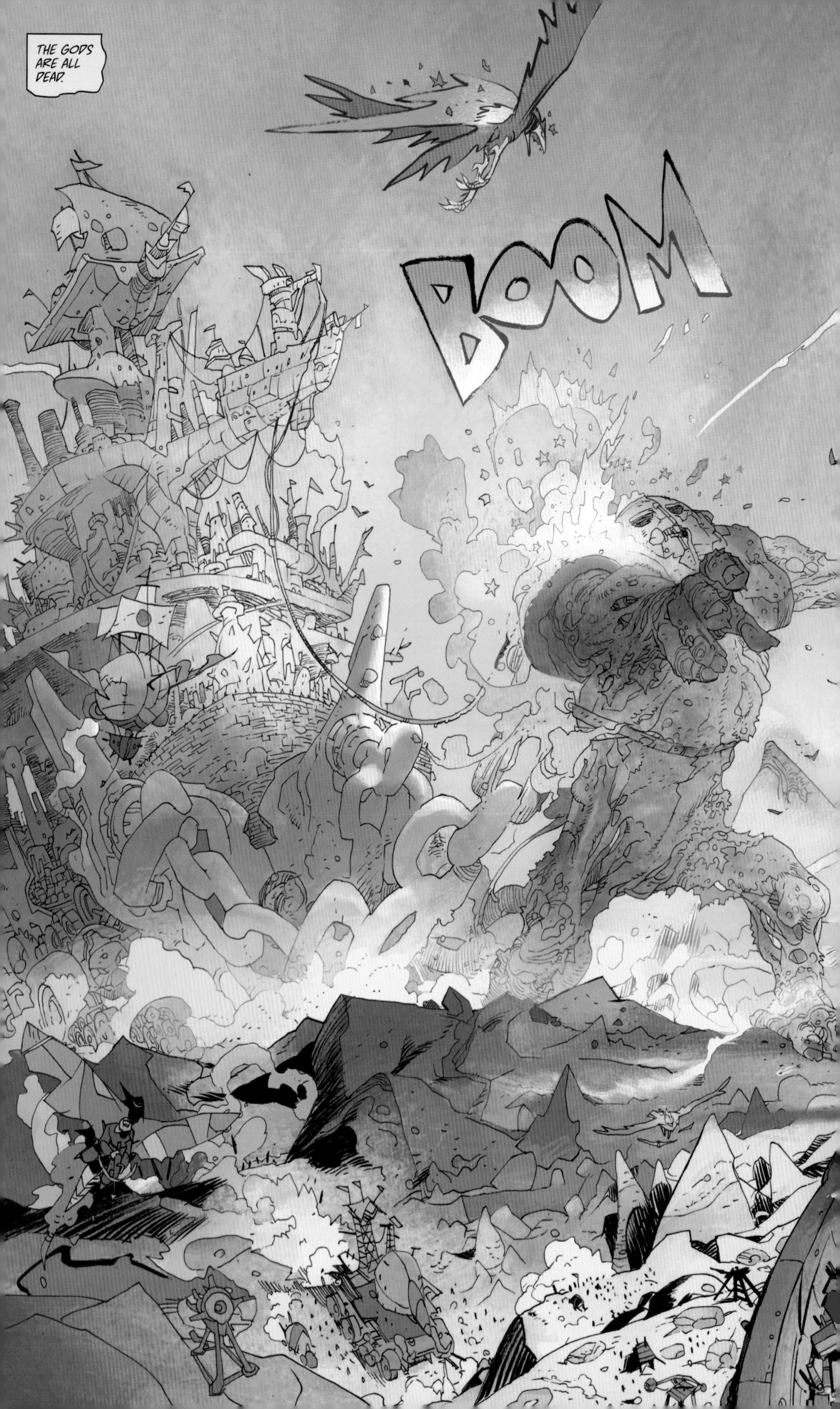
THE GODS ARE ALL DEAD.
BOOM

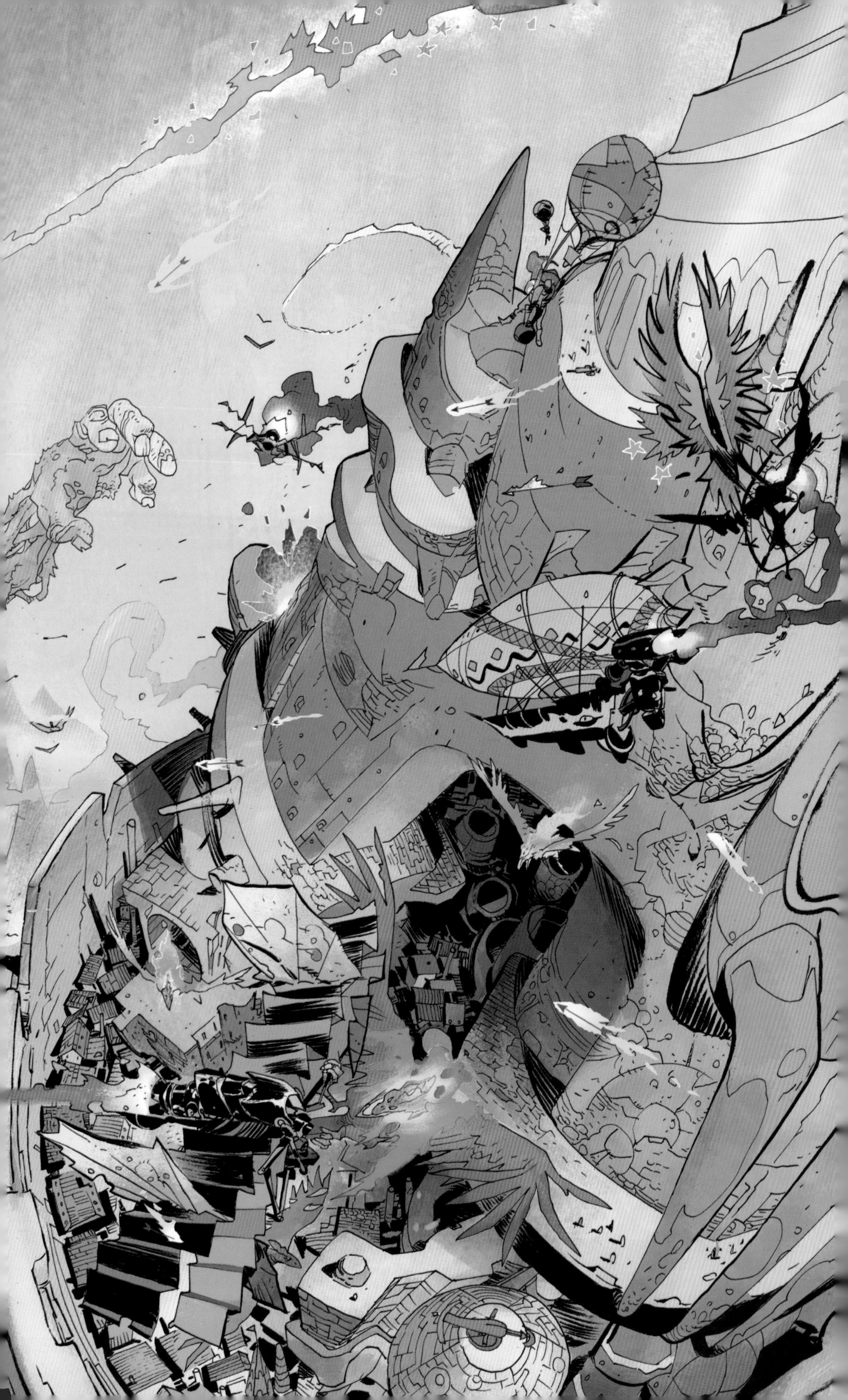

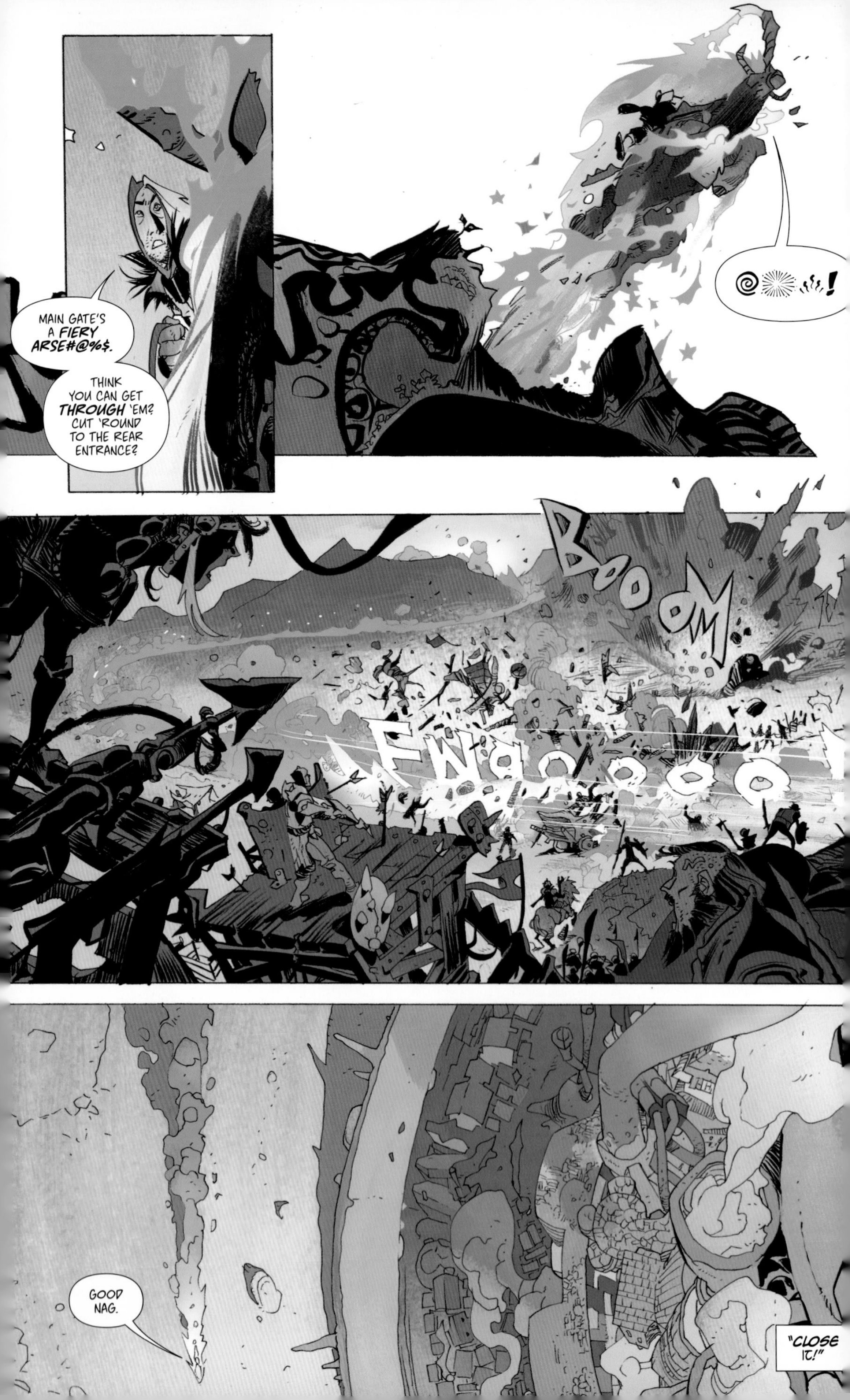

MAIN GATE'S A FIERY ARSE#@%$.
THINK YOU CAN GET THROUGH 'EM? CUT 'ROUND TO THE REAR ENTRANCE?
!
BOOOM
FWOOOOOO
GOOD NAG.
"CLOSE IT!"

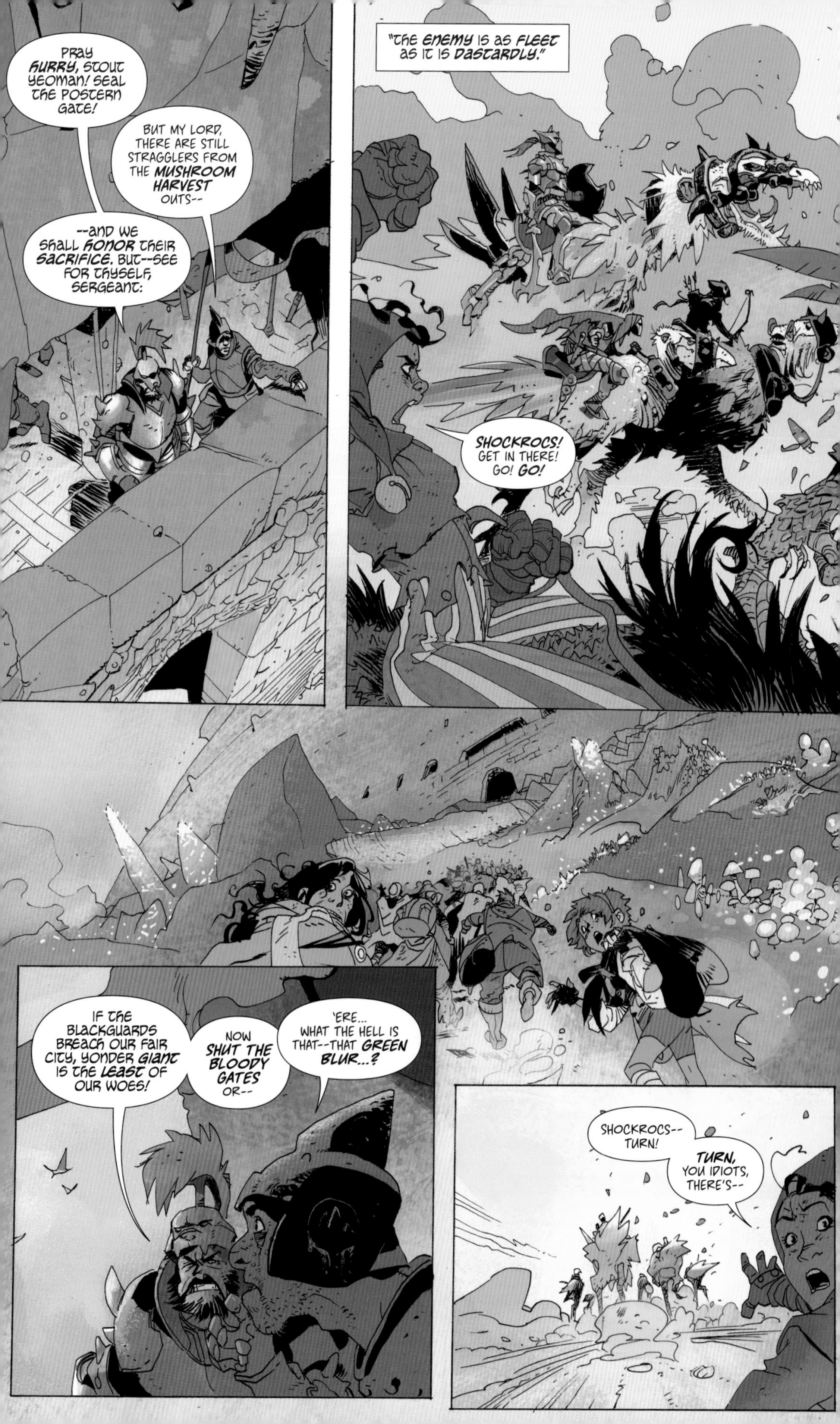
PRAY HURRY, STOUT YEOMAN! SEAL THE POSTERN GATE!
BUT MY LORD, THERE ARE STILL STRAGGLERS FROM THE MUSHROOM HARVEST OUTS--
--AND WE SHALL HONOR THEIR SACRIFICE. BUT--SEE FOR THYSELF, SERGEANT:
"THE ENEMY IS AS FLEET AS IT IS DASTARDLY."
SHOCKROCS! GET IN THERE! GO! GO!
IF THE BLACKGUARDS BREACH OUR FAIR CITY, YONDER GIANT IS THE LEAST OF OUR WOES!
NOW SHUT THE BLOODY GATES OR--
'ERE... WHAT THE HELL IS THAT--THAT GREEN BLUR...?
SHOCKROCS-- TURN!
TURN, YOU IDIOTS, THERE'S--

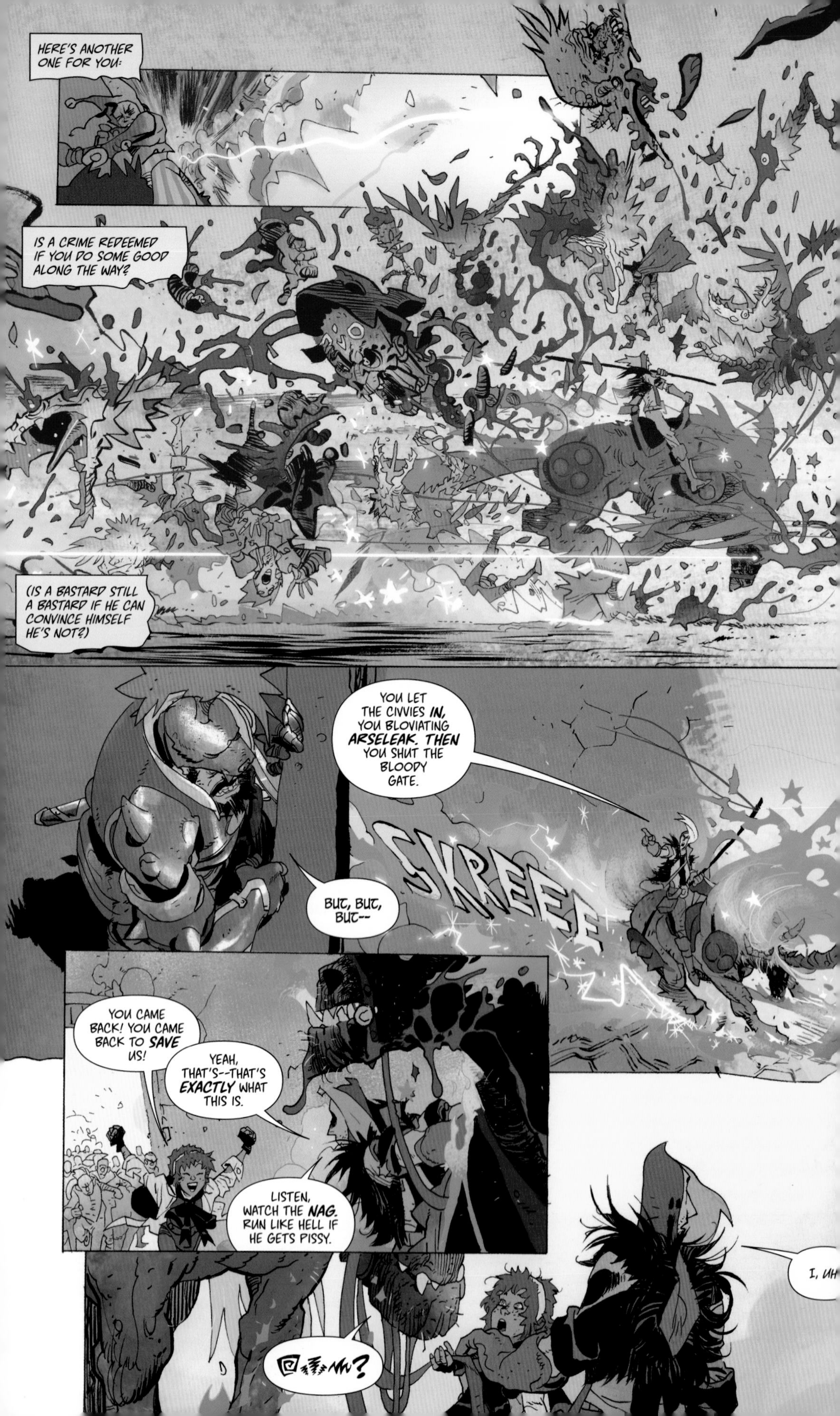
HERE'S ANOTHER ONE FOR YOU:
IS A CRIME REDEEMED IF YOU DO SOME GOOD ALONG THE WAY?
(IS A BASTARD STILL A BASTARD IF HE CAN CONVINCE HIMSELF HE'S NOT?)
YOU LET THE CIVVIES IN, YOU BLOVIATING ARSELEAK. THEN YOU SHUT THE BLOODY GATE.
BUT, BUT, BUT--
SKREEE
YOU CAME BACK! YOU CAME BACK TO SAVE US!
YEAH, THAT'S--THAT'S EXACTLY WHAT THIS IS.
LISTEN, WATCH THE NAG. RUN LIKE HELL IF HE GETS PISSY.
I, UH

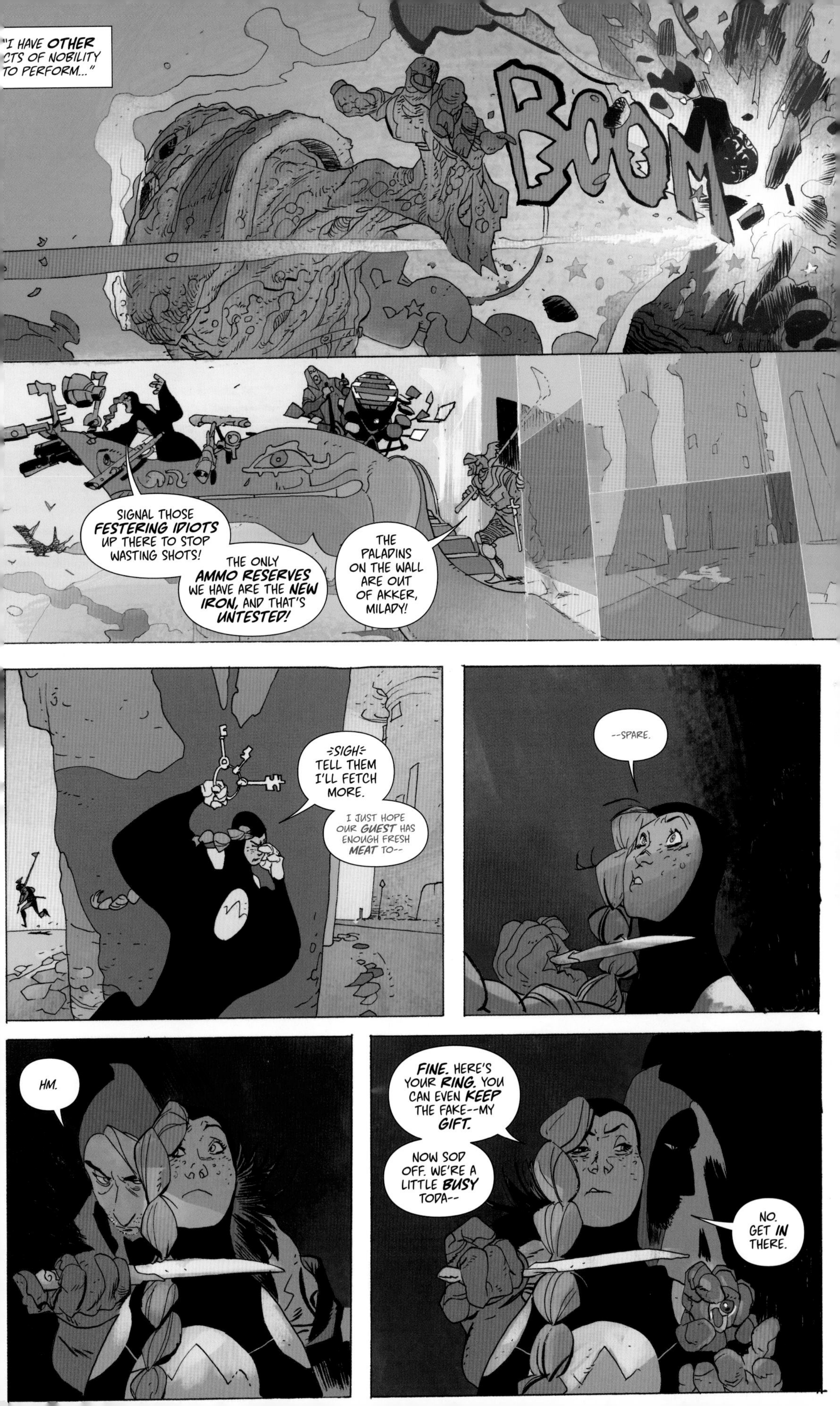
"I HAVE OTHER
CTS OF NOBILITY
TO PERFORM..."
BOOM
SIGNAL THOSE FESTERING IDIOTS UP THERE TO STOP WASTING SHOTS!
THE ONLY AMMO RESERVES WE HAVE ARE THE NEW IRON, AND THAT'S UNTESTED!
THE PALADINS ON THE WALL ARE OUT OF AKKER, MILADY!
SIGH TELL THEM I'LL FETCH MORE.
I JUST HOPE OUR GUEST HAS ENOUGH FRESH MEAT TO--
--SPARE.
HM.
FINE. HERE'S YOUR RING. YOU CAN EVEN KEEP THE FAKE--MY GIFT.
NOW SOD OFF. WE'RE A LITTLE BUSY TODA--
NO. GET IN THERE.

BUT THE **QUESTIONS** SPREAD LIKE A **POX.**

Y-YOU **CAN'T.** PLEASE.

I DON'T WANT IT **ALL.** JUST A--I DUNNO--A **LEG.** MAYBE AN **ARM.**

I'M NOT **DONE** HERE.

I TRY TO FIND THE MIDDLE PATH, SERKA. TO MIND MY OWN BUSINESS. TO KEEP THINGS SIMPLE.

LIKE: IS IT WRONG TO STEAL FROM THE UNJUST?

DOES SELF-AWARENESS MITIGATE GUILT?

IT DOESN'T GROW BACK **FAST ENOUGH!** Y-YOU'D **DEPRIVE** US! YOU **MONSTER!**

YOU BUTCHER AN **IMMORTAL** EVERY NIGHT JUST TO CLING TO **POWER,** LADY. LET'S NOT GET INTO **NAME-CALLING.**

AND WHAT GOOD'S A CONSCIENCE AT **ALL,** IN A WORLD THIS BROKEN?

A CUT OHHH A NEW CUT MAKE IT **CURVING** A SMILE A SMILE LIKE A RAINBOW **PAIN** IS MY DREAM NOW

...

YOU WOULDN'T **JUDGE US** IF YOU KNEW WHO CONTROLLED THAT GIANT.

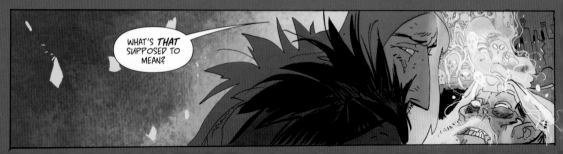

WHAT'S **THAT** SUPPOSED TO MEAN?

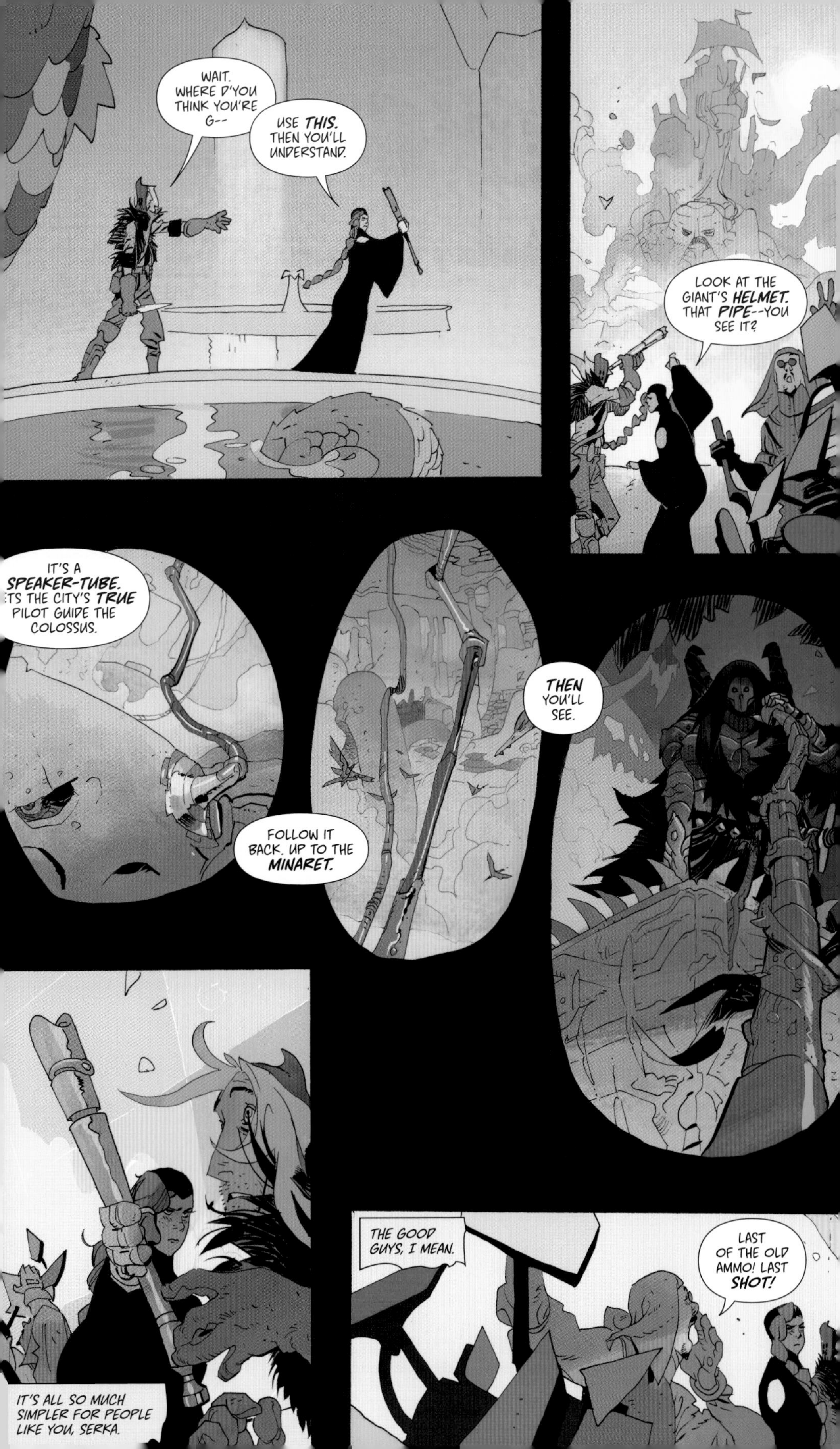
WAIT. WHERE D'YOU THINK YOU'RE G--
USE THIS. THEN YOU'LL UNDERSTAND.
LOOK AT THE GIANT'S HELMET. THAT PIPE--YOU SEE IT?
IT'S A SPEAKER-TUBE. ...ETS THE CITY'S TRUE PILOT GUIDE THE COLOSSUS.
FOLLOW IT BACK. UP TO THE MINARET.
THEN YOU'LL SEE.
IT'S ALL SO MUCH SIMPLER FOR PEOPLE LIKE YOU, SERKA.
THE GOOD GUYS, I MEAN.
LAST OF THE OLD AMMO! LAST SHOT!

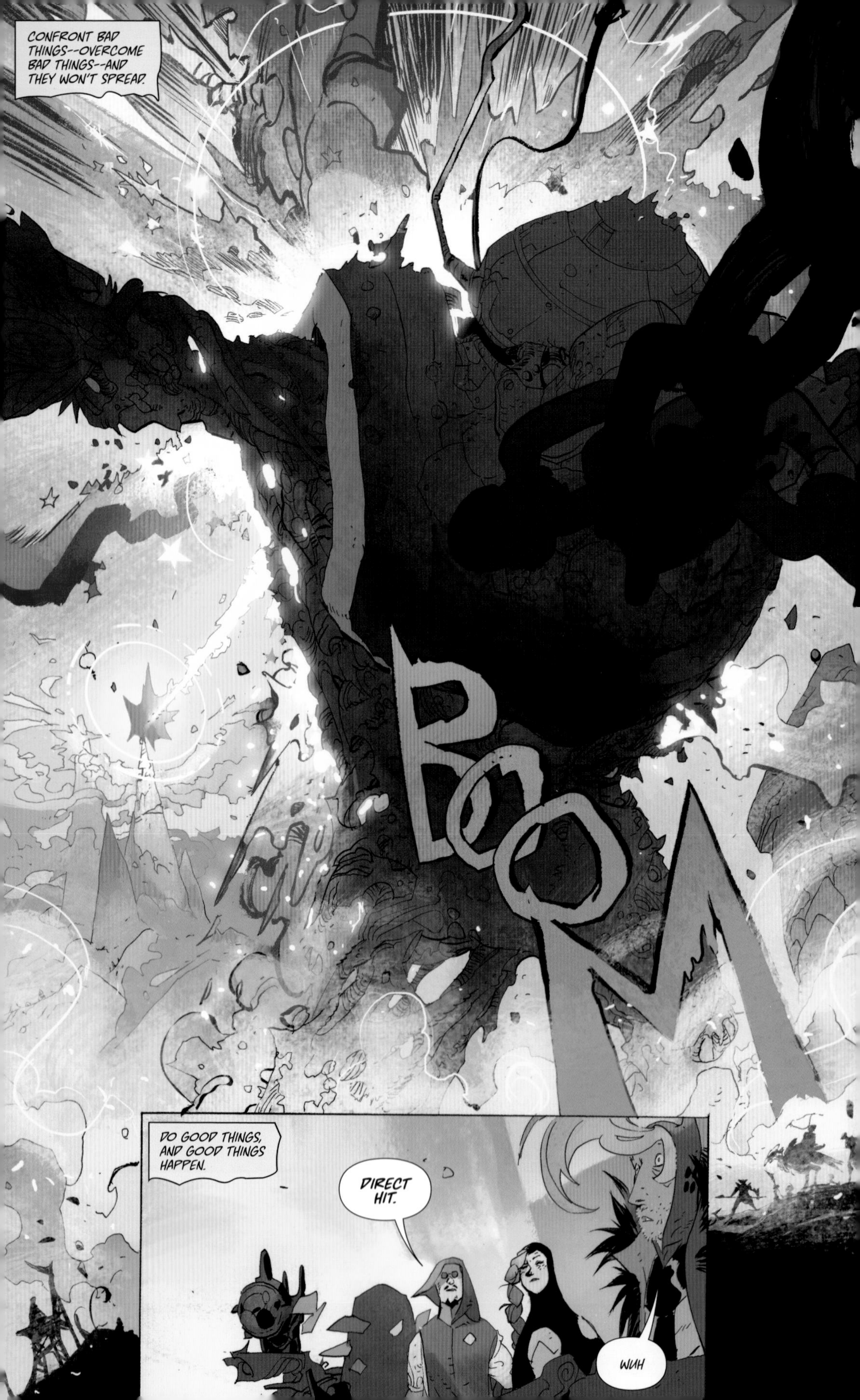
CONFRONT BAD THINGS--OVERCOME BAD THINGS--AND THEY WON'T SPREAD.
BOOM
DO GOOD THINGS, AND GOOD THINGS HAPPEN.
DIRECT HIT.
WUH

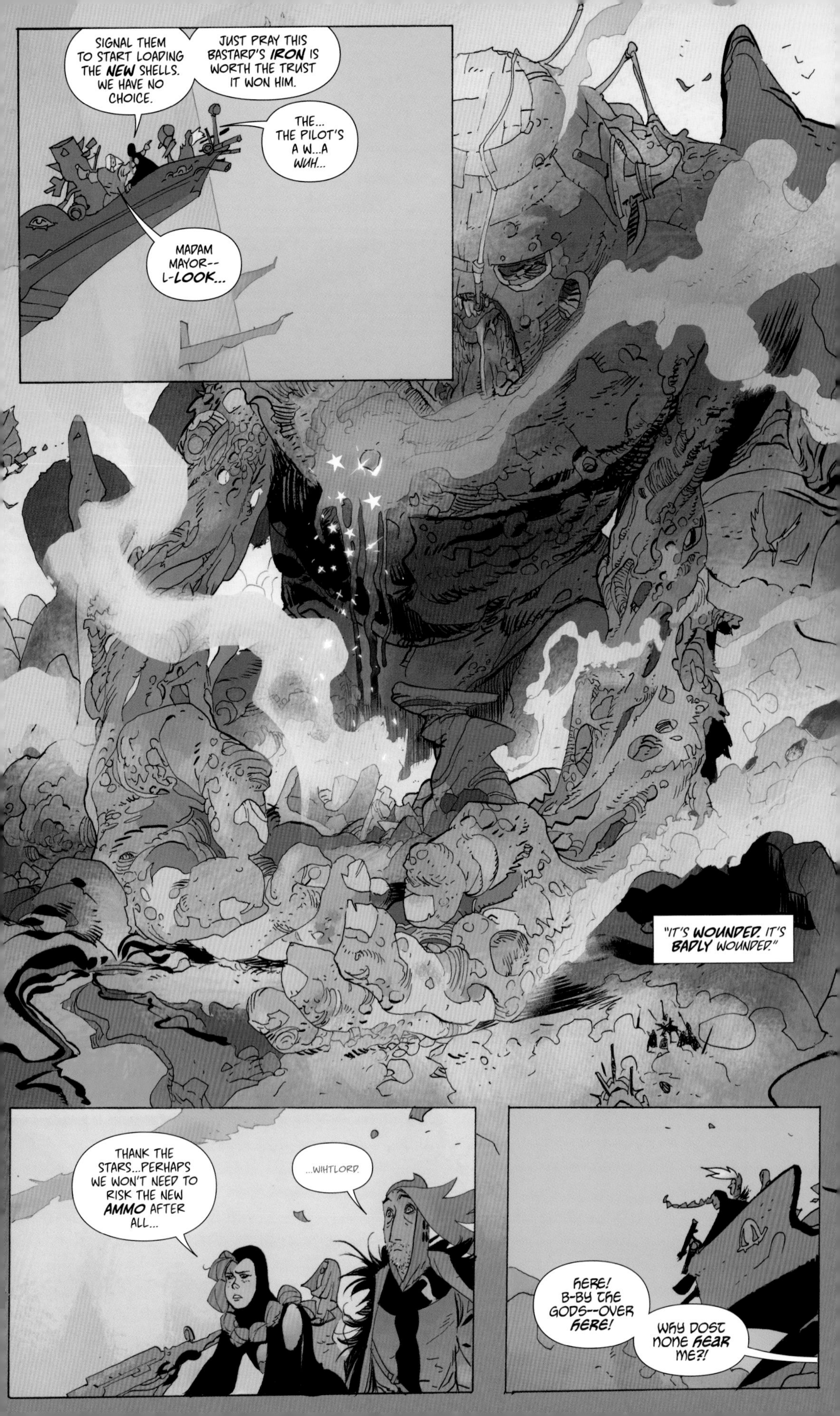
SIGNAL THEM TO START LOADING THE NEW SHELLS. WE HAVE NO CHOICE.
JUST PRAY THIS BASTARD'S IRON IS WORTH THE TRUST IT WON HIM.
THE... THE PILOT'S A W...A WUH...
MADAM MAYOR--L-LOOK...
"IT'S WOUNDED. IT'S BADLY WOUNDED."
THANK THE STARS...PERHAPS WE WON'T NEED TO RISK THE NEW AMMO AFTER ALL...
...WIHTLORD.
HERE! B-BY THE GODS--OVER HERE!
WHY DOST NONE HEAR ME?!

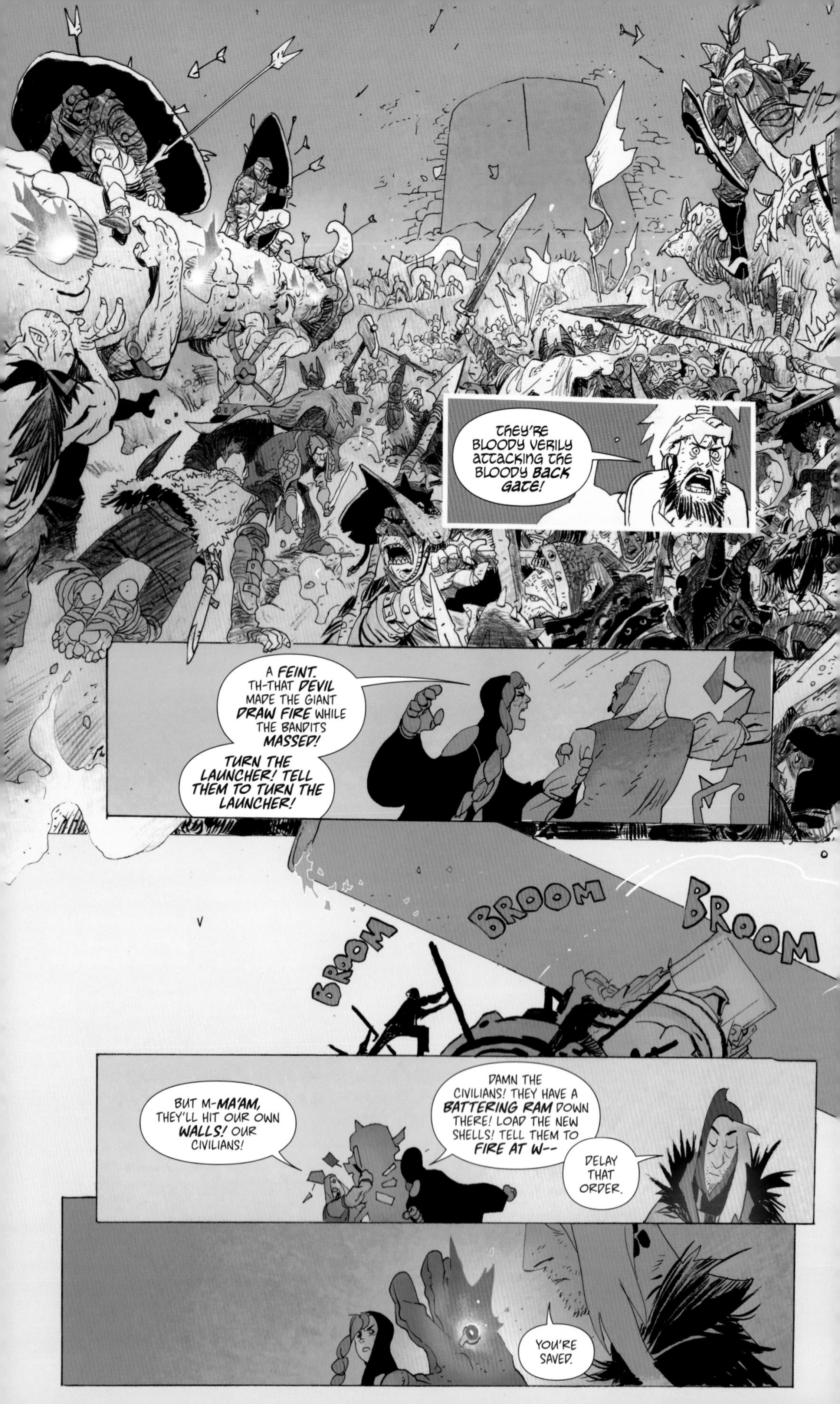
THEY'RE BLOODY VERILY ATTACKING THE BLOODY BACK GATE!
A FEINT. TH-THAT DEVIL MADE THE GIANT DRAW FIRE WHILE THE BANDITS MASSED!
TURN THE LAUNCHER! TELL THEM TO TURN THE LAUNCHER!
BROOM
BROOM
BROOM
BUT M-MA'AM, THEY'LL HIT OUR OWN WALLS! OUR CIVILIANS!
DAMN THE CIVILIANS! THEY HAVE A BATTERING RAM DOWN THERE! LOAD THE NEW SHELLS! TELL THEM TO FIRE AT W--
DELAY THAT ORDER.
YOU'RE SAVED.

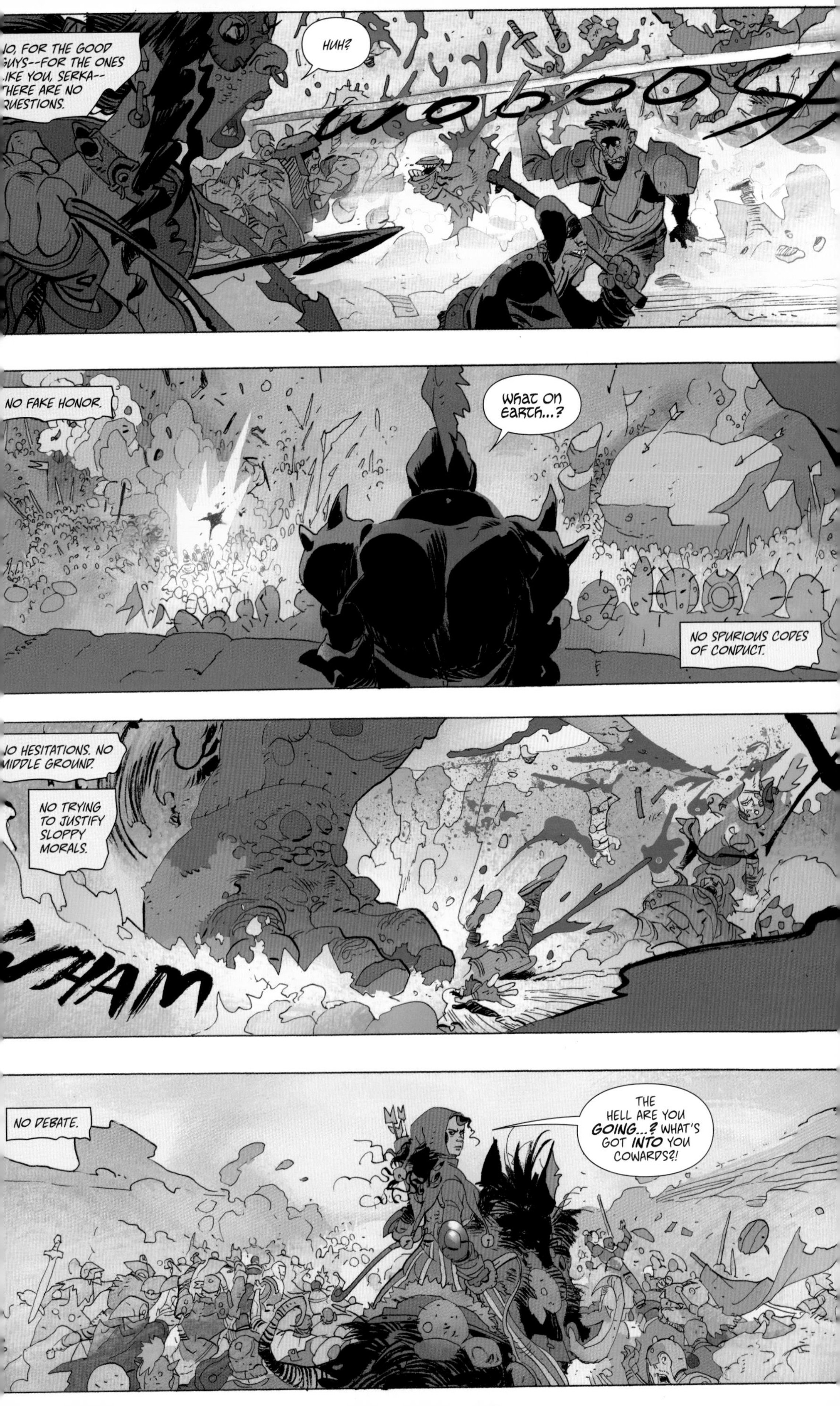

NO, FOR THE GOOD GUYS--FOR THE ONES LIKE YOU, SERKA--THERE ARE NO QUESTIONS.
HUH?
WOBOOOSH
NO FAKE HONOR.
WHAT ON EARTH...?
NO SPURIOUS CODES OF CONDUCT.
NO HESITATIONS. NO MIDDLE GROUND.
NO TRYING TO JUSTIFY SLOPPY MORALS.
SHAM
NO DEBATE.
THE HELL ARE YOU **GOING...?** WHAT'S GOT **INTO** YOU COWARDS?!

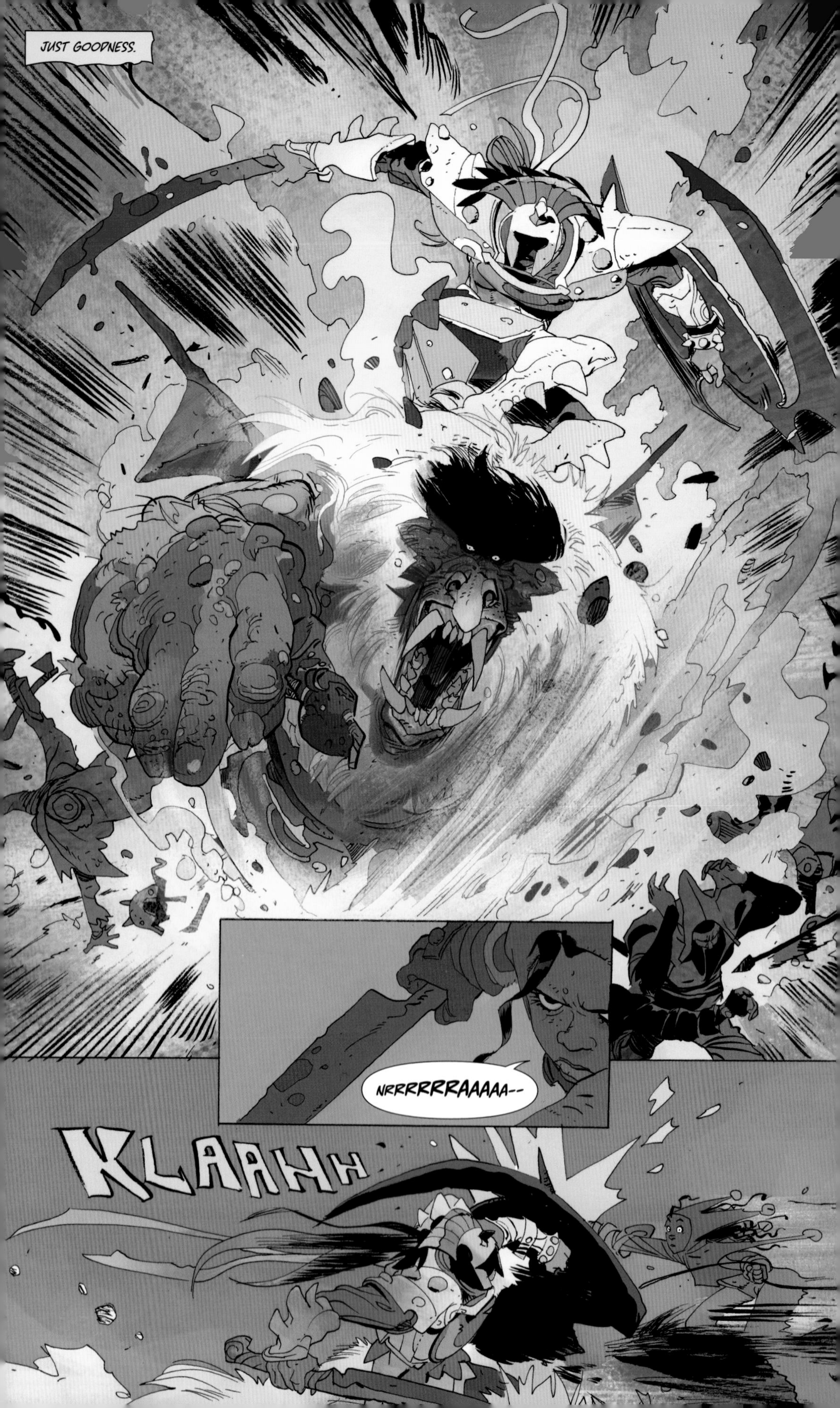
JUST GOODNESS.
NRRRRRRAAAAA--
KLAAHH

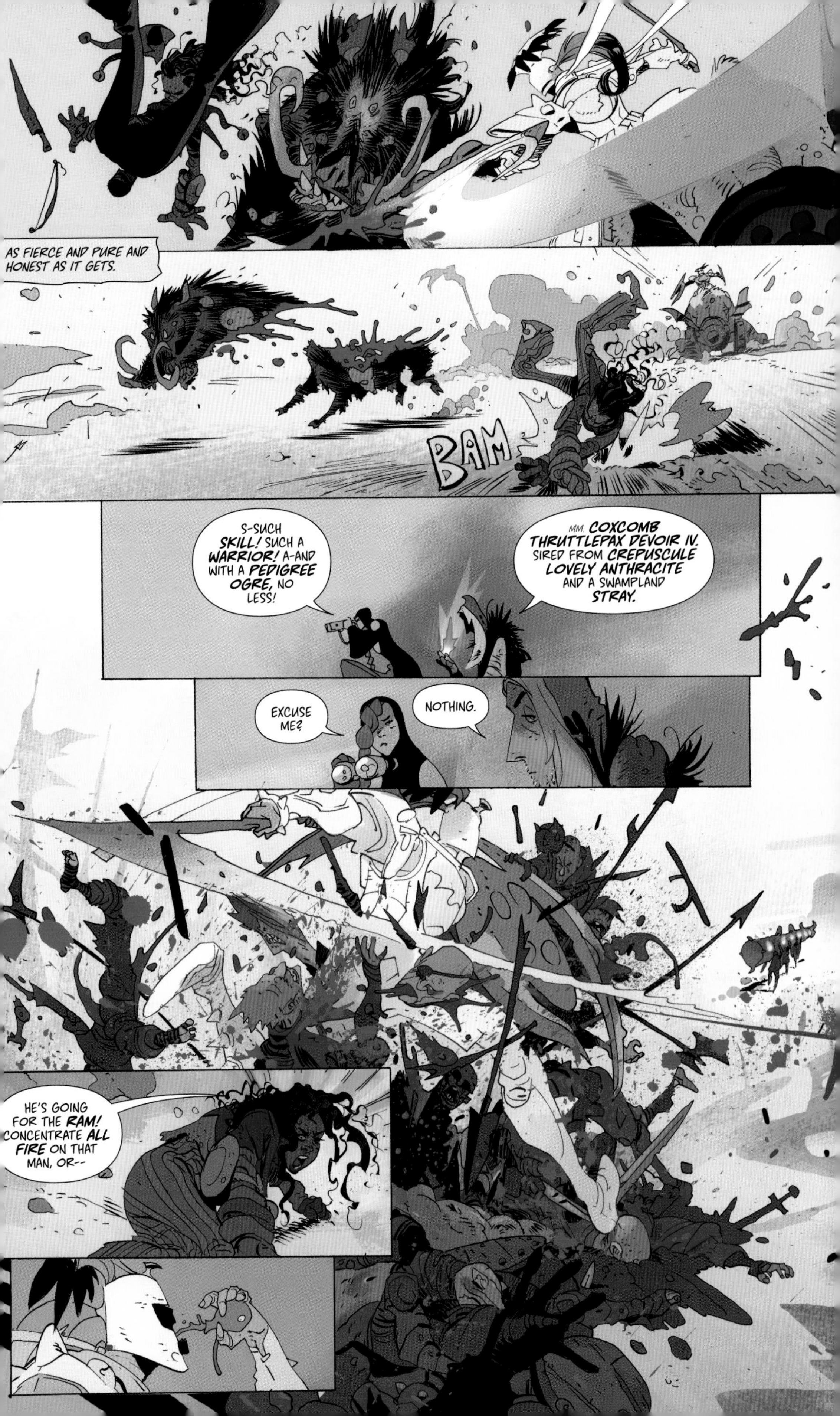

AS FIERCE AND PURE AND HONEST AS IT GETS.
BAM
S-SUCH SKILL! SUCH A WARRIOR! A-AND WITH A PEDIGREE OGRE, NO LESS!
MM. COXCOMB THRUTTLEPAX DEVOIR IV. SIRED FROM CREPUSCULE LOVELY ANTHRACITE AND A SWAMPLAND STRAY.
EXCUSE ME?
NOTHING.
HE'S GOING FOR THE RAM! CONCENTRATE ALL FIRE ON THAT MAN, OR--

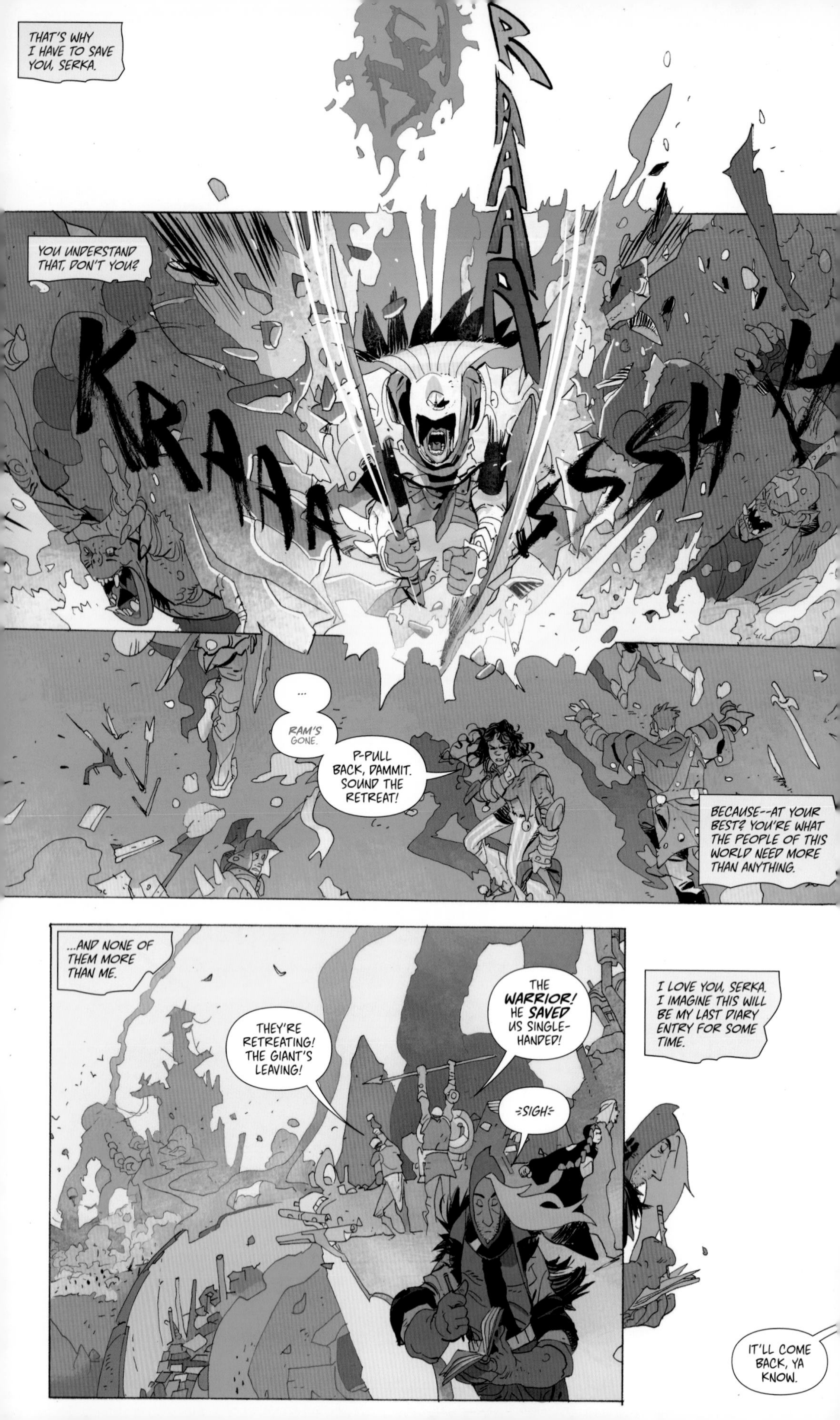
THAT'S WHY I HAVE TO SAVE YOU, SERKA.
RRAAAA
YOU UNDERSTAND THAT, DON'T YOU?
KRAAAASSSHH
...
RAM'S GONE.
P-PULL BACK, DAMMIT. SOUND THE RETREAT!
BECAUSE--AT YOUR BEST? YOU'RE WHAT THE PEOPLE OF THIS WORLD NEED MORE THAN ANYTHING.
...AND NONE OF THEM MORE THAN ME.
THEY'RE RETREATING! THE GIANT'S LEAVING!
THE WARRIOR! HE SAVED US SINGLE-HANDED!
SIGH
I LOVE YOU, SERKA. I IMAGINE THIS WILL BE MY LAST DIARY ENTRY FOR SOME TIME.
IT'LL COME BACK, YA KNOW.

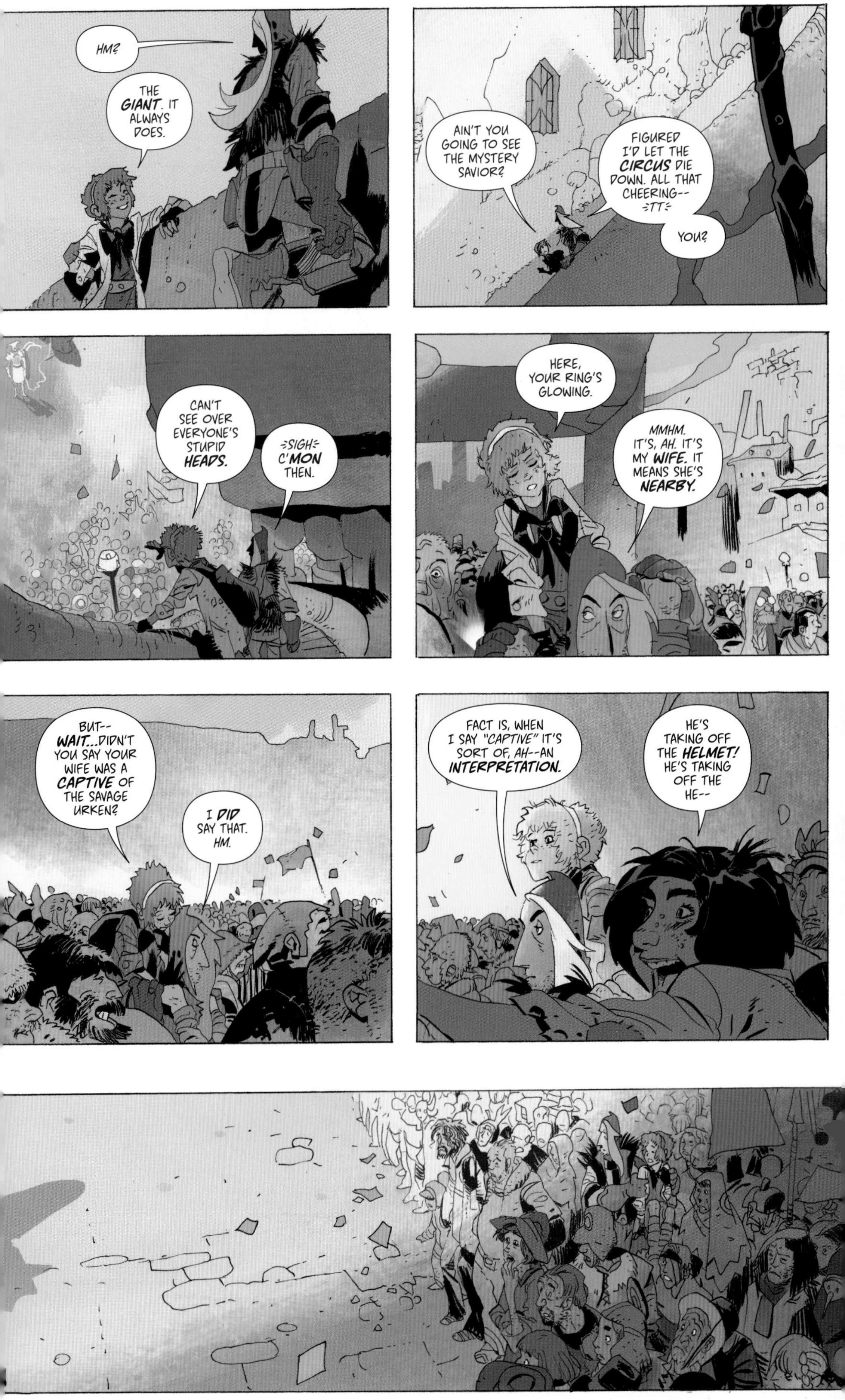
HM?
THE GIANT. IT ALWAYS DOES.
AIN'T YOU GOING TO SEE THE MYSTERY SAVIOR?
FIGURED I'D LET THE CIRCUS DIE DOWN. ALL THAT CHEERING-- =TT=
YOU?
CAN'T SEE OVER EVERYONE'S STUPID HEADS.
=SIGH= C'MON THEN.
HERE, YOUR RING'S GLOWING.
MMHM. IT'S, AH. IT'S MY WIFE. IT MEANS SHE'S NEARBY.
BUT-- WAIT...DIDN'T YOU SAY YOUR WIFE WAS A CAPTIVE OF THE SAVAGE URKEN?
I DID SAY THAT. HM.
FACT IS, WHEN I SAY "CAPTIVE" IT'S SORT OF, AH--AN INTERPRETATION.
HE'S TAKING OFF THE HELMET! HE'S TAKING OFF THE HE--

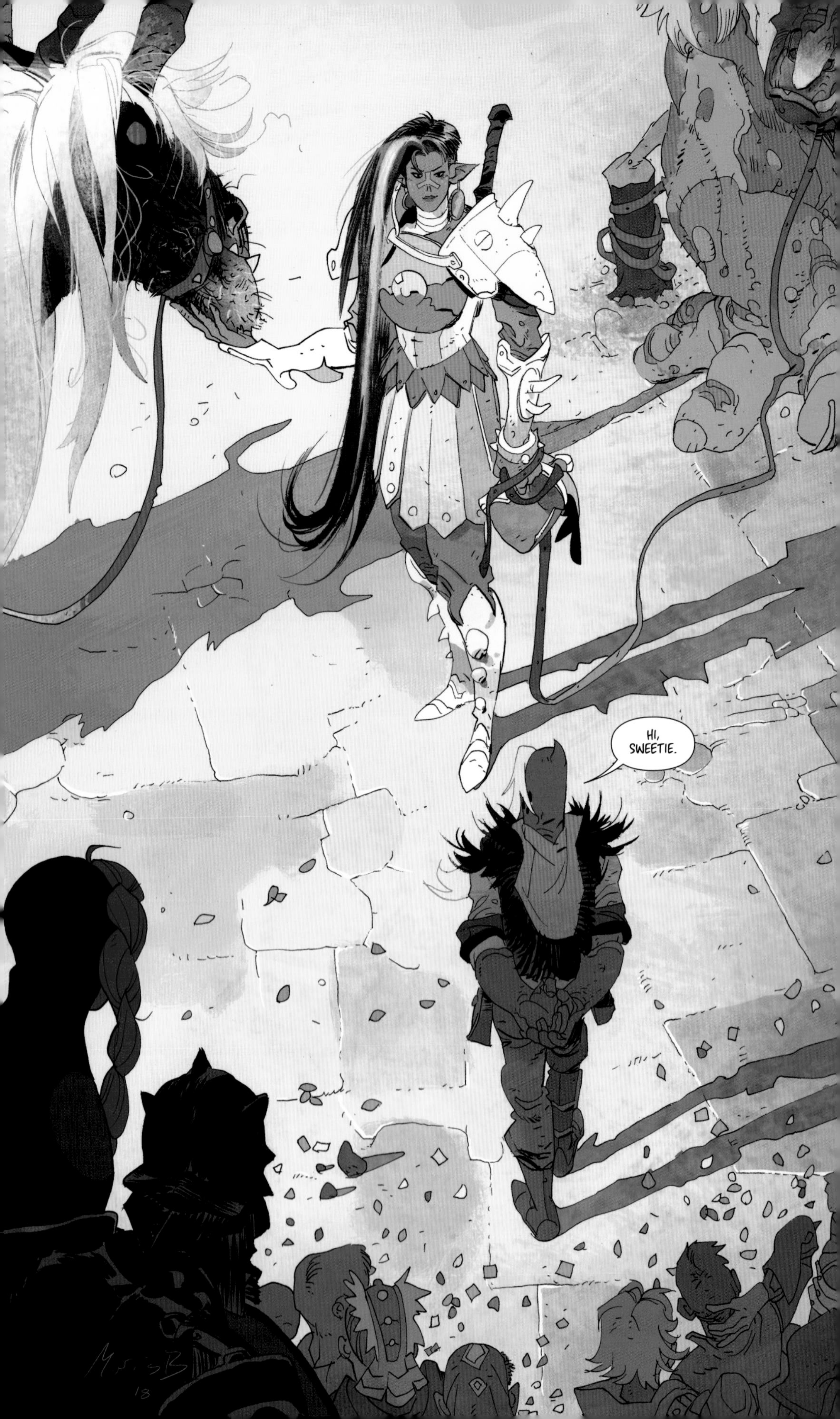
HI, SWEETIE.

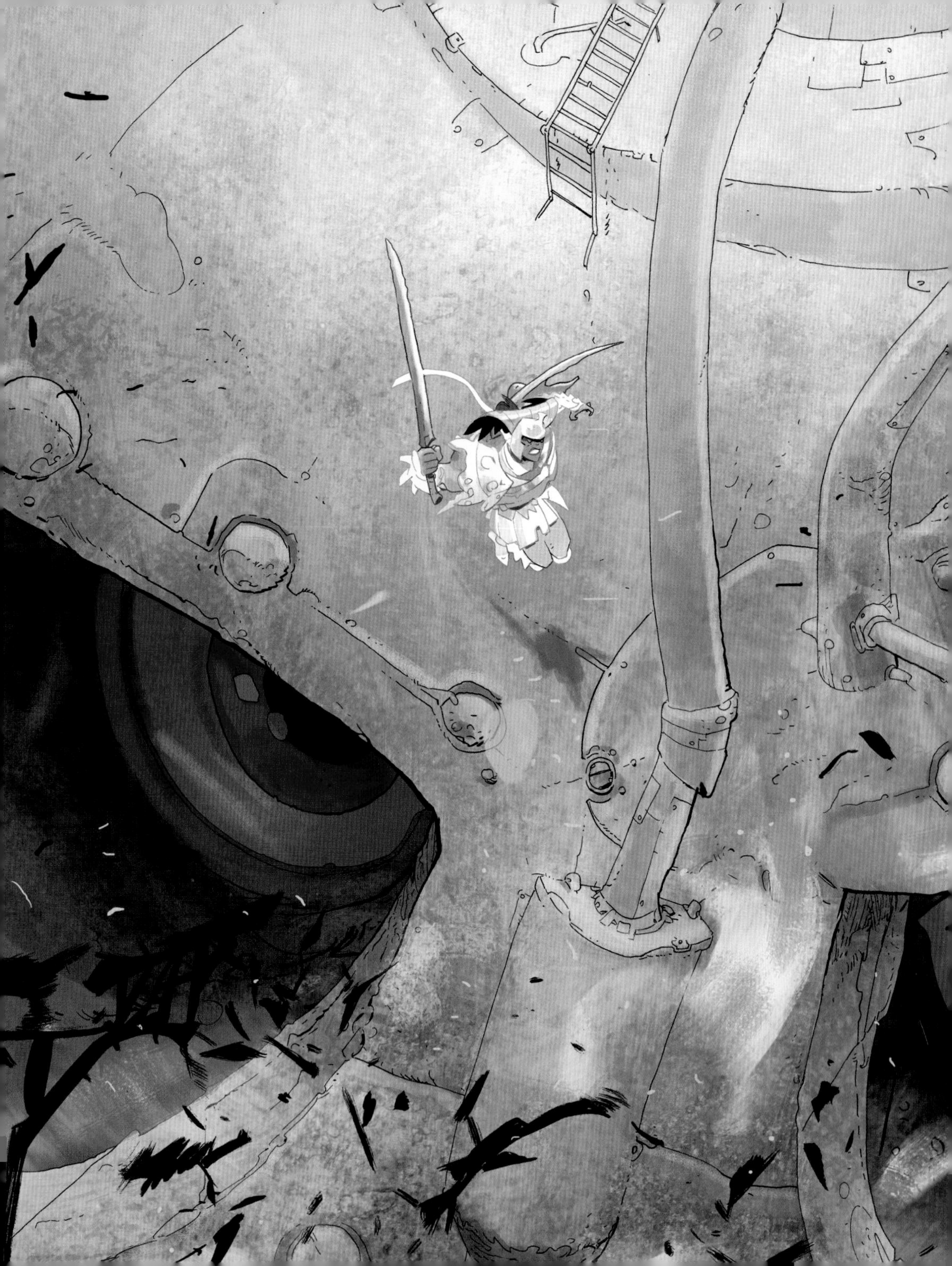

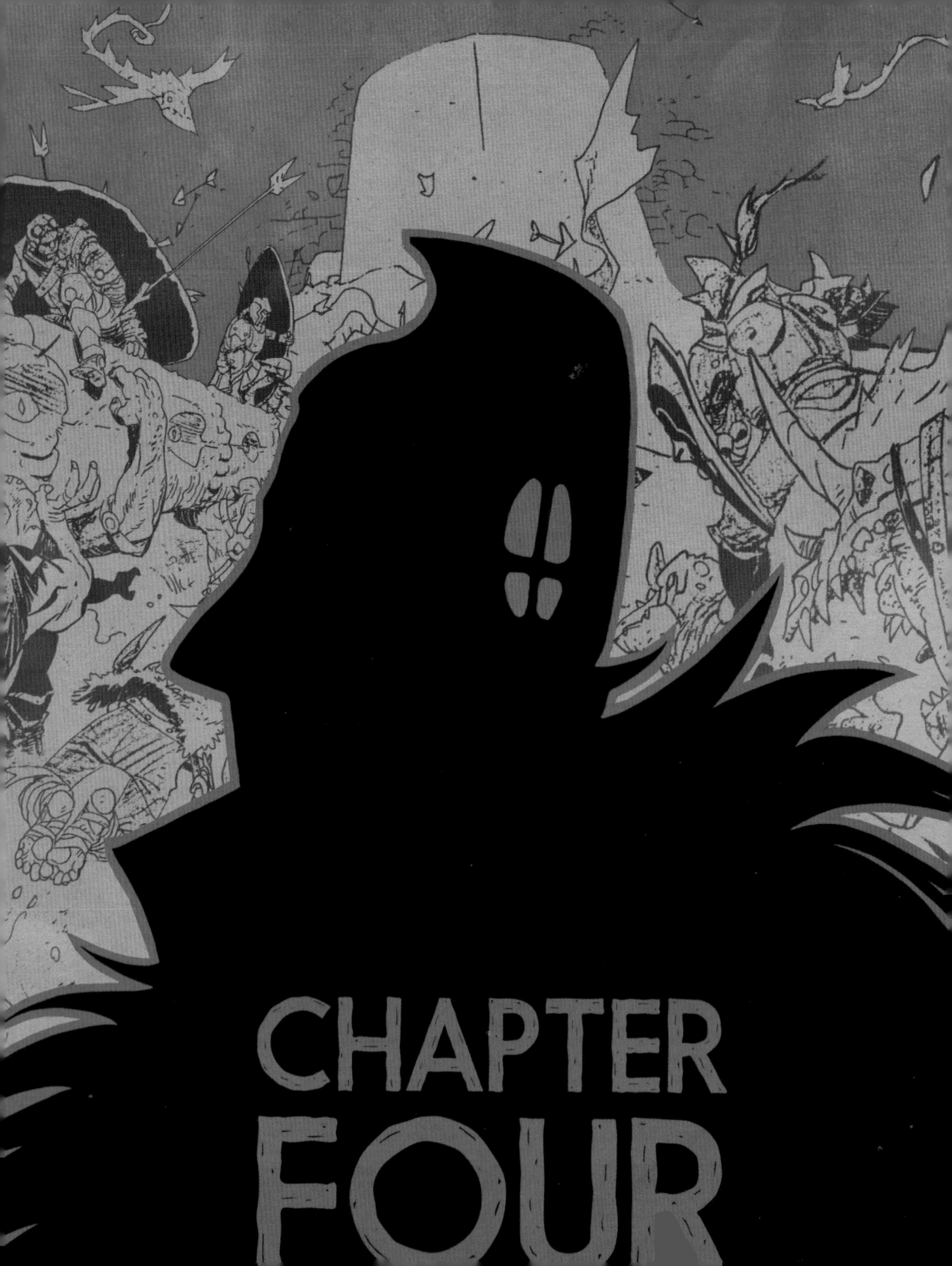
CHAPTER
FOUR

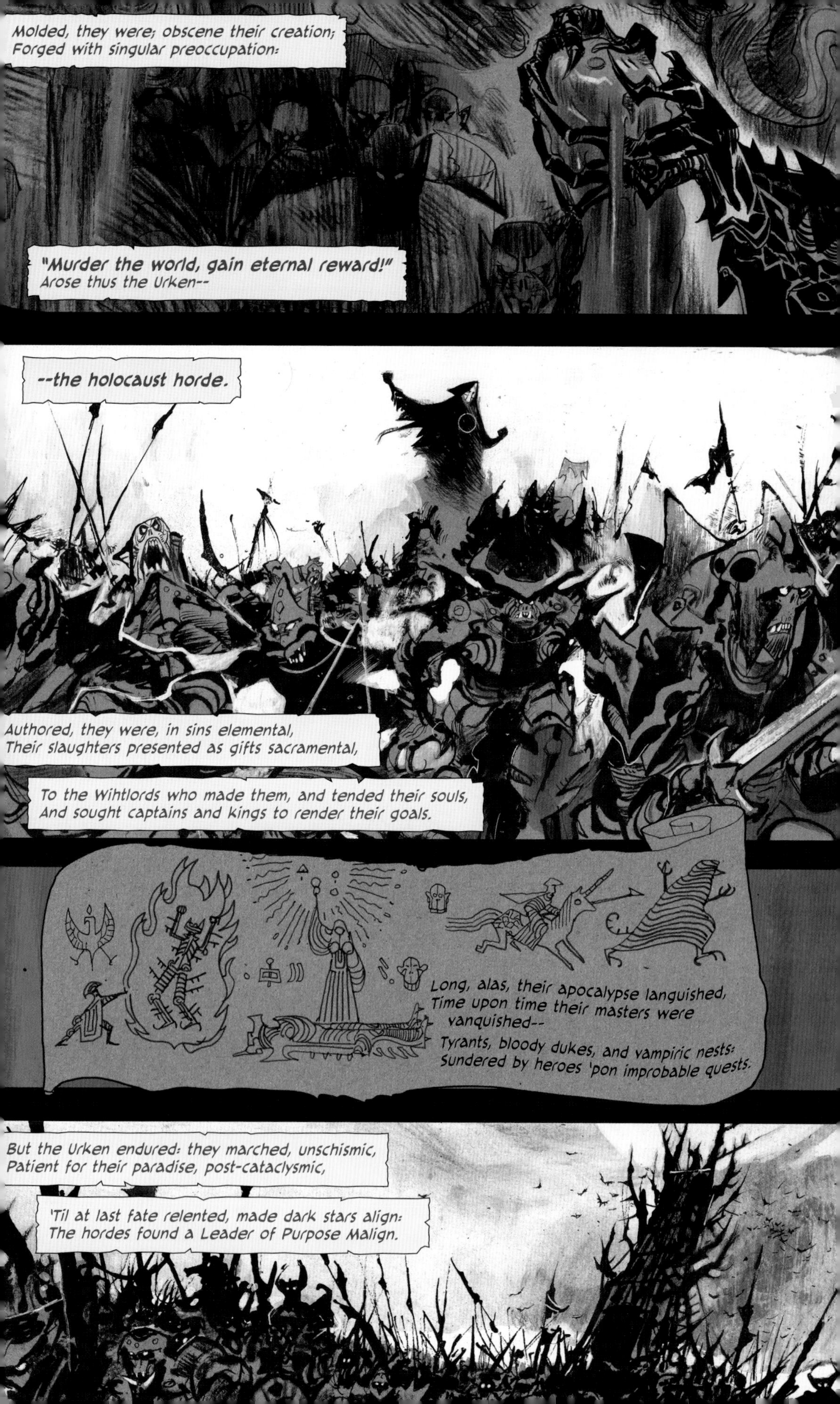
Molded, they were; obscene their creation; Forged with singular preoccupation:
"Murder the world, gain eternal reward!" Arose thus the Urken--
--the holocaust horde.
Authored, they were, in sins elemental, Their slaughters presented as gifts sacramental,
To the Wihtlords who made them, and tended their souls, And sought captains and kings to render their goals.
Long, alas, their apocalypse languished, Time upon time their masters were vanquished--
Tyrants, bloody dukes, and vampiric nests: Sundered by heroes 'pon improbable quests.
But the Urken endured: they marched, unschismic, Patient for their paradise, post-cataclysmic,
'Til at last fate relented, made dark stars align: The hordes found a Leader of Purpose Malign.

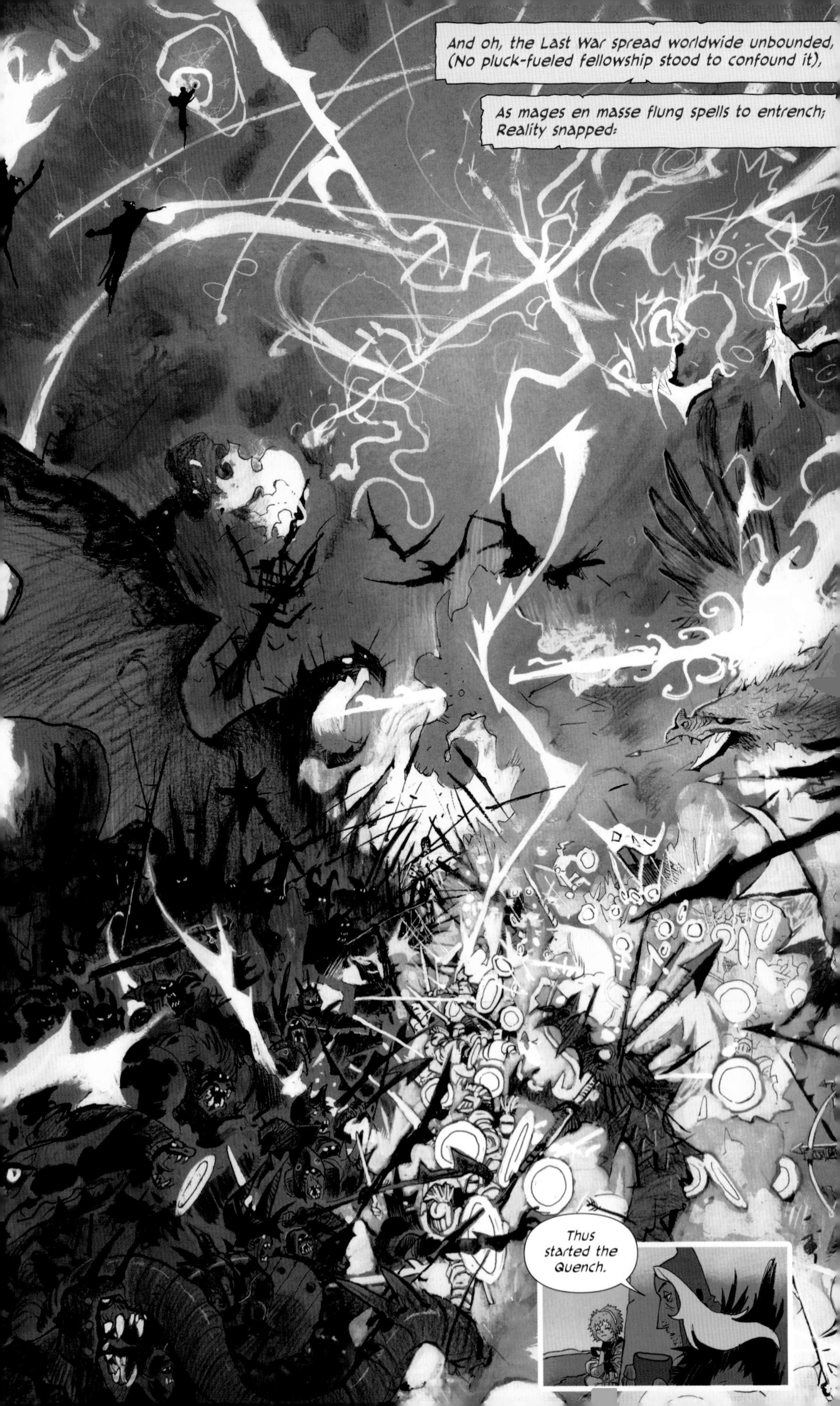

And oh, the Last War spread worldwide unbounded,
(No pluck-fueled fellowship stood to confound it),
As mages en masse flung spells to entrench;
Reality snapped:
Thus started the Quench.

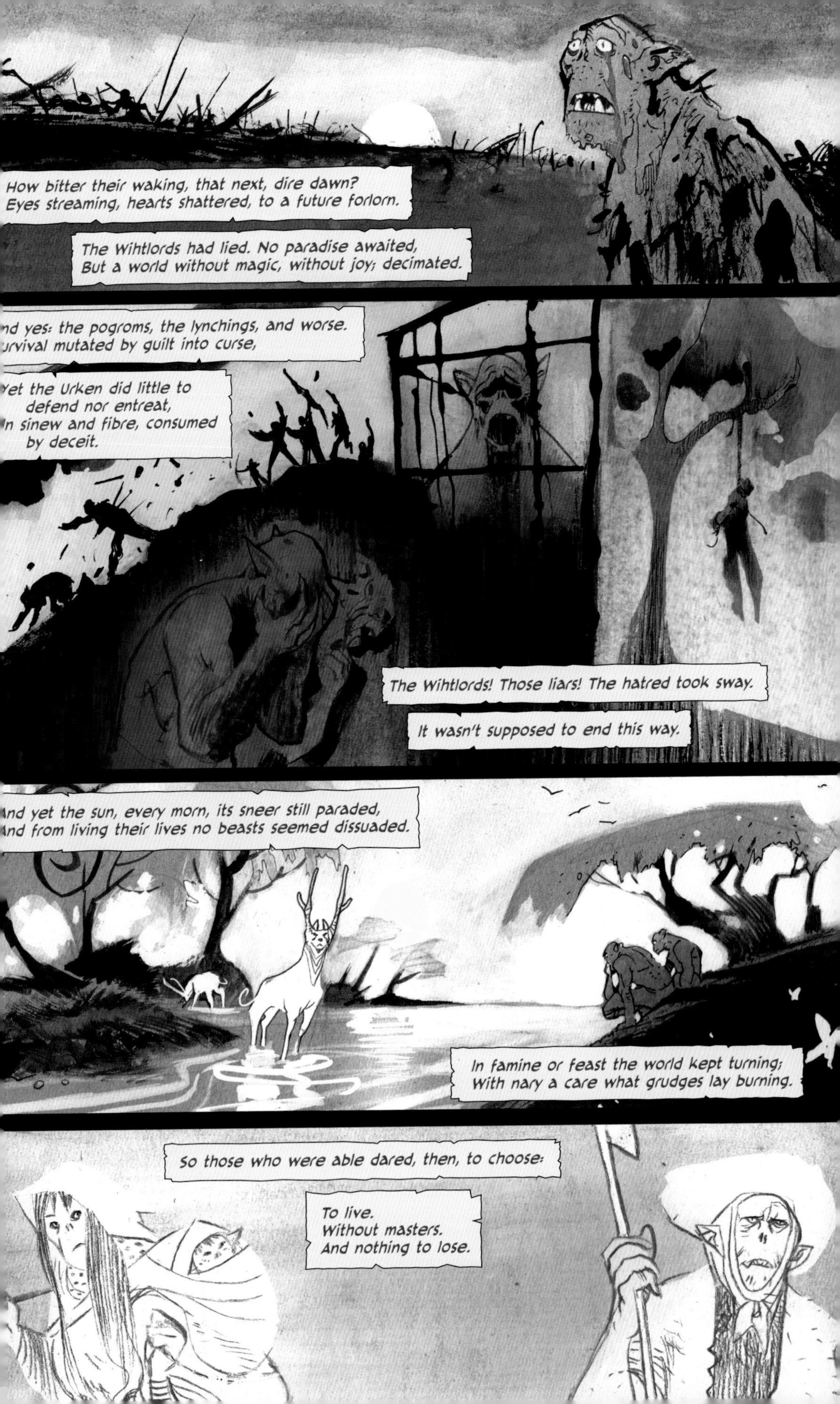
How bitter their waking, that next, dire dawn?
Eyes streaming, hearts shattered, to a future forlorn.
The Wihtlords had lied. No paradise awaited,
But a world without magic, without joy; decimated.
nd yes: the pogroms, the lynchings, and worse.
urvival mutated by guilt into curse,
Yet the Urken did little to defend nor entreat,
n sinew and fibre, consumed by deceit.
The Wihtlords! Those liars! The hatred took sway.
It wasn't supposed to end this way.
And yet the sun, every morn, its sneer still paraded,
And from living their lives no beasts seemed dissuaded.
In famine or feast the world kept turning;
With nary a care what grudges lay burning.
So those who were able dared, then, to choose:
To live.
Without masters.
And nothing to lose.

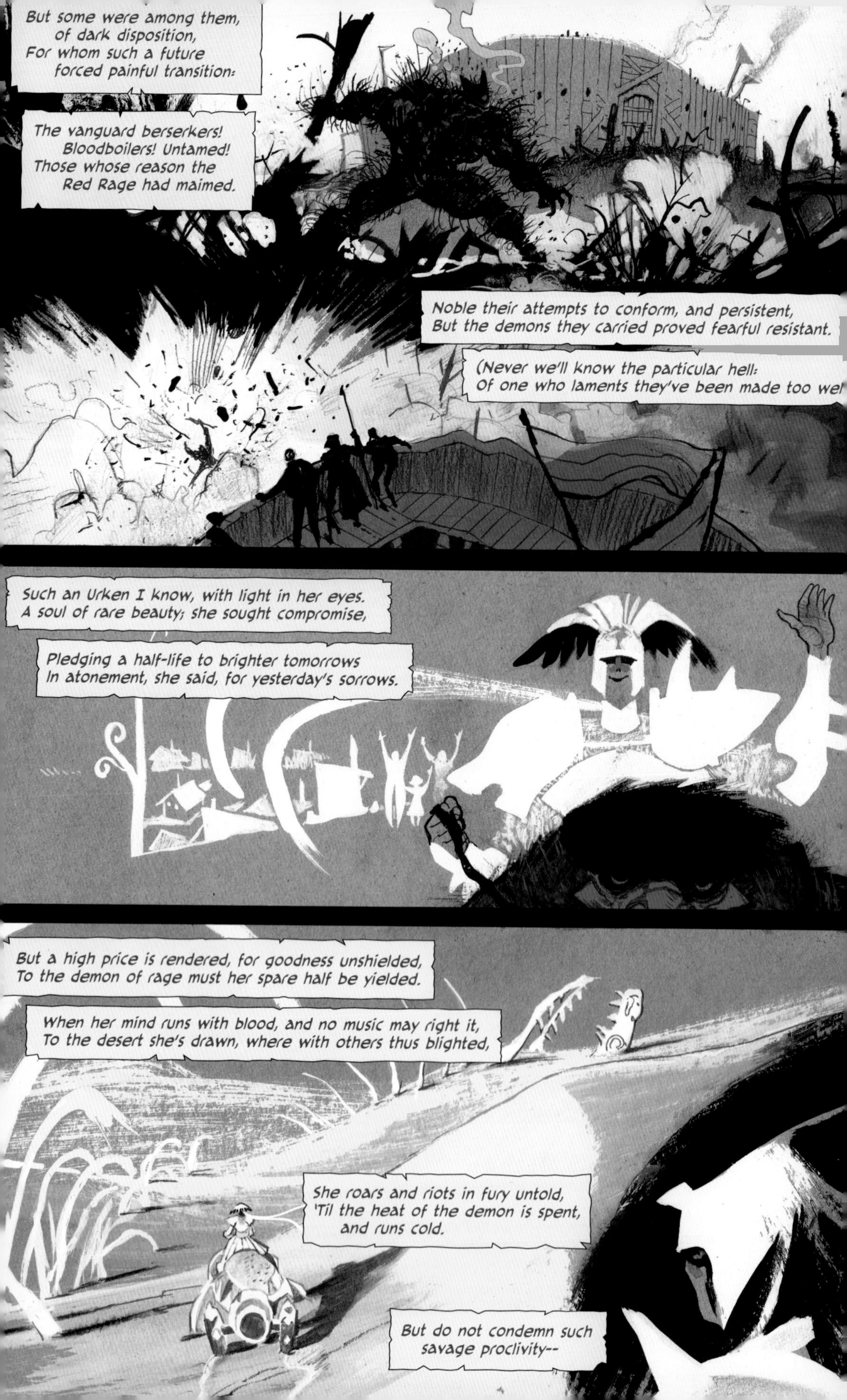
But some were among them, of dark disposition, For whom such a future forced painful transition:
The vanguard berserkers! Bloodboilers! Untamed! Those whose reason the Red Rage had maimed.
Noble their attempts to conform, and persistent, But the demons they carried proved fearful resistant.
(Never we'll know the particular hell: Of one who laments they've been made too we
Such an Urken I know, with light in her eyes. A soul of rare beauty; she sought compromise,
Pledging a half-life to brighter tomorrows In atonement, she said, for yesterday's sorrows.
But a high price is rendered, for goodness unshielded, To the demon of rage must her spare half be yielded.
When her mind runs with blood, and no music may right it, To the desert she's drawn, where with others thus blighted,
She roars and riots in fury untold, 'Til the heat of the demon is spent, and runs cold.
But do not condemn such savage proclivity--

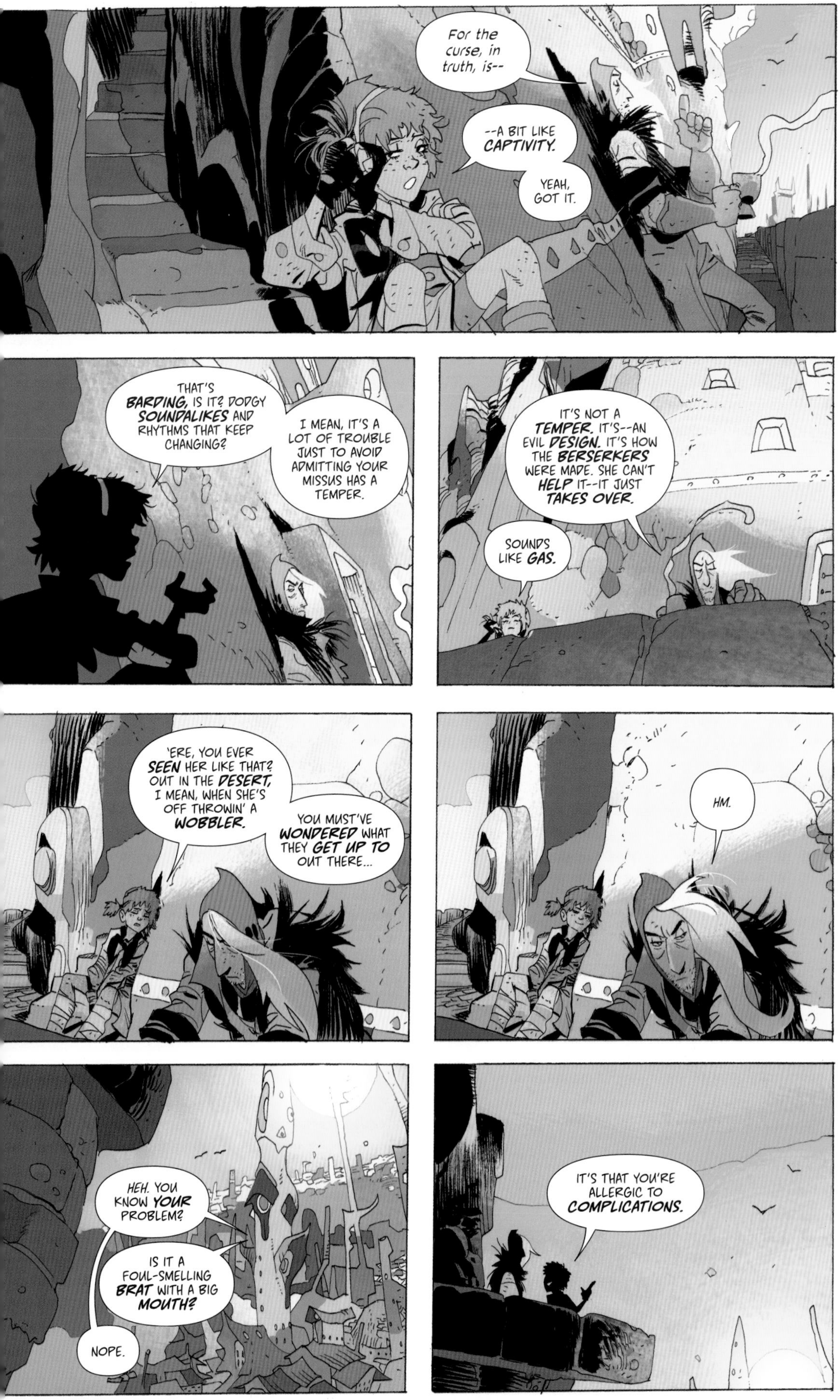
For the curse, in truth, is--
--A BIT LIKE CAPTIVITY.
YEAH, GOT IT.
THAT'S BARDING, IS IT? DODGY SOUNDALIKES AND RHYTHMS THAT KEEP CHANGING?
I MEAN, IT'S A LOT OF TROUBLE JUST TO AVOID ADMITTING YOUR MISSUS HAS A TEMPER.
IT'S NOT A TEMPER. IT'S--AN EVIL DESIGN. IT'S HOW THE BERSERKERS WERE MADE. SHE CAN'T HELP IT--IT JUST TAKES OVER.
SOUNDS LIKE GAS.
'ERE, YOU EVER SEEN HER LIKE THAT? OUT IN THE DESERT, I MEAN, WHEN SHE'S OFF THROWIN' A WOBBLER.
YOU MUST'VE WONDERED WHAT THEY GET UP TO OUT THERE...
HM.
HEH. YOU KNOW YOUR PROBLEM?
IS IT A FOUL-SMELLING BRAT WITH A BIG MOUTH?
NOPE.
IT'S THAT YOU'RE ALLERGIC TO COMPLICATIONS.

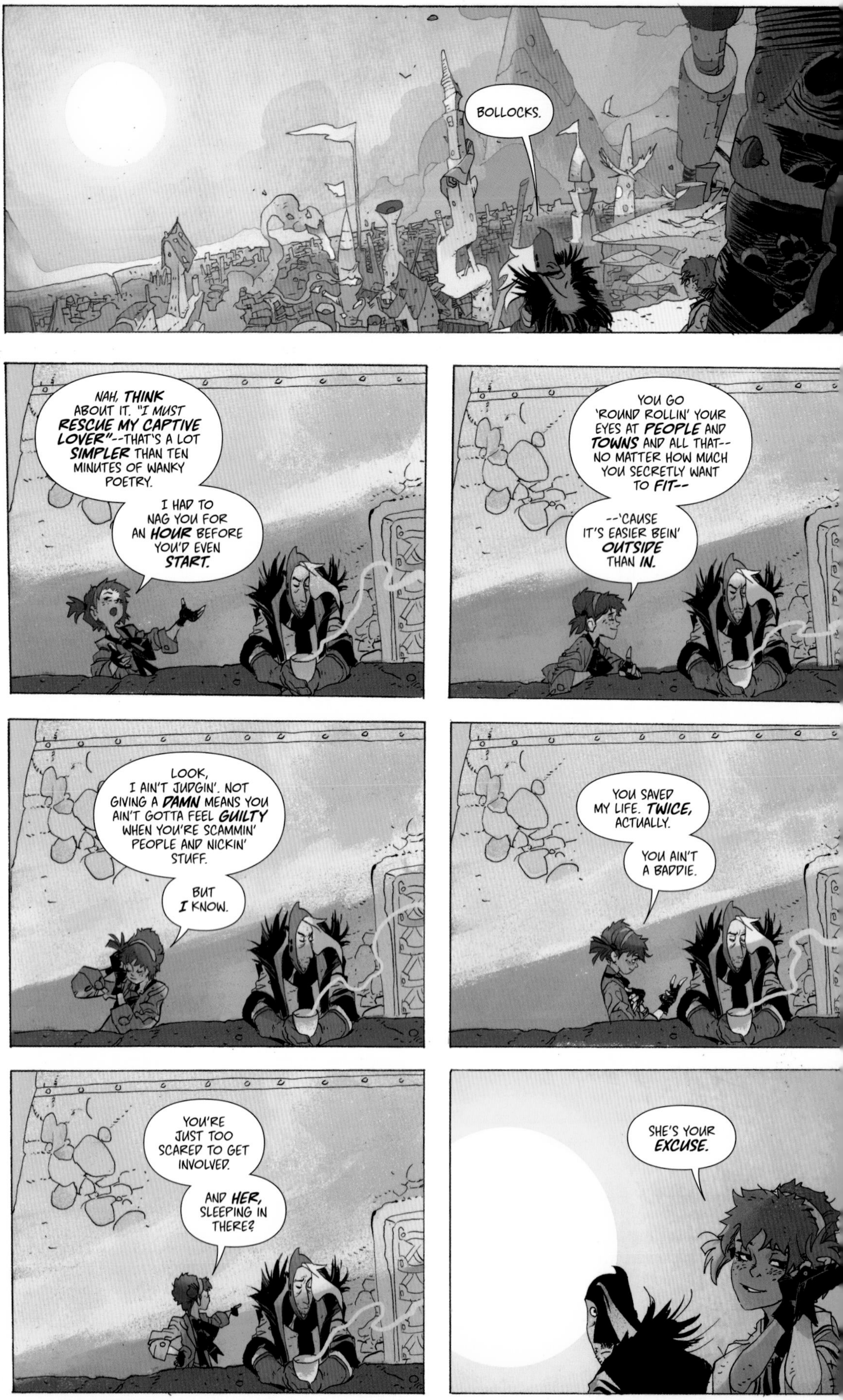
BOLLOCKS.
NAH, THINK ABOUT IT. "I MUST RESCUE MY CAPTIVE LOVER"--THAT'S A LOT SIMPLER THAN TEN MINUTES OF WANKY POETRY.
I HAD TO NAG YOU FOR AN HOUR BEFORE YOU'D EVEN START.
YOU GO 'ROUND ROLLIN' YOUR EYES AT PEOPLE AND TOWNS AND ALL THAT--NO MATTER HOW MUCH YOU SECRETLY WANT TO FIT--
--'CAUSE IT'S EASIER BEIN' OUTSIDE THAN IN.
LOOK, I AIN'T JUDGIN'. NOT GIVING A DAMN MEANS YOU AIN'T GOTTA FEEL GUILTY WHEN YOU'RE SCAMMIN' PEOPLE AND NICKIN' STUFF.
BUT I KNOW.
YOU SAVED MY LIFE. TWICE, ACTUALLY.
YOU AIN'T A BADDIE.
YOU'RE JUST TOO SCARED TO GET INVOLVED.
AND HER, SLEEPING IN THERE?
SHE'S YOUR EXCUSE.

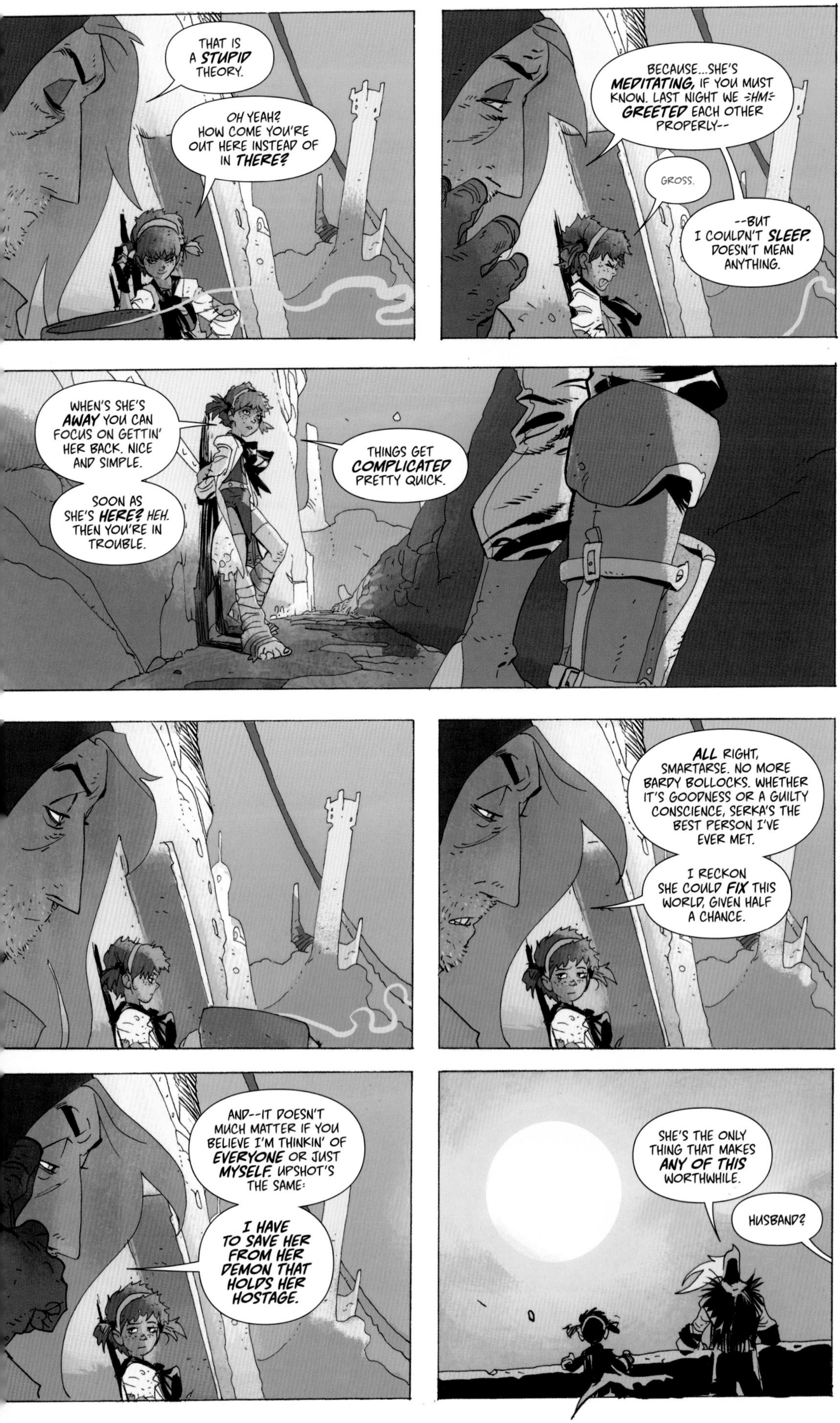
THAT IS A STUPID THEORY.
OH YEAH? HOW COME YOU'RE OUT HERE INSTEAD OF IN THERE?
BECAUSE...SHE'S MEDITATING, IF YOU MUST KNOW. LAST NIGHT WE =HM= GREETED EACH OTHER PROPERLY--
GROSS.
--BUT I COULDN'T SLEEP. DOESN'T MEAN ANYTHING.
WHEN'S SHE'S AWAY YOU CAN FOCUS ON GETTIN' HER BACK. NICE AND SIMPLE.
SOON AS SHE'S HERE? HEH. THEN YOU'RE IN TROUBLE.
THINGS GET COMPLICATED PRETTY QUICK.
ALL RIGHT, SMARTARSE. NO MORE BARDY BOLLOCKS. WHETHER IT'S GOODNESS OR A GUILTY CONSCIENCE, SERKA'S THE BEST PERSON I'VE EVER MET.
I RECKON SHE COULD FIX THIS WORLD, GIVEN HALF A CHANCE.
AND--IT DOESN'T MUCH MATTER IF YOU BELIEVE I'M THINKIN' OF EVERYONE OR JUST MYSELF. UPSHOT'S THE SAME:
I HAVE TO SAVE HER FROM HER DEMON THAT HOLDS HER HOSTAGE.
SHE'S THE ONLY THING THAT MAKES ANY OF THIS WORTHWHILE.
HUSBAND?

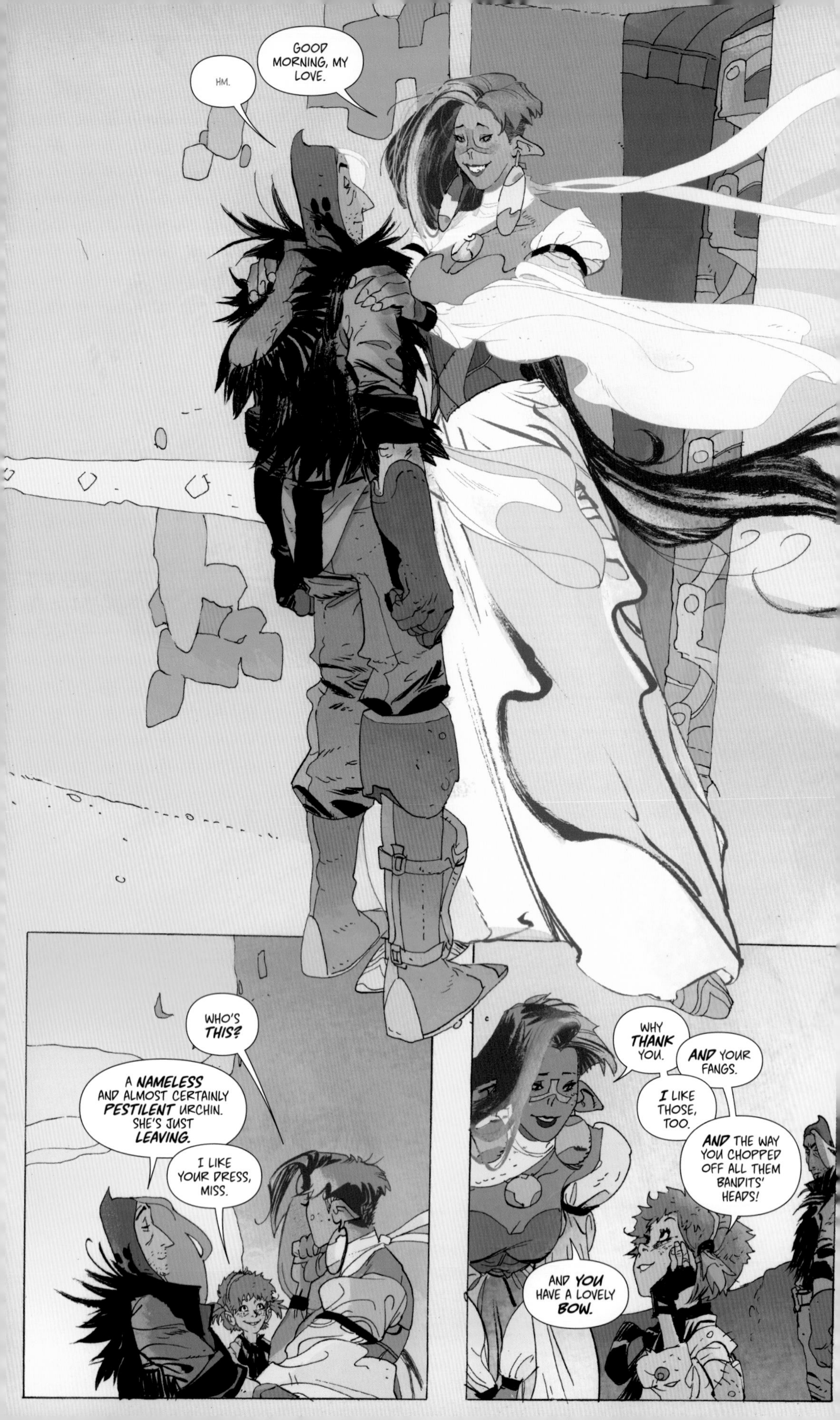
HM.
GOOD MORNING, MY LOVE.
WHO'S THIS?
A NAMELESS AND ALMOST CERTAINLY PESTILENT URCHIN. SHE'S JUST LEAVING.
I LIKE YOUR DRESS, MISS.
WHY THANK YOU.
AND YOUR FANGS.
I LIKE THOSE, TOO.
AND THE WAY YOU CHOPPED OFF ALL THEM BANDITS' HEADS!
AND YOU HAVE A LOVELY BOW.

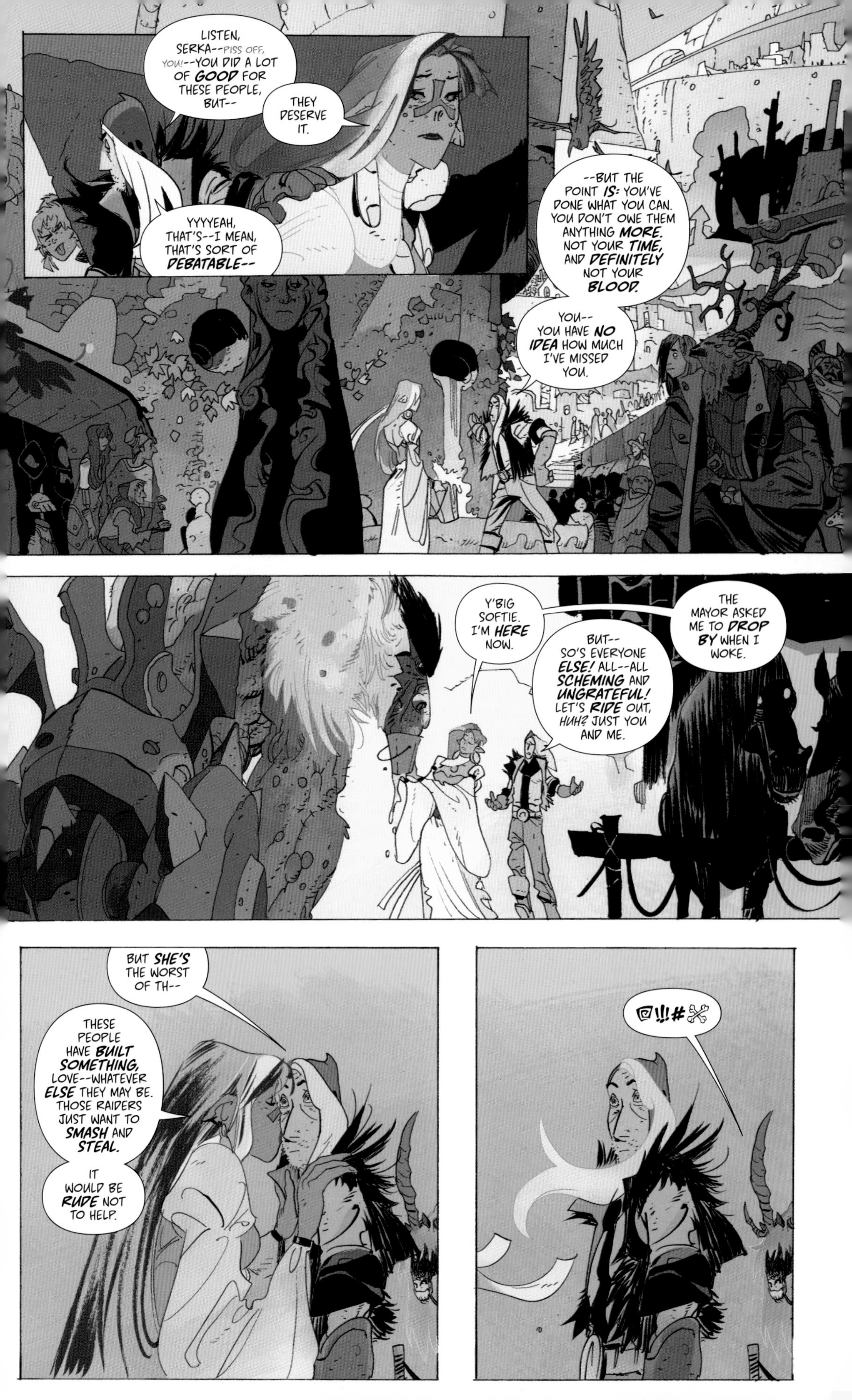

LISTEN, SERKA--PISS OFF, YOU!--YOU DID A LOT OF GOOD FOR THESE PEOPLE, BUT--
THEY DESERVE IT.
YYYYEAH, THAT'S--I MEAN, THAT'S SORT OF DEBATABLE--
--BUT THE POINT IS: YOU'VE DONE WHAT YOU CAN. YOU DON'T OWE THEM ANYTHING MORE. NOT YOUR TIME, AND DEFINITELY NOT YOUR BLOOD.
YOU-- YOU HAVE NO IDEA HOW MUCH I'VE MISSED YOU.
Y'BIG SOFTIE. I'M HERE NOW.
BUT-- SO'S EVERYONE ELSE! ALL--ALL SCHEMING AND UNGRATEFUL! LET'S RIDE OUT, HUH? JUST YOU AND ME.
THE MAYOR ASKED ME TO DROP BY WHEN I WOKE.
BUT SHE'S THE WORST OF TH--
THESE PEOPLE HAVE BUILT SOMETHING, LOVE--WHATEVER ELSE THEY MAY BE. THOSE RAIDERS JUST WANT TO SMASH AND STEAL.
IT WOULD BE RUDE NOT TO HELP.
@!!!#

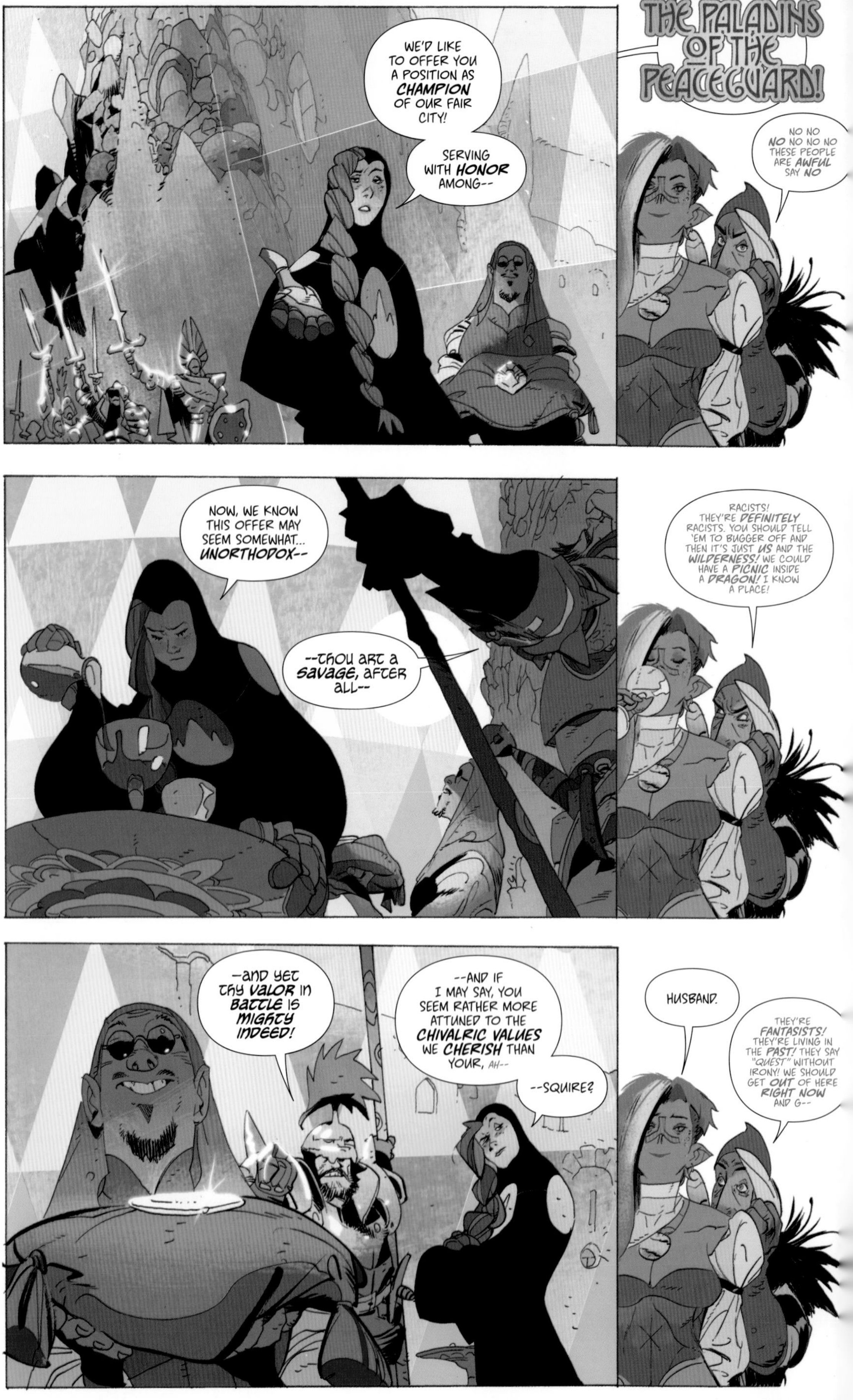
WE'D LIKE TO OFFER YOU A POSITION AS CHAMPION OF OUR FAIR CITY!
SERVING WITH HONOR AMONG--
THE PALADINS OF THE PEACEGUARD!
NO NO NO NO NO NO THESE PEOPLE ARE AWFUL SAY NO
NOW, WE KNOW THIS OFFER MAY SEEM SOMEWHAT... UNORTHODOX--
--THOU ART A SAVAGE, AFTER ALL--
RACISTS! THEY'RE DEFINITELY RACISTS. YOU SHOULD TELL 'EM TO BUGGER OFF AND THEN IT'S JUST US AND THE WILDERNESS! WE COULD HAVE A PICNIC INSIDE A DRAGON! I KNOW A PLACE!
--AND YET THY VALOR IN BATTLE IS MIGHTY INDEED!
--AND IF I MAY SAY, YOU SEEM RATHER MORE ATTUNED TO THE CHIVALRIC VALUES WE CHERISH THAN YOUR, AH--
--SQUIRE?
HUSBAND.
THEY'RE FANTASISTS! THEY'RE LIVING IN THE PAST! THEY SAY "QUEST" WITHOUT IRONY! WE SHOULD GET OUT OF HERE RIGHT NOW AND G--

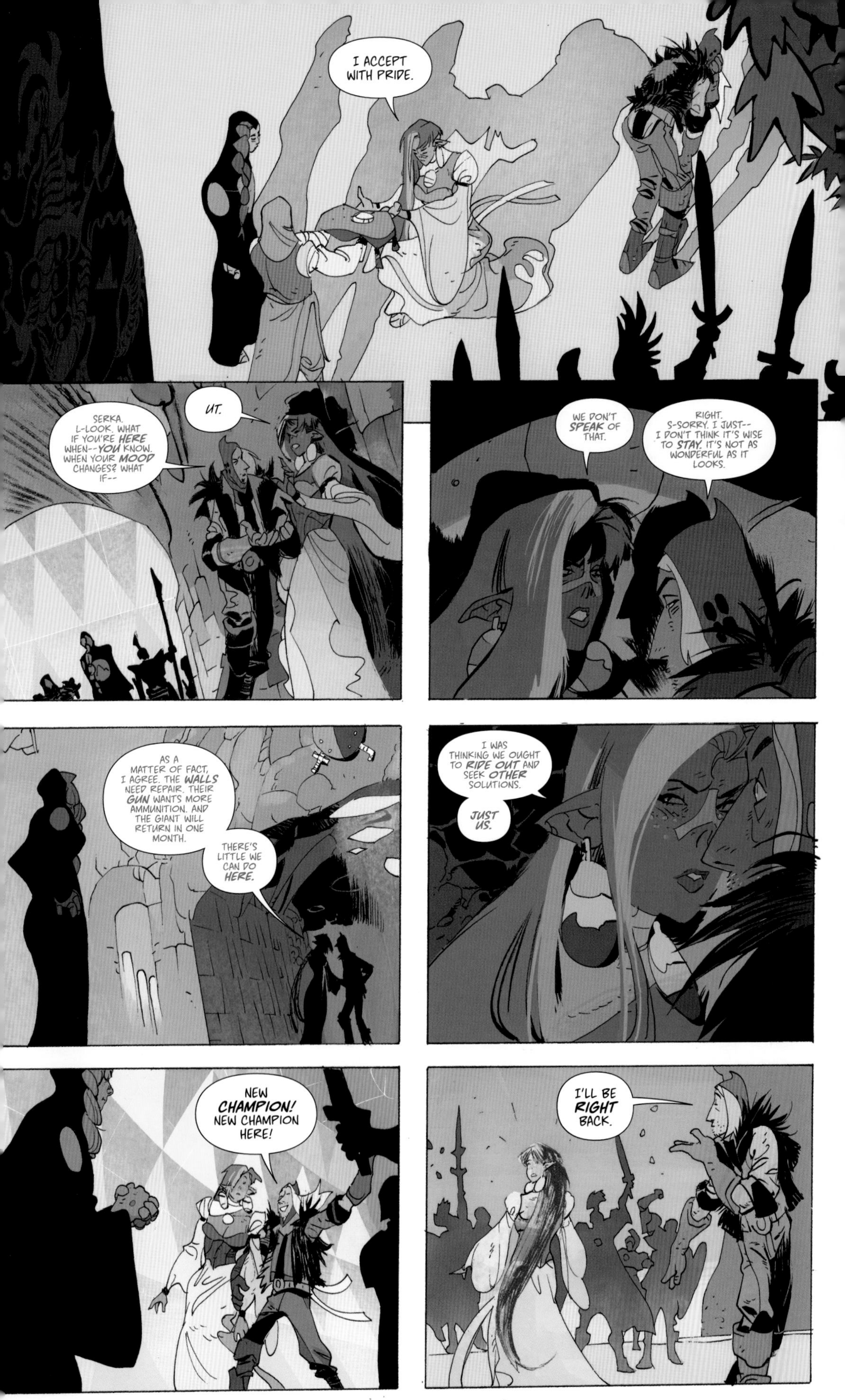
I ACCEPT WITH PRIDE.
SERKA. L-LOOK. WHAT IF YOU'RE HERE WHEN--YOU KNOW. WHEN YOUR MOOD CHANGES? WHAT IF--
UT.
WE DON'T SPEAK OF THAT.
RIGHT. S-SORRY. I JUST-- I DON'T THINK IT'S WISE TO STAY. IT'S NOT AS WONDERFUL AS IT LOOKS.
AS A MATTER OF FACT, I AGREE. THE WALLS NEED REPAIR. THEIR GUN WANTS MORE AMMUNITION. AND THE GIANT WILL RETURN IN ONE MONTH.
THERE'S LITTLE WE CAN DO HERE.
I WAS THINKING WE OUGHT TO RIDE OUT AND SEEK OTHER SOLUTIONS.
JUST US.
NEW CHAMPION! NEW CHAMPION HERE!
I'LL BE RIGHT BACK.

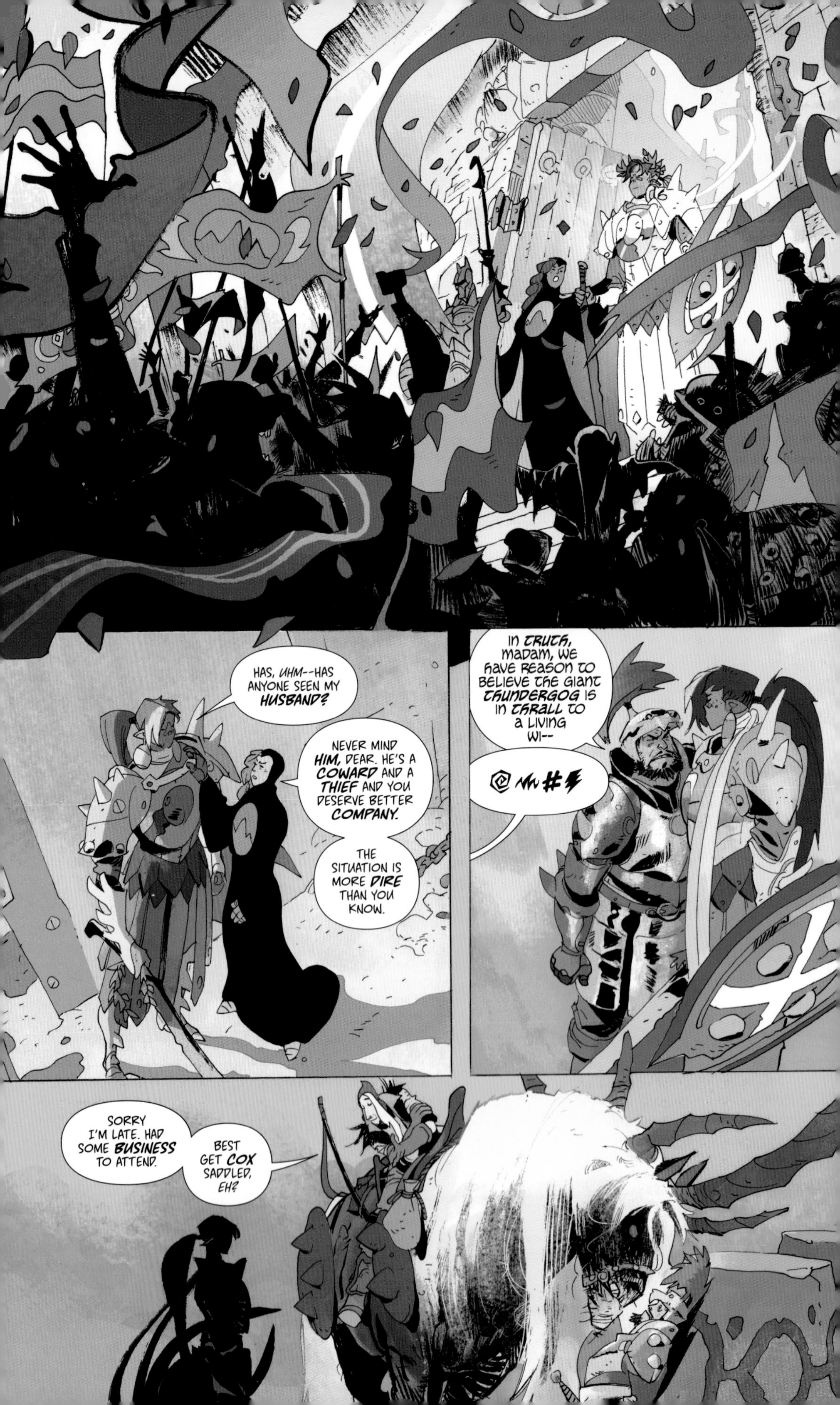
HAS, UHM--HAS ANYONE SEEN MY HUSBAND?
NEVER MIND HIM, DEAR. HE'S A COWARD AND A THIEF AND YOU DESERVE BETTER COMPANY.
THE SITUATION IS MORE DIRE THAN YOU KNOW.
IN TRUTH, MADAM, WE HAVE REASON TO BELIEVE THE GIANT THUNDERGOG IS IN THRALL TO A LIVING WI--
SORRY I'M LATE. HAD SOME BUSINESS TO ATTEND.
BEST GET COX SADDLED, EH?

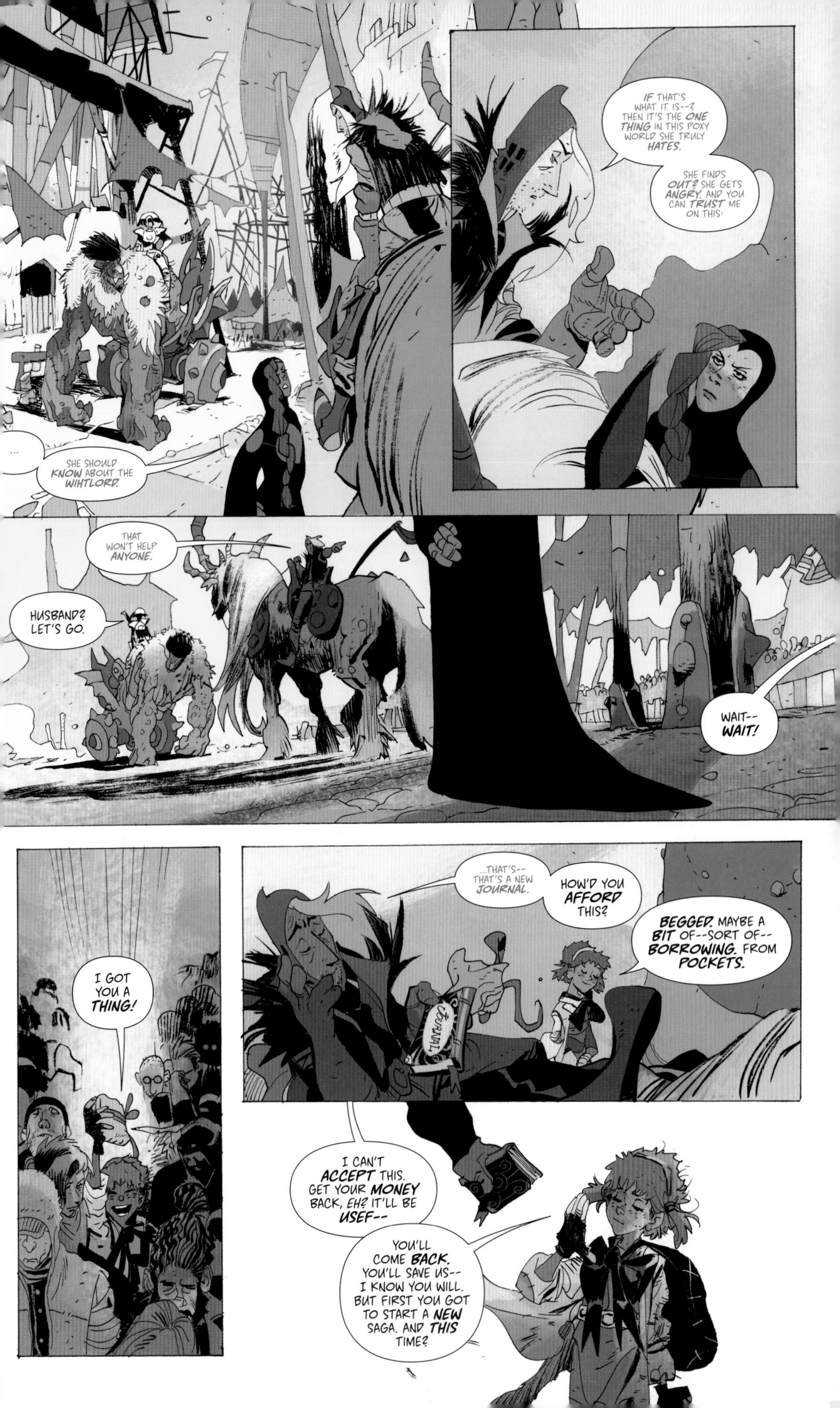

...
SHE SHOULD KNOW ABOUT THE WIHTLORD.
IF THAT'S WHAT IT IS--? THEN IT'S THE ONE THING IN THIS POXY WORLD SHE TRULY HATES.
SHE FINDS OUT? SHE GETS ANGRY. AND YOU CAN TRUST ME ON THIS:
THAT WON'T HELP ANYONE.
HUSBAND? LET'S GO.
WAIT-- WAIT!
I GOT YOU A THING!
...THAT'S-- THAT'S A NEW JOURNAL.
HOW'D YOU AFFORD THIS?
BEGGED. MAYBE A BIT OF--SORT OF-- BORROWING. FROM POCKETS.
JOURNAL
I CAN'T ACCEPT THIS. GET YOUR MONEY BACK, EH? IT'LL BE USEF--
YOU'LL COME BACK. YOU'LL SAVE US-- I KNOW YOU WILL. BUT FIRST YOU GOT TO START A NEW SAGA. AND THIS TIME?

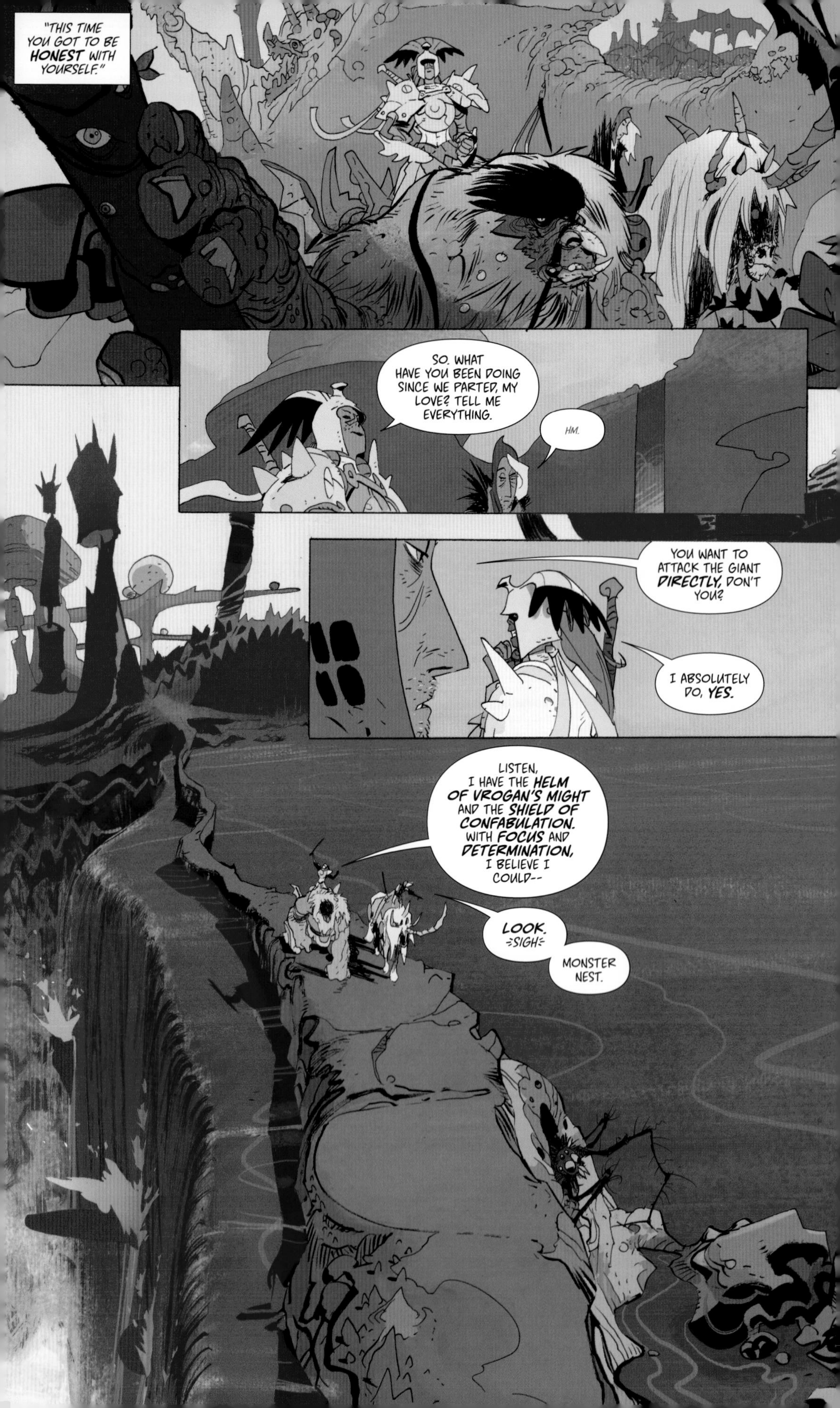
"THIS TIME YOU GOT TO BE HONEST WITH YOURSELF."
SO. WHAT HAVE YOU BEEN DOING SINCE WE PARTED, MY LOVE? TELL ME EVERYTHING.
HM.
YOU WANT TO ATTACK THE GIANT DIRECTLY, DON'T YOU?
I ABSOLUTELY DO, YES.
LISTEN, I HAVE THE HELM OF VROGAN'S MIGHT AND THE SHIELD OF CONFABULATION. WITH FOCUS AND DETERMINATION, I BELIEVE I COULD--
LOOK. SIGH
MONSTER NEST.

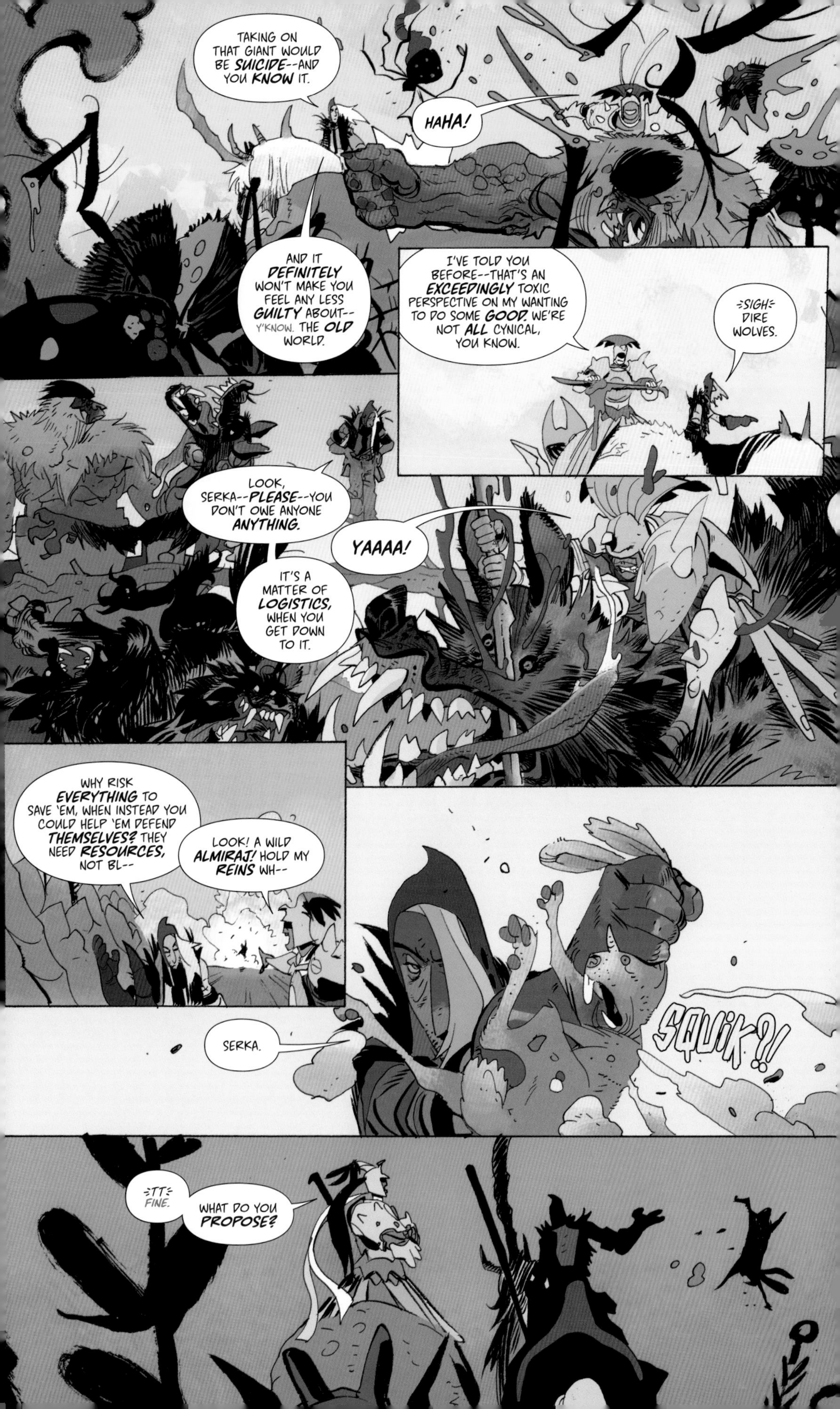
TAKING ON THAT GIANT WOULD BE SUICIDE--AND YOU KNOW IT.
HAHA!
AND IT DEFINITELY WON'T MAKE YOU FEEL ANY LESS GUILTY ABOUT-- Y'KNOW. THE OLD WORLD.
I'VE TOLD YOU BEFORE--THAT'S AN EXCEEDINGLY TOXIC PERSPECTIVE ON MY WANTING TO DO SOME GOOD. WE'RE NOT ALL CYNICAL, YOU KNOW.
SIGH DIRE WOLVES.
LOOK, SERKA--PLEASE--YOU DON'T OWE ANYONE ANYTHING.
YAAAA!
IT'S A MATTER OF LOGISTICS, WHEN YOU GET DOWN TO IT.
WHY RISK EVERYTHING TO SAVE 'EM, WHEN INSTEAD YOU COULD HELP 'EM DEFEND THEMSELVES? THEY NEED RESOURCES, NOT BL--
LOOK! A WILD ALMIRAJ! HOLD MY REINS WH--
SERKA.
SQUIK?!
TT FINE.
WHAT DO YOU PROPOSE?

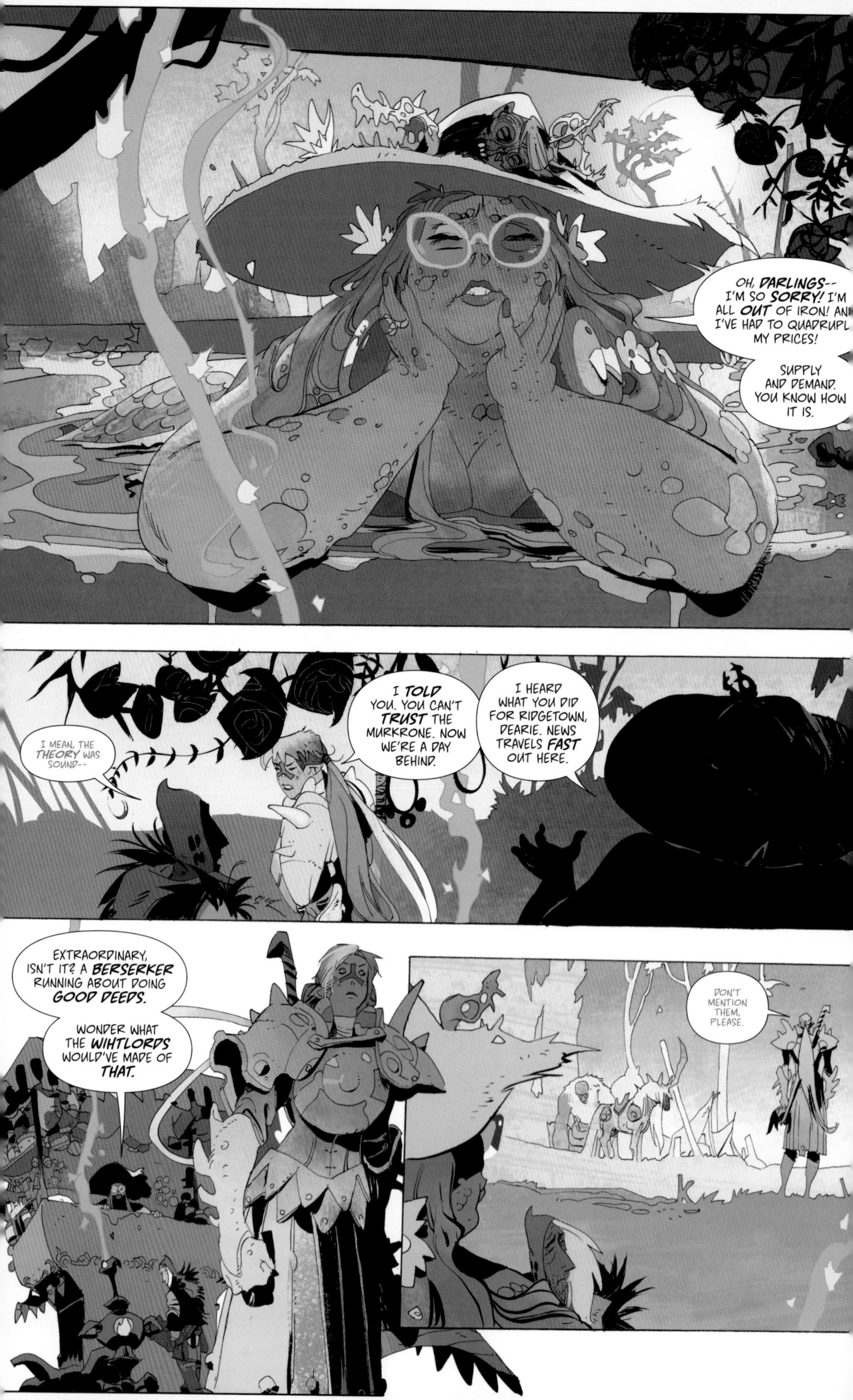
OH, DARLINGS-- I'M SO SORRY! I'M ALL OUT OF IRON! AN I'VE HAD TO QUADRUPL MY PRICES!
SUPPLY AND DEMAND. YOU KNOW HOW IT IS.
I MEAN, THE THEORY WAS SOUND--
I TOLD YOU. YOU CAN'T TRUST THE MURKRONE. NOW WE'RE A DAY BEHIND.
I HEARD WHAT YOU DID FOR RIDGETOWN, DEARIE. NEWS TRAVELS FAST OUT HERE.
EXTRAORDINARY, ISN'T IT? A BERSERKER RUNNING ABOUT DOING GOOD DEEDS.
WONDER WHAT THE WIHTLORDS WOULD'VE MADE OF THAT.
DON'T MENTION THEM, PLEASE.

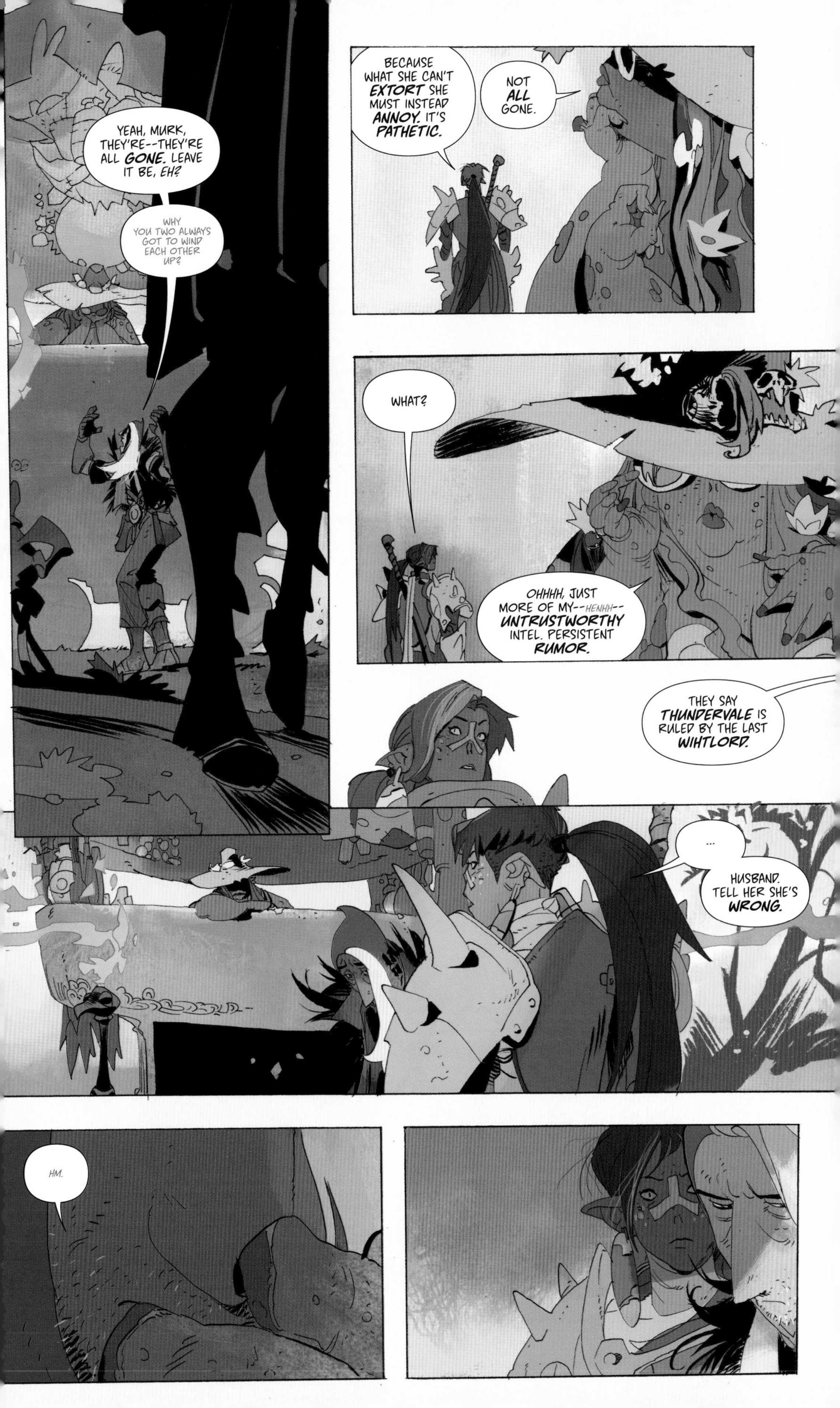
YEAH, MURK, THEY'RE--THEY'RE ALL GONE. LEAVE IT BE, EH?
WHY YOU TWO ALWAYS GOT TO WIND EACH OTHER UP?
BECAUSE WHAT SHE CAN'T EXTORT SHE MUST INSTEAD ANNOY. IT'S PATHETIC.
NOT ALL GONE.
WHAT?
OHHHH, JUST MORE OF MY--HENHH--UNTRUSTWORTHY INTEL. PERSISTENT RUMOR.
THEY SAY THUNDERVALE IS RULED BY THE LAST WIHTLORD.
...
HUSBAND. TELL HER SHE'S WRONG.
HM.

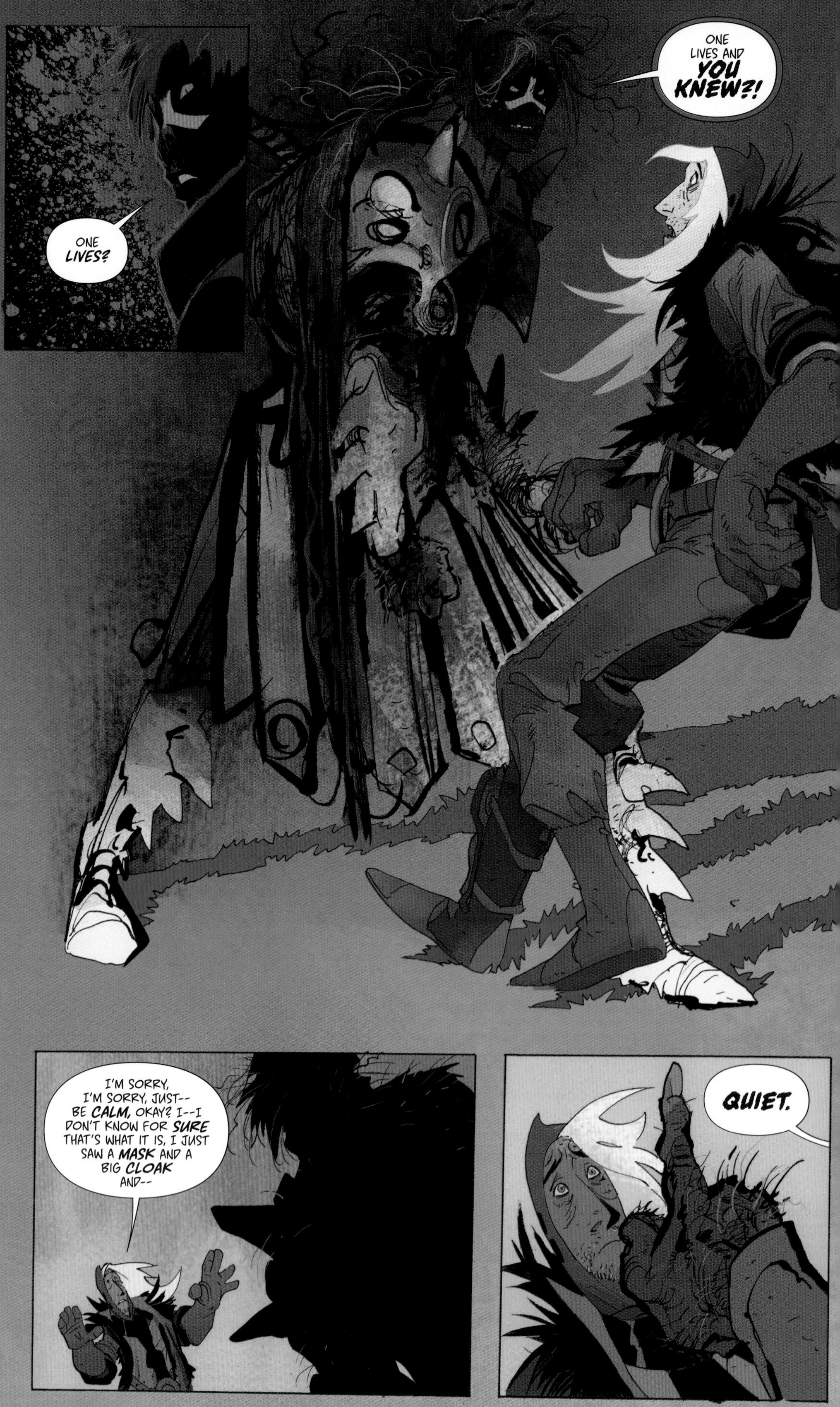
ONE LIVES?
ONE LIVES AND YOU KNEW?!
I'M SORRY, I'M SORRY, JUST-- BE CALM, OKAY? I--I DON'T KNOW FOR SURE THAT'S WHAT IT IS, I JUST SAW A MASK AND A BIG CLOAK AND--
QUIET.

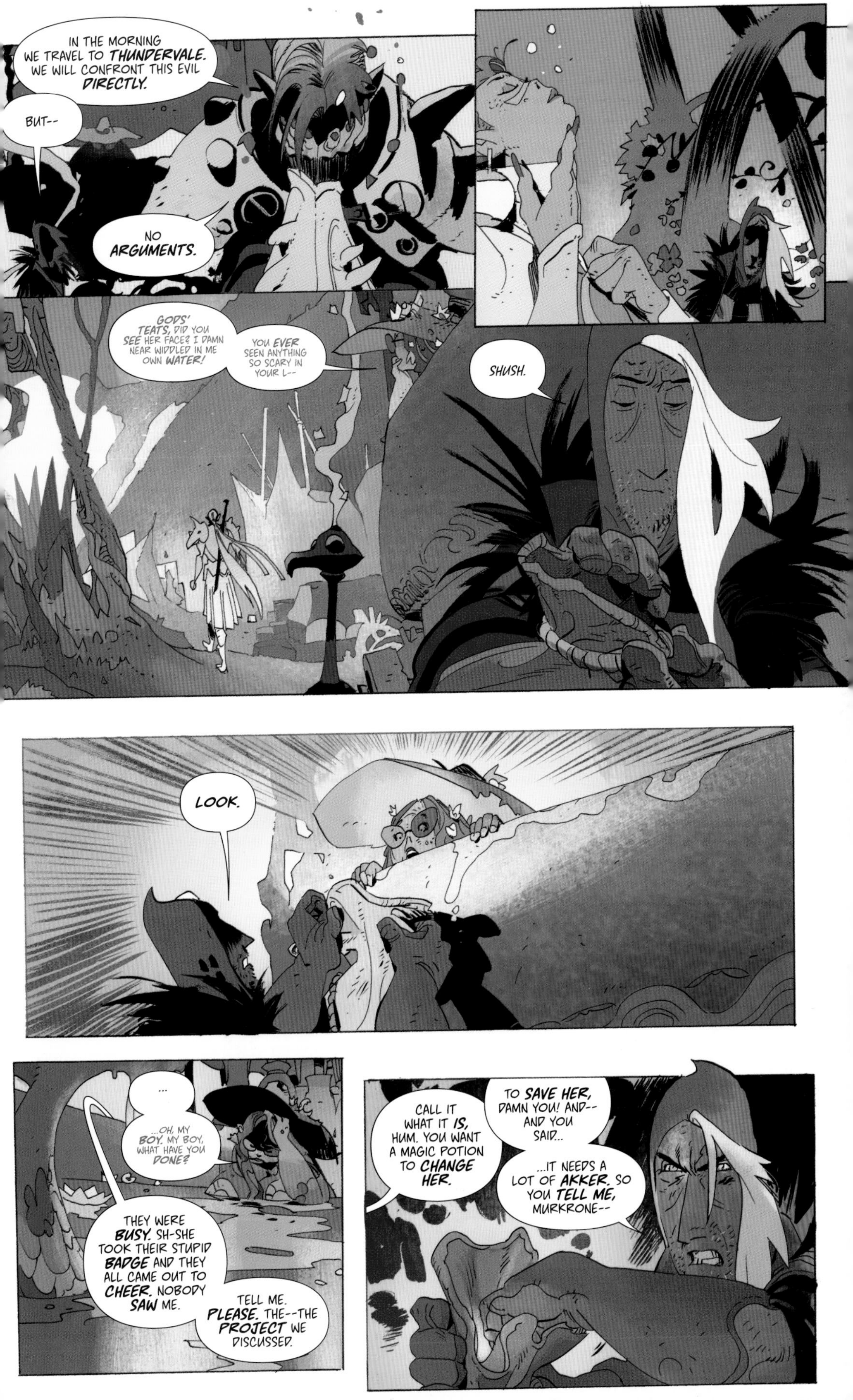
IN THE MORNING WE TRAVEL TO THUNDERVALE. WE WILL CONFRONT THIS EVIL DIRECTLY.
BUT--
NO ARGUMENTS.
GODS' TEATS, DID YOU SEE HER FACE? I DAMN NEAR WIDDLED IN ME OWN WATER!
YOU EVER SEEN ANYTHING SO SCARY IN YOUR L--
SHUSH.
LOOK.
...
...OH, MY BOY. MY BOY, WHAT HAVE YOU DONE?
THEY WERE BUSY. SH-SHE TOOK THEIR STUPID BADGE AND THEY ALL CAME OUT TO CHEER. NOBODY SAW ME.
TELL ME. PLEASE. THE--THE PROJECT WE DISCUSSED.
CALL IT WHAT IT IS, HUM. YOU WANT A MAGIC POTION TO CHANGE HER.
TO SAVE HER, DAMN YOU! AND--AND YOU SAID...
...IT NEEDS A LOT OF AKKER. SO YOU TELL ME, MURKRONE--

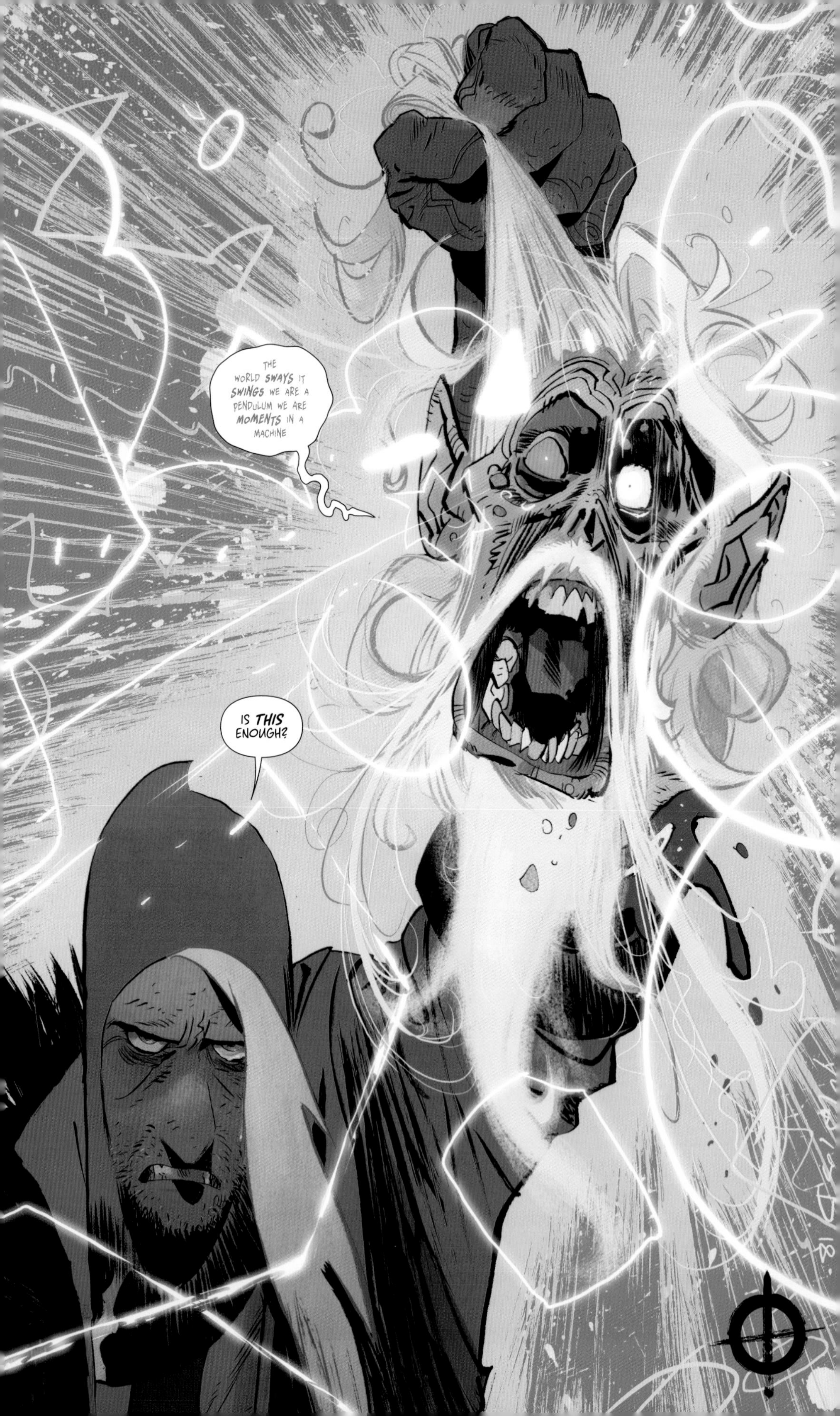
THE WORLD SWAYS IT SWINGS WE ARE A PENDULUM WE ARE MOMENTS IN A MACHINE
IS THIS ENOUGH?

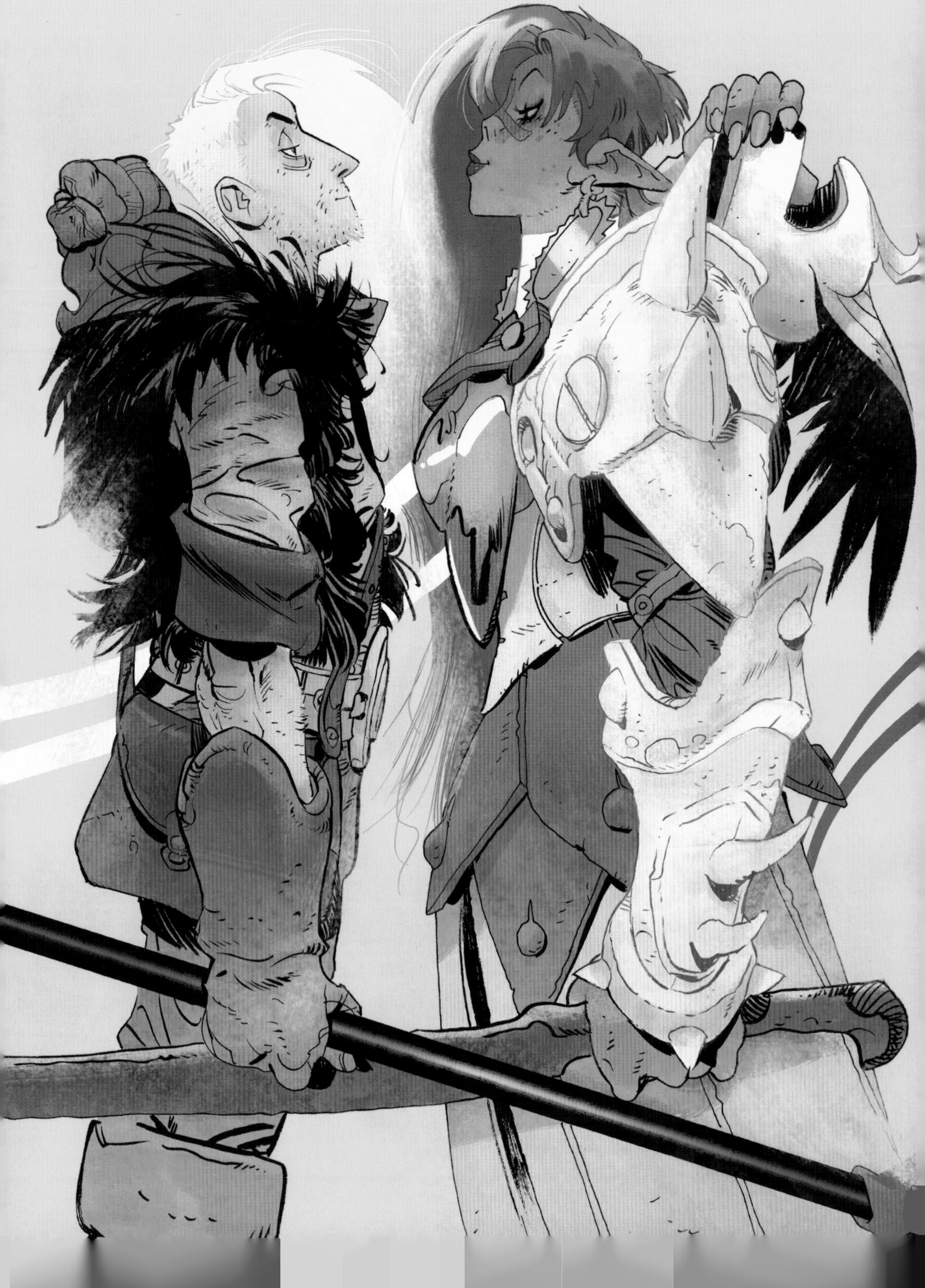

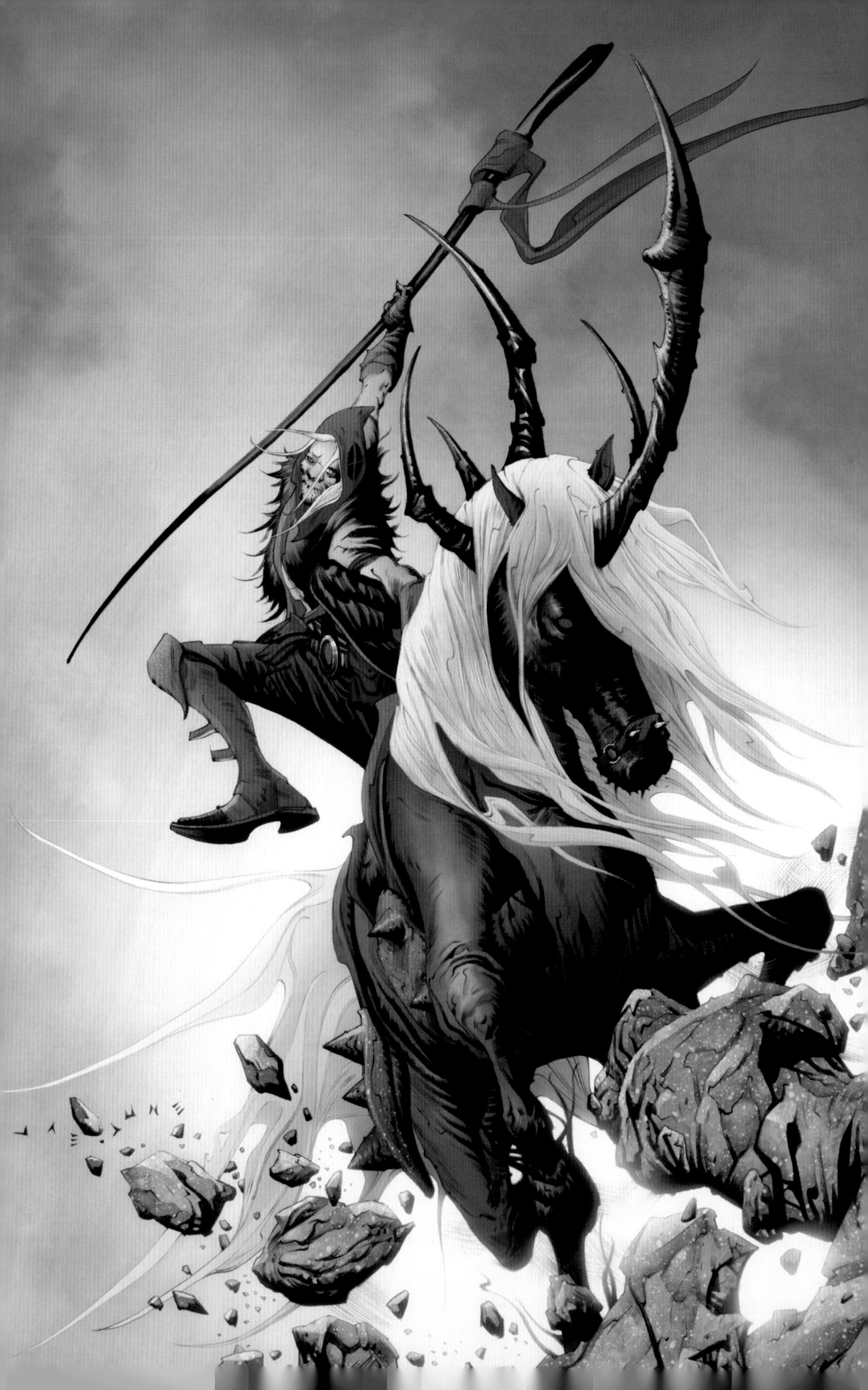

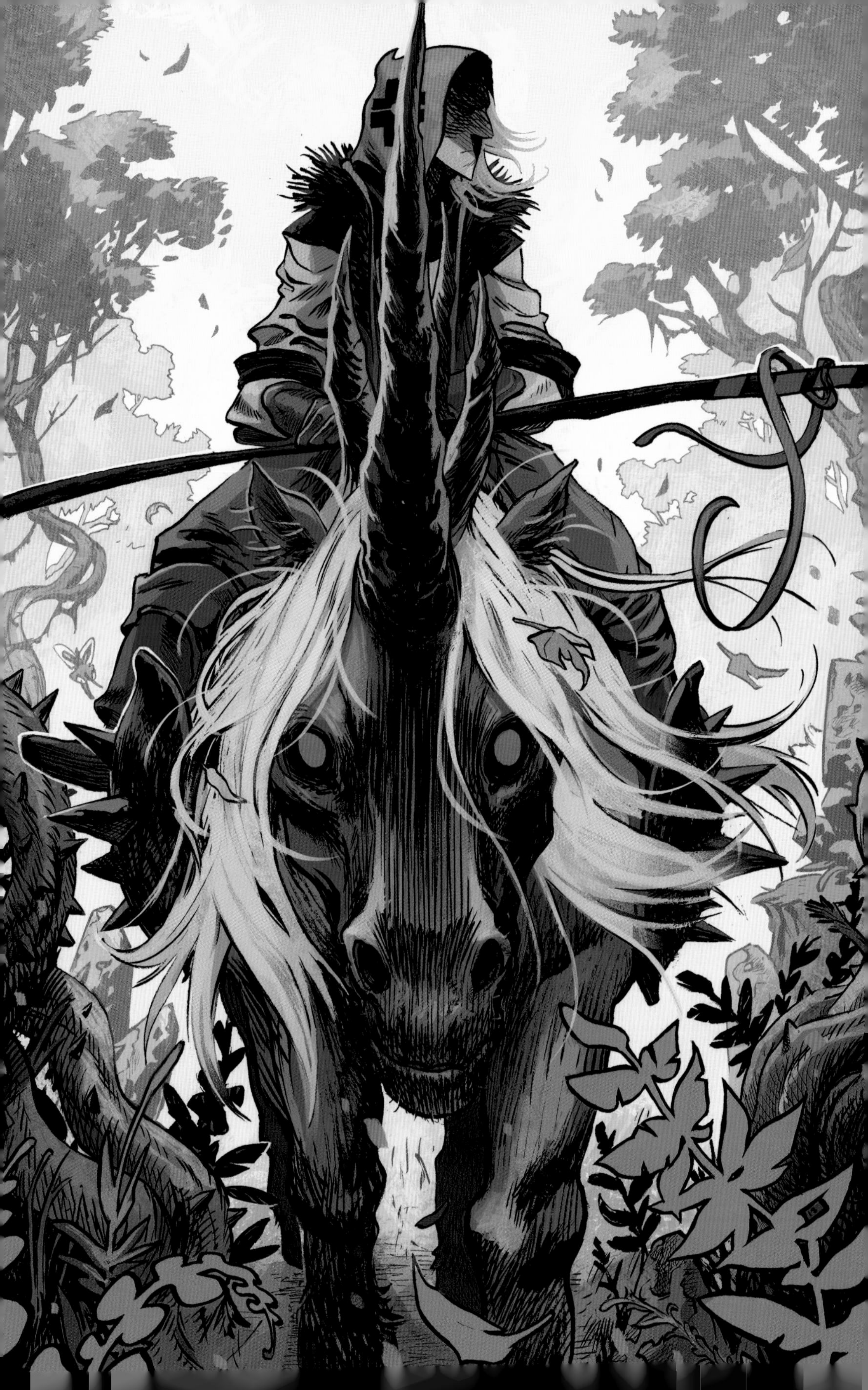

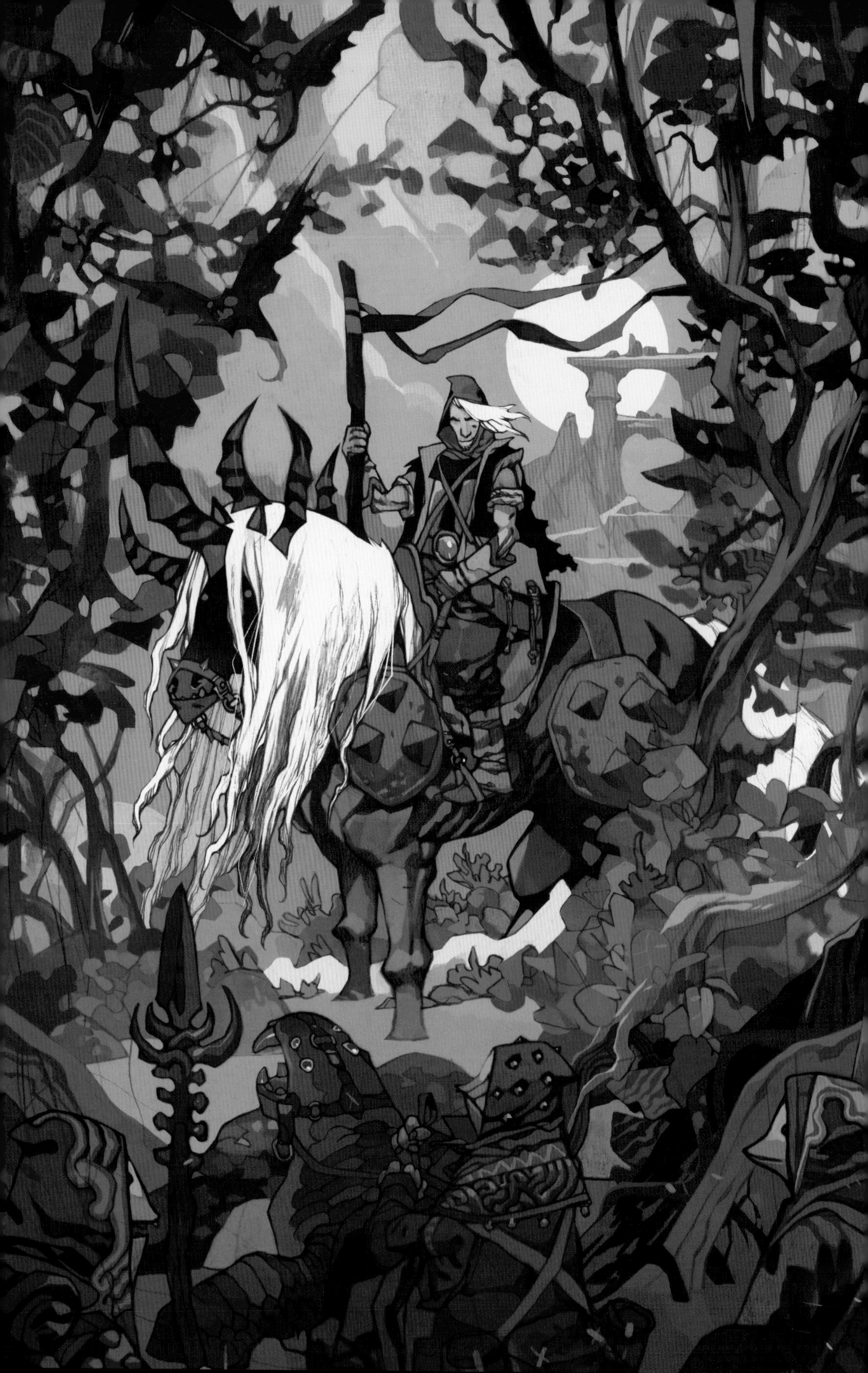

ISSUE ONE 2ND PRINT COVER BY **JAKUB REBELKA**

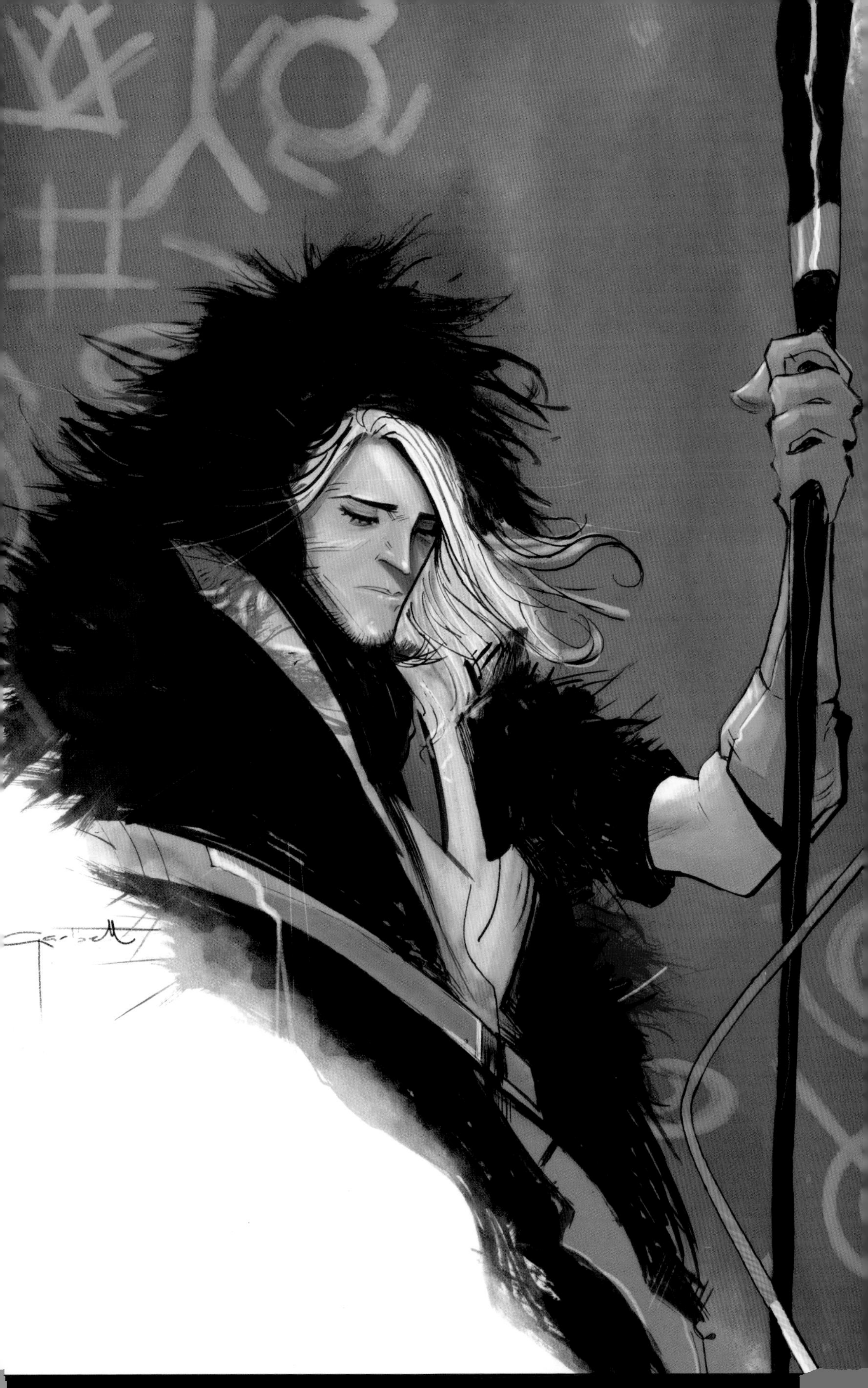

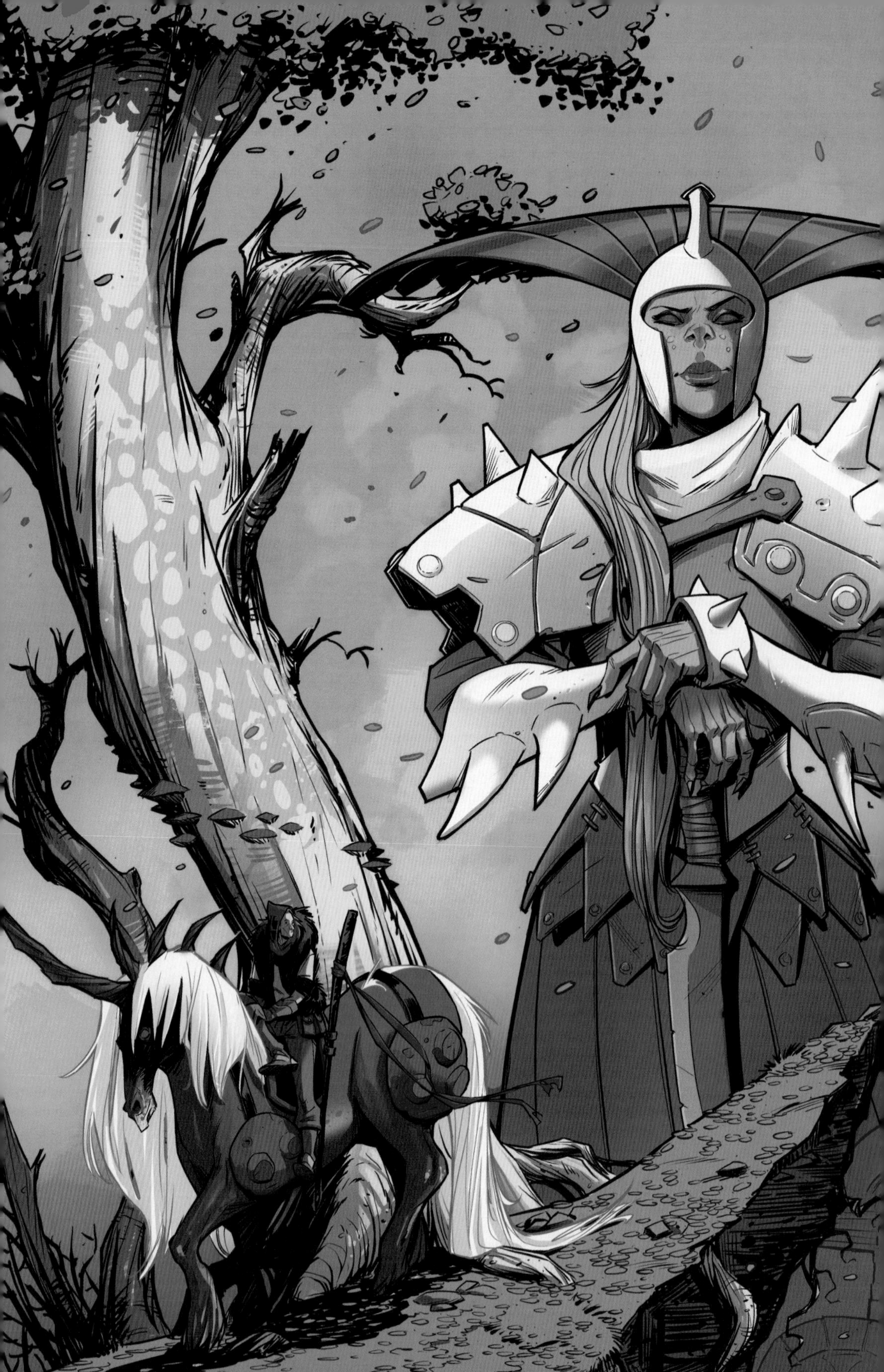

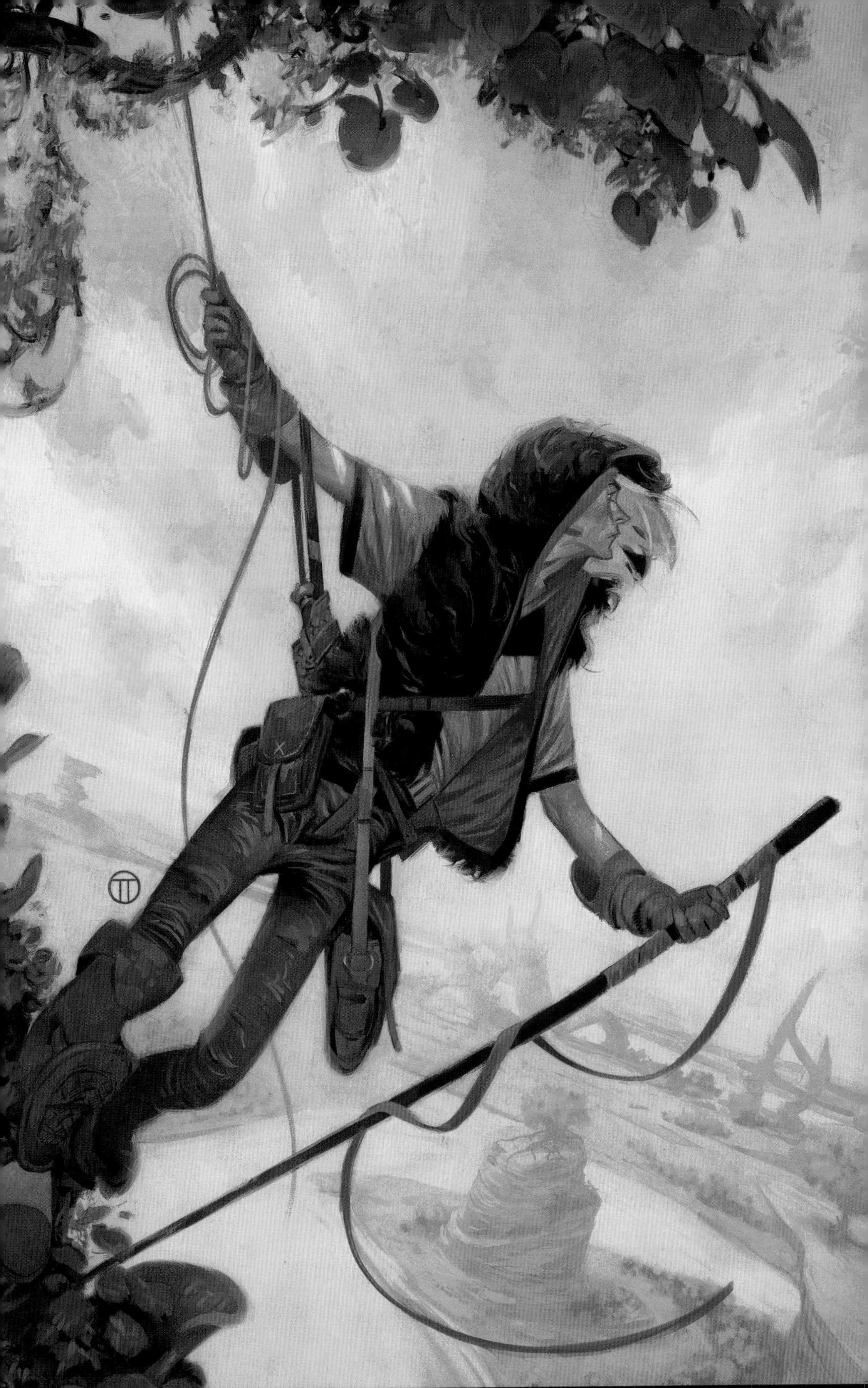

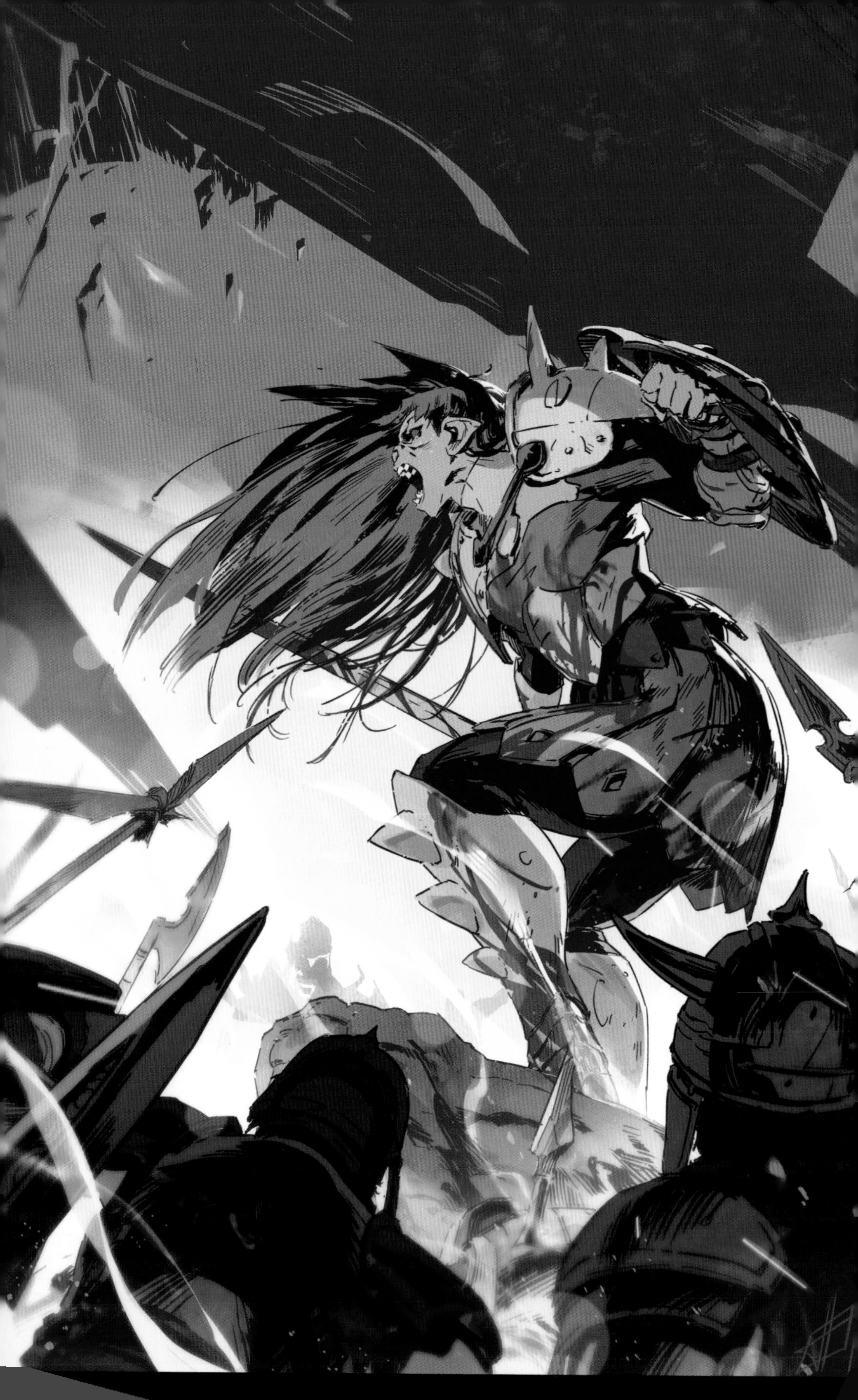

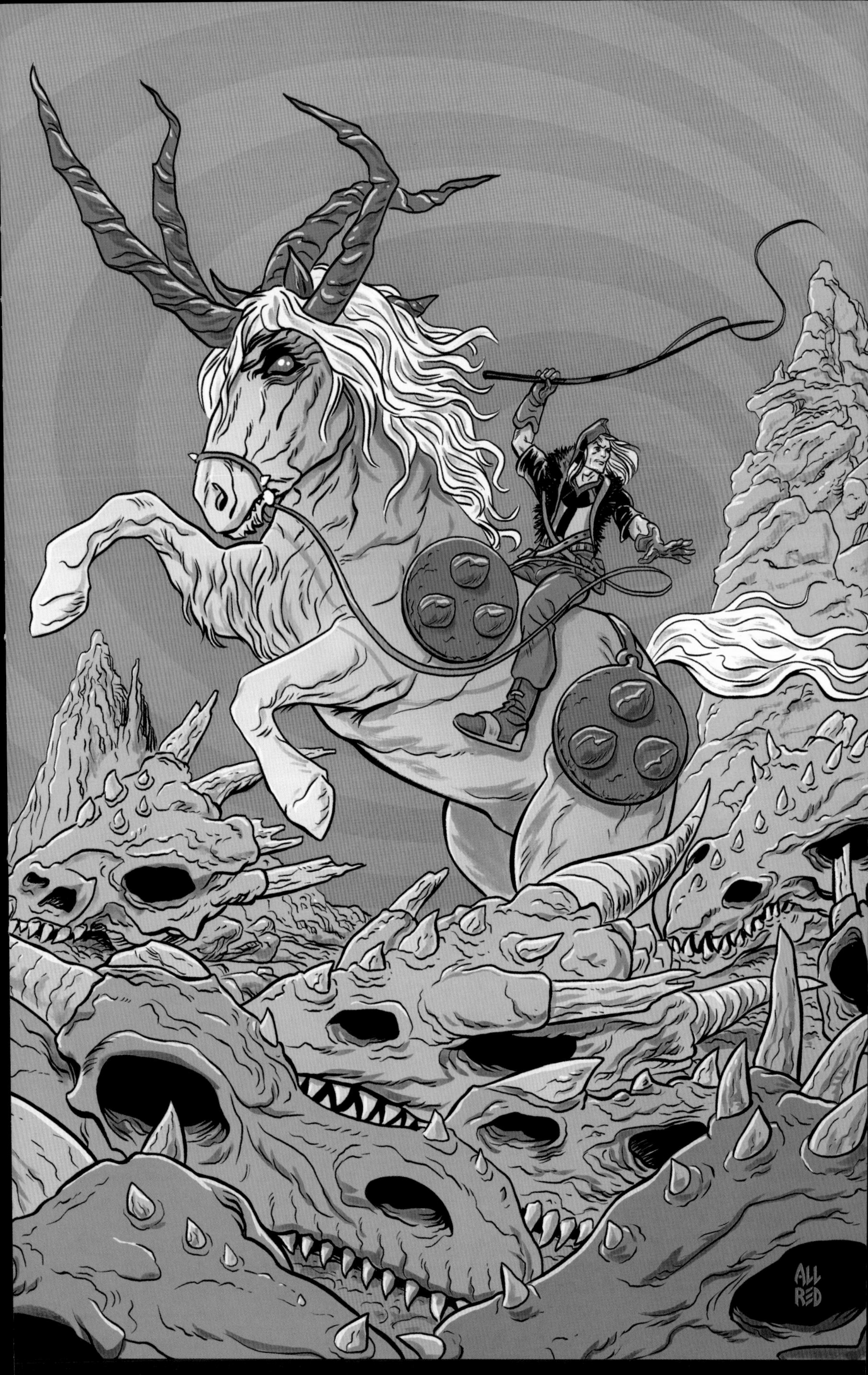
ALLRED

ISSUE FOUR COVER BY **MICHAEL ALLRED**
WITH COLORS BY **LAURA ALLRED**

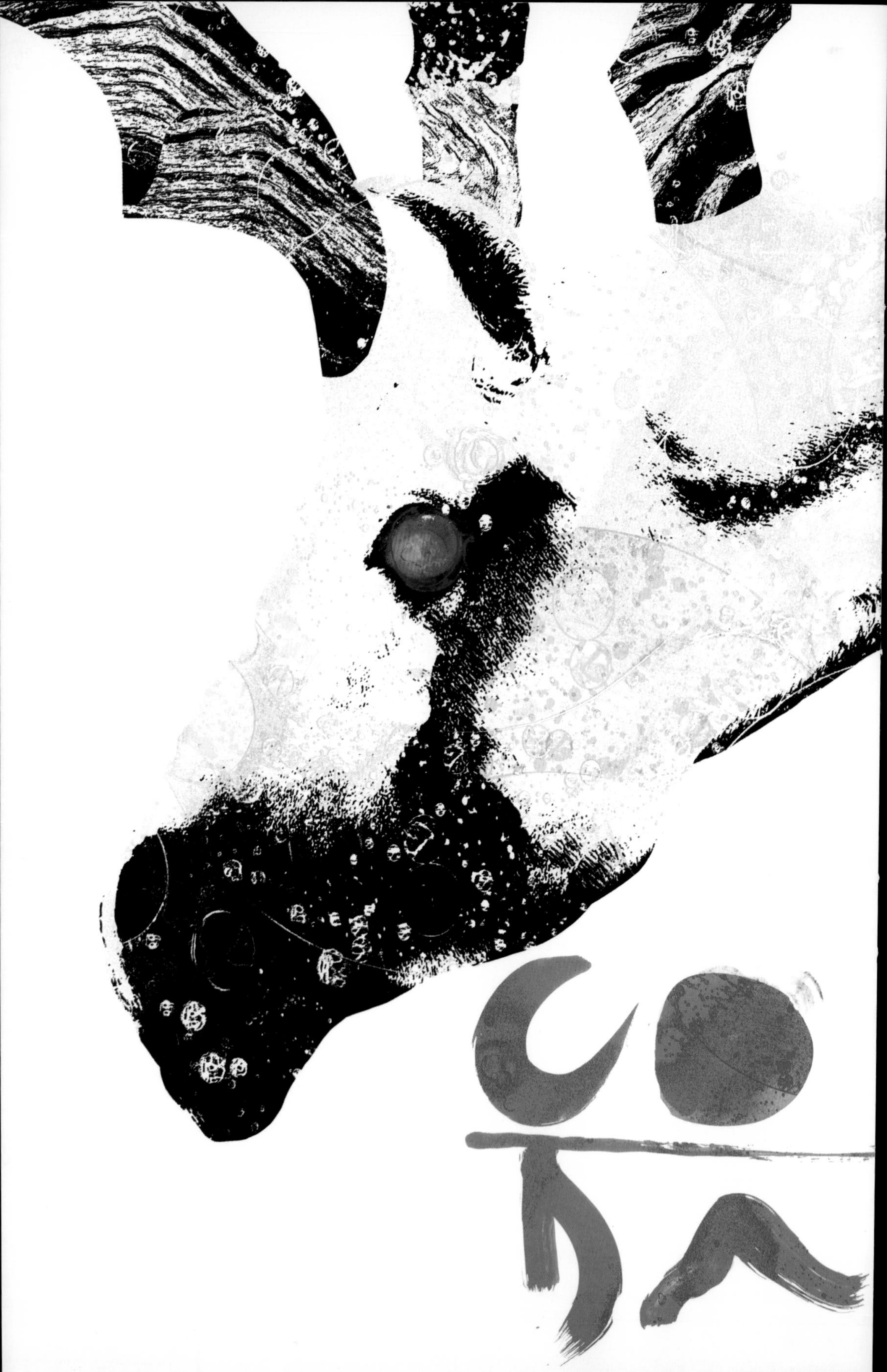
CODA

ISSUE FOUR VARIANT COVER BY **JAY SHAW**

THE WORLD OF

CODA™

BEFORE + AFTER

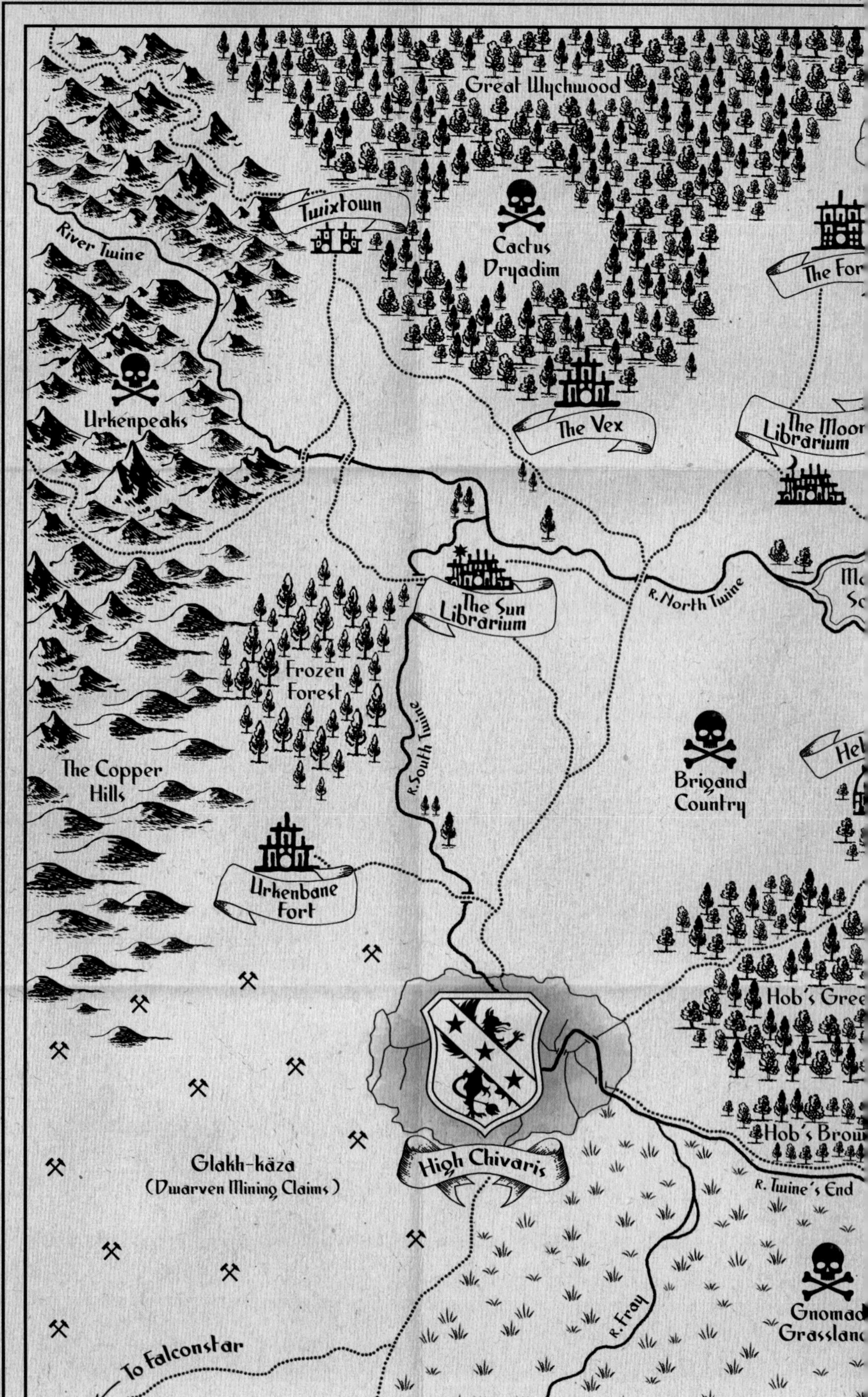
Great Wychwood
Twixtown
Cactus Dryadim
River Twine
Urkenpeaks
The Vex
The Moon Librarium
The Sun Librarium
R. North Twine
Frozen Forest
The Copper Hills
R. South Twine
Brigand Country
Urkenbane Fort
Hob's Gree
Hob's Brow
High Chivaris
R. Twine's End
Glakh-kāza
(Dwarven Mining Claims)
R. Fray
Gnomad Grasslan
To Falconstar

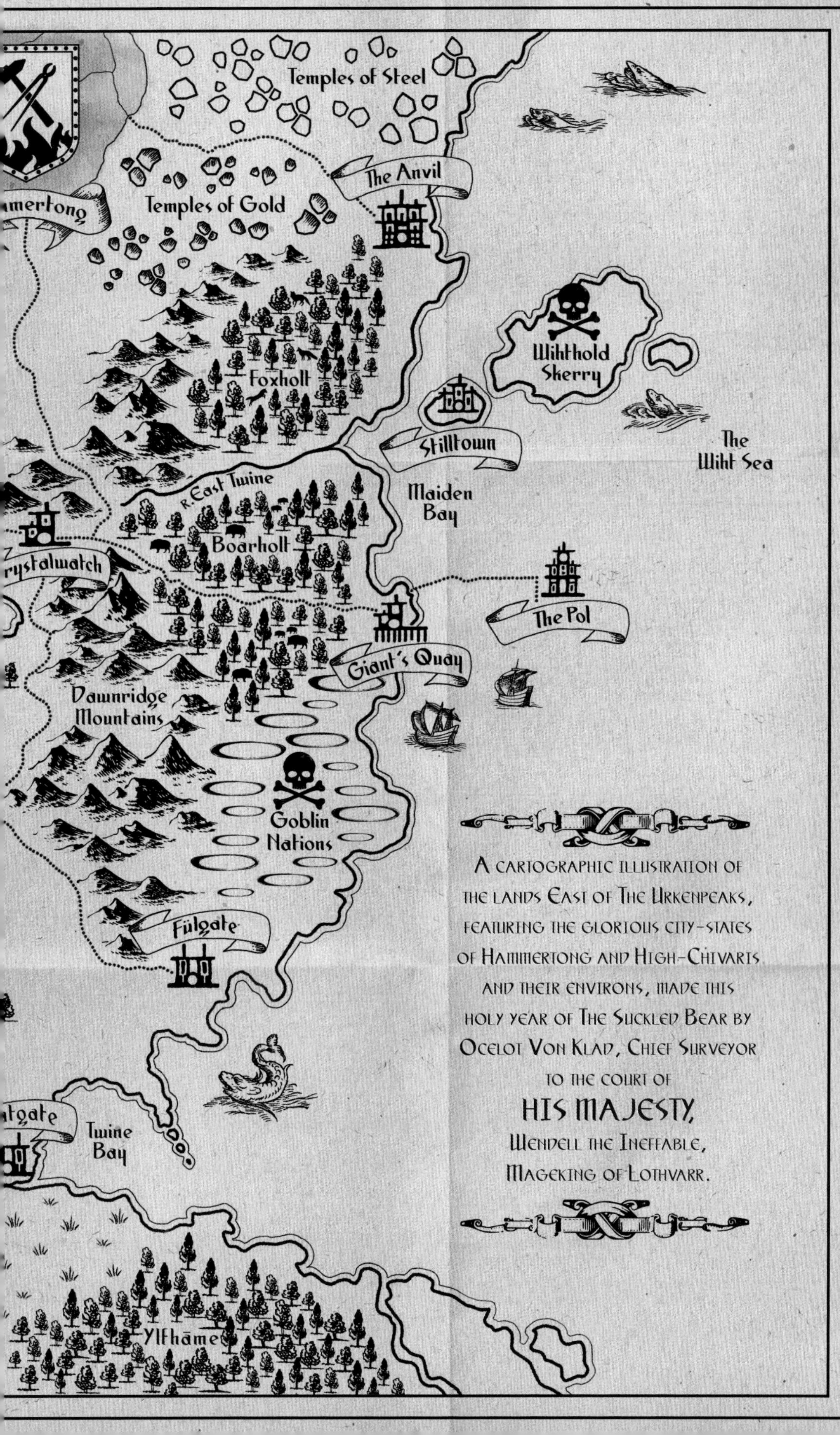
Temples of Steel
The Anvil
Temples of Gold
Foxholt
Wihthold Skerry
Stilltown
The Wiht Sea
R. East Twine
Maiden Bay
Boarholt
The Pol
Giant's Quay
Dawnridge Mountains
Goblin Nations
Fülgate
Twine Bay
Ylfhame
A cartographic illustration of the lands East of The Urkenpeaks, featuring the glorious city-states of Hammertong and High-Chivaris and their environs, made this holy year of The Suckled Bear by Ocelot Von Klad, Chief Surveyor to the court of
HIS MAJESTY,
Wendell the Ineffable,
Mageking of Lothvarr.

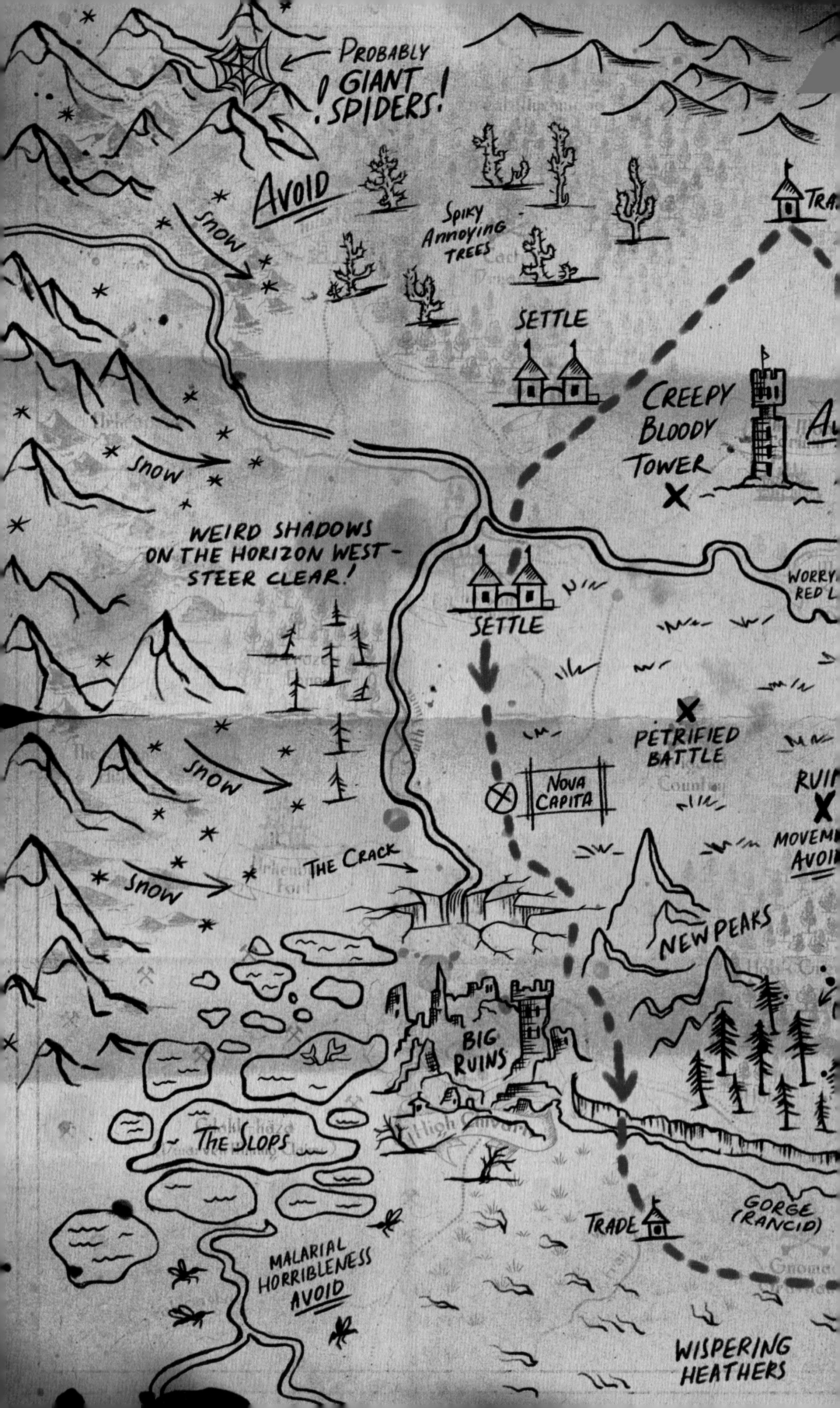
PROBABLY GIANT SPIDERS!
AVOID
SNOW
SPIKY ANNOYING TREES
SETTLE
CREEPY BLOODY TOWER
SNOW
WEIRD SHADOWS ON THE HORIZON WEST - STEER CLEAR!
SETTLE
PETRIFIED BATTLE
SNOW
NOVA CAPITA
SNOW
THE CRACK
NEW PEAKS
BIG RUINS
THE SLOPS
GORGE (RANCID)
TRADE
MALARIAL HORRIBLENESS AVOID
WISPERING HEATHERS

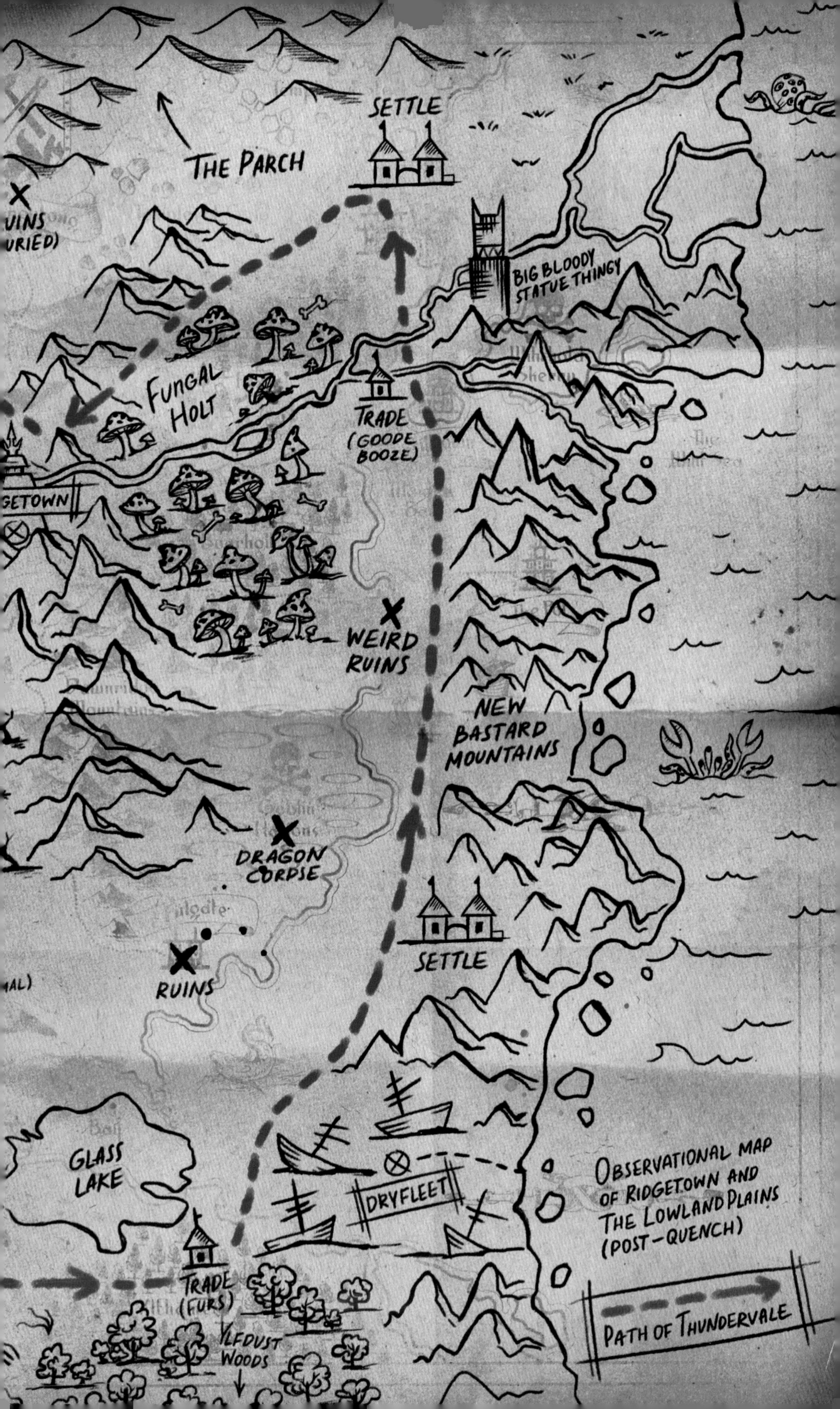
THE PARCH
SETTLE
UINS
URIED)
BIG BLOODY STATUE THINGY
FUNGAL HOLT
TRADE (GOODE BOOZE)
GETOWN
WEIRD RUINS
NEW BASTARD MOUNTAINS
DRAGON CORPSE
SETTLE
RUINS
AL)
GLASS LAKE
DRYFLEET
OBSERVATIONAL MAP OF RIDGETOWN AND THE LOWLAND PLAINS (POST-QUENCH)
TRADE (FURS)
ELFDUST WOODS
PATH OF THUNDERVALE

ABOUT THE AUTHORS

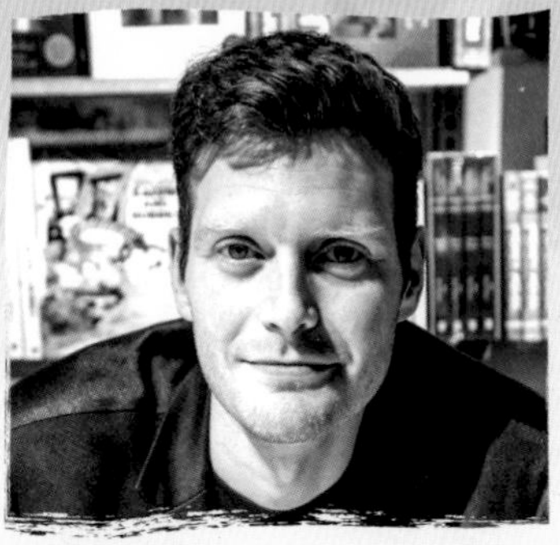

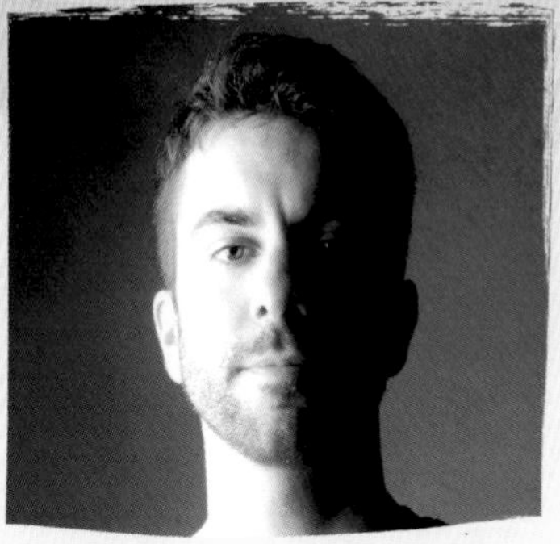

Simon Spurrier is a writer of actual words. His comic book credits stretch from *2000AD* and *Judge Dredd* to *X-Men Legacy*, *Suicide Squad*, and *Star Wars*. His creator-owned books include *Cry Havoc*, *Angelic*, and Eisner Nominee *The Spire*. He's published several prose novels, including *Contract* and *A Serpent Uncoiled*. His absurdist-noir novella *Unusual Concentrations* was shortlisted for the Shirley Jackson Award and is available online. He is currently working on new television and comic book projects. He lives in the south of Britain and normally isn't very good at writing about himself in the third person, but I think this time I'm actually doing pretty well.

Matías Bergara was born and still lives in the curious little country of Uruguay. He's been illustrating comics, book covers, and video game art ever since leaving a college career in literature. Most of his published work was created for Latin America and Europe, so he's a recent arrival on U.S. titles such as *Sons of Anarchy* (BOOM!, 2014) and *Cannibal* (Image, 2016).

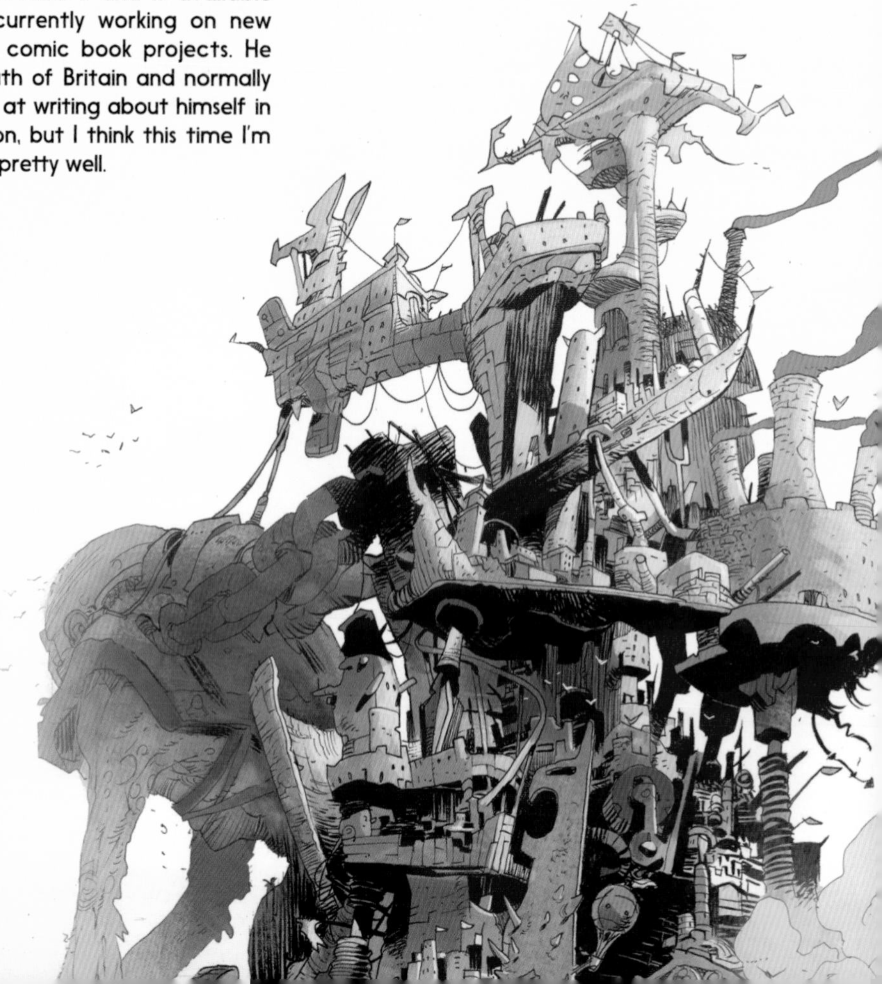